INFAMOUS PLAYERS

INFAMOUS PLAYERS

A Tale of Movies, the Mob (and Sex)

PETER BART

WEINSTEIN
BOOKS

ISBN: 978-1-60286-139-8

First Edition
10   9   8   7   6   5   4   3   2   1

Contents

PROLOGUE   *vii*

INTRODUCTION   *xi*

ACKNOWLEDGMENTS   *xiii*

CHAPTER 1
Taking the Leap   *1*

CHAPTER 2
The Tenuous Team   *24*

CHAPTER 3
The Salon   *39*

CHAPTER 4
The Boss's Bombs   *45*

CHAPTER 5
Lovers   *66*

CHAPTER 6
Modus Sexualis   83

CHAPTER 7
The Bad Guys   96

CHAPTER 8
Breaking the Mold   114

CHAPTER 9
Hard Lessons   130

CHAPTER 10
Rising Stars   153

CHAPTER 11
Unholy Alliances   185

CHAPTER 12
The Outlaws   200

CHAPTER 13
The Glitz Machine   233

CHAPTER 14
Reckoning   248

PARAMOUNT SLATE OF FILMS   *262*

Prologue

The projection room was dark except for the surreal images dancing across the screen. There were twenty plush seats, but I was the room's only occupant. The voices of the two actors on the screen resonated in the empty room as they enacted their scene over and over again but their performances were utterly robotic, as though they were channeling lines that were completely alien to their inner thoughts.

I was watching rushes, or dailies, as they are called, and I was alone because none of my colleagues were willing to share this ordeal. I was the most junior member of the executive staff and hence was delegated this dubious responsibility. The scene I was reviewing had been shot two days earlier and would ultimately become a key moment in a lavishly expensive movie titled *Darling Lili*.

It starred Julie Andrews and Rock Hudson, playing lovers brought together in France amid the rigors of World War I. And that, indeed, was the problem that I was observing—Andrews and Hudson as lovers. According to the script,

Andrews, a spy, was assigned to seduce Hudson, an American war hero, to elicit important war secrets, but their supposedly steamy love scene had as much fizzle as day-old beer.

Julie Andrews, totally believable as the faithful governess in *Mary Poppins*, was never a threat to Marilyn Monroe as a sex goddess. As for Hudson, his predilection for men was becoming widely suspected in Hollywood. Their mutual disinterest, if not distaste, was abundantly visible in take after take as they embraced and kissed and then, when the director yelled "cut," they wiped their lips and breathed a sigh of relief. The director, Blake Edwards, was Andrews's husband, and he obviously empathized with his wife's dilemma, but still, the scene was an important one, and a semblance of passion had to be generated, irrespective of how many takes it would require.

I watched five takes and could not cope with any more. As I exited, I noticed the door to the projection booth was ajar. "Those two really have the 'hots' for each other," called out the projectionist, his tone heavy with sarcasm.

I smiled, but I also found myself wincing. What was I doing here? How did I reach the point in my alleged career when I was witnessing two stars feign passion—actors who clearly wanted nothing to do with each other?

Had my life become this surreal?

I would find myself asking that question again some four years later at perhaps the defining moment of my Paramount odyssey. After a tortured period of preproduction, *The Godfather* was about to start shooting in New York. The fortunes of the fabled studio rested in the hands of Francis Coppola and his balky star, Marlon Brando. The corporate apparatchiks at Paramount's parent company, Gulf & Western, were openly skeptical about the project. Their nervousness was shared by representatives of New York's Italian community who believed that the movie would reflect badly on them, and they were making their feelings felt in a variety of ways. A bomb threat forced the evacuation of the Gulf & Western headquarters building on 58th Street. Robert Evans received a threatening phone call. A committee from an Italian-American group demanded to read the script, and members of one of the prominent Mafia families sent out word that they wanted to be involved in the casting process.

Charles Bluhdorn, the chairman of the G & W conglomerate, was in a frenzy of anxiety, and Evans shared his agitation because he was receiving admonitions of caution from his new best friend, Henry Kissinger, the top adviser to President Nixon. Ponderous and reserved, Kissinger had become a fairly regular visitor to Evans's house, and Evans was seeing to it that his evenings were spent in the company of beautiful women. Kissinger had been on edge about the impact of column items identifying him with Evans, but now, as word of Mafia pressures leaked to the press, his concerns took on an added dimension.

The rumblings about *The Godfather* worried Charles Bluhdorn for still another reason. Even as his company was producing a movie about the Mafia, he was in negotiation with financiers who had close ties to the mob community—ties that were more obvious, if not to Bluhdorn, to government investigators.

So this was, in a sense, a perfect storm. The studio was exposing the Mafia at the very time when its corporate parents were engaged in dealings with them. And meanwhile, the top power player in the Nixon administration was partying at the home of the chief of production.

Again I wondered, how did I get to this place?

Introduction

This book is about the interplay of triumph and failure. In the years between 1967 and 1975, the motion pictures flowing from the Paramount studio were arguably among the most distinguished, and idiosyncratic, of any that emerged from any company in the recent history of the movie industry.

Yet during the same period, Paramount was surely the most eccentric studio in the annals of Hollywood—an assessment based on runaway budgets, chaotic distribution, management infighting, an absence of strategy, and the recurring presence of criminal influences over company policy.

I played an integral role in both the success and the chaos. This is my story of how I got there.

As I relate my various studio imbroglios on the following pages, I describe and allude to many films, some of them memorable, others eminently forgettable. In either case I want to make it clear that I did not write or direct or produce any of these films. The movie business has more than its share of credit grabbers, and I do not aspire to membership in that fraternity. I am proud to have been present at the creation of films like *The Godfather* or *Rosemary's Baby*, but I do not claim responsibility for their success. My role was that of advocate and promulgator. I was part of the process, but I was not the final process. I often advanced the relationships and propelled the deals, but I did not sign the checks. I was neither the filmmaker nor the CEO, but I was lucky to be there at a moment of great achievement and great confusion, and I managed to contribute to both.

Most relevant to this book, I was an experienced observer. And I hope my observations will contribute to a greater understanding of that time, and of the unique characters who populated it.

Acknowledgments

This book would not have happened without the prodding and encouragement of Harvey Weinstein, without the enduring loyalty and friendship of Robert Evans, and without the love and resourcefulness, both editorial, and technological, of my wife, Phyllis.

CHAPTER 1

Taking the Leap

In 1967 at age thirty-five, being of sound mind and body, I accepted a job as an executive of a film studio. At that moment I believed my new position at Paramount Pictures would be a great adventure. If indeed it turned out to be a nightmare rather than an adventure, my tenure at the very least would provide the basis for a first-person account of my trip to the dark side. At the time, I was a staff reporter for the *New York Times*, so the alternative seemed perfectly practical. A career misstep could at least result in a compelling book. It never occurred to me that the book would finally emerge four decades later.

In fact, the Paramount experience was to last for eight years and prove to be both adventure and nightmare. During my studio odyssey some of the seminal films of the era would emerge from the studio slate—movies that would help define the nation's pop culture.

Yet I learned to accept the perverse fact that, while the films embodied boldness and vision, the studio culture that fostered them represented a mix of greed and corporate nihilism.

The filmmakers who shaped *The Godfather, Rosemary's Baby, Love Story, Harold and Maude*, and *Goodbye, Columbus* learned to feed off the studio as a black hole of conflict and corruption. The darkness helped bring forth the light.

The movies of the sixties and seventies have been scrupulously and skillfully analyzed by critics, but my aim in this book is to provide some insight into the players and processes of this robust moment of film history. My purpose is neither to sentimentalize this period nor to expose its confusion and venality, but rather to provide a glimpse of the realities that existed behind the tattered corporate curtain.

While Hollywood has always been buffeted by conflicting forces, the studios of this decade were peopled by a bizarre mix of creators and exploiters, some intent on redefining the aesthetic of cinema, others intent solely on personal enrichment.

The machinery of filmmaking had broken down, the dream factories were impoverished, and shrewd operators realized that where there was desperation there was also great opportunity.

Enterprising young filmmakers had also discovered that, where they were once confronted by closed doors, they were now being courted by studio executives. Similarly, financial players, some with criminal ties, found Hollywood to be suddenly open to funding schemes, no matter how esoteric. Indeed, not since the era of the Great Depression had the underworld so successfully infiltrated mainstream Hollywood or exercised such influence on the films being made and the people making them. Ironically, at the very time that *The Godfather* was portraying how the mob was embracing capitalism, the Mafia was also embracing Hollywood.

And as all this became apparent to me, I found myself wondering, how in hell did I find myself in this battle zone? What had impelled me to wander in?

The answer: a lethal mixture of ambition and curiosity, with a good measure of cultural wanderlust thrown in. Plus, my voyage would not be a lonely one. My friend, Bob Evans, was journeying with me, and we shared the foreboding that the odds might be stacked against us.

At the time I embarked on my Paramount journey I was content with the progress of my reporting career. I had worked my way through reporting stints on the *Wall Street Journal* and the *Chicago Sun-Times* before scoring my job on the *Times*, which in my mind represented the zenith of the newspaper business. My metabolism seemed perfectly attuned to the rhythms of newspaper work and to the noise of the newsroom (reporters still yelled "Copy!" in those days as the typewriters hummed).

From the first moment I walked into the *Times* newsroom, I felt a surge of exhilaration. This was, indeed, my playing field. And I knew instinctively that I could make it work for me.

The *Times* I joined was a rather genteel, WASPy environment led by men whom I looked on as journalist-statesmen— Turner Catledge, Clifton Daniel, Frank Adams, and Claude Sitton. Daniel, the managing editor, was suave and silver-haired and wore immaculately tailored dark blue suits made for him in London. He addressed me always as "Mr. Bart" and our dialogues were more akin to those of student and headmaster.

For four years my beat on the *Times* consisted of writing six columns a week that bore the title "Advertising." The assignment appealed to me because I had the freedom to select my own stories, on topics that extended well beyond the normal intrigues of ad agencies.

The media business is exhaustively covered in today's *Times*, but that was not case in the midsixties, which meant that my column was free to explore the foibles of magazines (the *Saturday Evening Post* was declining into oblivion), network television (CBS under Jim Aubrey and Mike Dann was dominating the ratings with the help of Jackie Gleason and Lucille Ball), and other strands of the pop culture. The ad agencies themselves were undergoing a mini-revolution, with the old school agencies like Ted Bates and BBD & O under assault from imaginative new players like Doyle Dane Bernbach and a rejuvenated Young & Rubicam. This was the moment of the brilliant Volkswagen campaign that shouted "Lemon!" and exhorted buyers to "Think small."

Though a corner of my brain told me that my journalistic aims should focus on Washington or a foreign assignment, I loved both the pace and autonomy of my media beat. I was married, had a young daughter, and had lucked into a small but bright one-bedroom apartment tucked into an elegant town house on East 82nd Street just off Madison Avenue. I was also churning out a steady stream of freelance articles for *Harper's*, *Esquire*, and the old *Saturday Review*—so many pieces, in fact, that Clifton Daniel admonished me that the *New York Times Magazine* had first call on my services.

Shortly after the reprimand, Daniel summoned me for a further meeting. While the *Times* liked my work on the column, the editors had decided I was ready for a new beat, he said. The reporters stationed both in Los Angeles and San Francisco were close to retirement age, Daniel said, and the *Times* felt that there were compelling stories in California that might be probed by a younger journalist.

As we talked, I became aware of the intriguing subtext to his remarks. The traditional attitude of the *Times* was that New York was the center of the universe both in terms of economic power and pop culture, but now a new "scene" was emerging on the West Coast. The components of that scene, however, remained opaque to the *Times*.

In short, the *Times* was worried that it was losing touch with the crosscurrents of midsixties America, both culturally and politically. Our tastes and proclivities were increasingly difficult to read. Vietnam and the civil rights movement had pre-empted the political agenda. In entertainment, even as Julie Andrews was winning an Oscar for *Mary Poppins*, the Jefferson Airplane was making its debut at the Matrix in San Francisco and the Beatles were opening at Shea Stadium. Hollywood was still banking on Elvis Presley movies and chestnuts like *Anne of a Thousand Days*, but audiences were favoring *Bonnie and Clyde* and *Who's Afraid of Virginia Woolf?*

The bottom line: Would I move to Los Angeles, to become one of the *Times'* missionaries to the brave new world?

I replied that I needed to think it over. Though I had covered stories throughout the South for the *Wall Street Journal,* and had reported on murder and mayhem for the *Sun-Times* in Chicago, I had never been to California, nor had ever contemplated it. I was a New Yorker; I had grown up a city kid, albeit a rather privileged city kid with a second home on Martha's Vineyard. My parents had seen to it that I attended private school. My schoolboy friends were expected to go on to top colleges, but also feasted on the energy of the city.

My school days were spent in a 225-year-old structure called Friends Seminary. Amid all the *Sturm und Drang* of the city, this creaky, brick edifice on Rutherford Place on the Lower East Side seemed to possess its own serenity. Choosing a college to me was a no-brainer: I chose Swarthmore, eager to continue within the Quaker enclave.

Hence, New York represented many environments to me. I relished the energy and yet also knew where to find the pockets of peace. Would I trade in all this for California?

My initial instinct was to deliver a polite "no" to my courtly managing editor, mindful that *Times* editors do not like to hear that word. I described my dilemma one day to another young reporter on the paper, David Halberstam. We were both standing at the urinal in the men's room when I queried: "What happens when you give Clifton Daniel a 'no'?" Halberstam, then a droll, if somber-looking, young man, replied, "You probably end up holding a very small piece of what you're presently holding."

He was being funny, but he was also right. I realized I would be an idiot not to take the *Times* up on its offer. I would be writing about the world of surfers and rockers, about Governor Earl Warren and the Beach Boys and a young senator named Richard Nixon. And maybe I'd even sneak in an occasional piece about the radical changes taking place in Hollywood, though my national news editor, Claude Sitton, made it clear that Hollywood would not be a prime target. While the *Times* had had a full-time Hollywood correspondent for many years, the decision had been made to discontinue that beat. There were more important things to focus on in the fast-changing cauldron of California.

From the moment we unpacked, my wife and I both found ourselves enjoying that cauldron. New Yorkers were expected to complain that they missed the theater and hated the driving. But we liked our new cars (provided by the *Times*) as well as our rented house nestled near the rolling UCLA campus. We knew we were supposed to resent the smog; instead we basked in the sunshine.

Within days of settling in, however, our illusions about sunny Southern California were shattered with one phone call.

The voice from the national news desk sounded at once confused and a bit panicked: "There's an early report on the wires that race riots have broken out. They're setting fires. Do you see anything?"

"I live near the UCLA campus," I said. "All I see are palm trees. Are you sure this is about LA?"

"Some place called Watts."

I was stunned; I'd been staring at the map during my initial days in Los Angeles, but there was no sign of Watts.

Within hours I was to learn all about Watts and its riots, which had swept through downtown Los Angeles and were soon headed west. Within the next few days my car was to sustain three bullet holes and I was to be pinned down by gunfire on streets that in no way represented my image of Southern California.

In my initial weeks in Los Angeles I was realizing every young reporter's dream—big stories on page one. And once the Watts riots showed signs of subsiding, I was on a plane to San Francisco to report on that city's racial upheaval.

Ultimately a semblance of calm descended once again on California's major cities, and I found time to explore other sectors of my new beat. I wrote pieces about the impact of the real estate boom, the developing surfer culture, the gay baths in San Francisco, and the fast-rising California university system. I described the increasing problems of coexistence between California's robotic right-wing constituencies in Orange County and the radical activists of San Francisco. I even managed to sneak in some stories about Hollywood. To me, the big story in the movie business was not about glamour and glitz but rather its economic collapse. Television had simply eviscerated the movie audience—some 30 million filmgoers a week were now buying movie tickets versus 90 million a decade earlier. The studios had run out of money; they had also run out of ideas.

Hollywood's press agents were exasperated with the *Times* for no longer posting a full-time correspondent to cover the film scene. It was as though the nation's most important newspaper was saying "movies don't matter anymore," which was partially true. I found time to do an occasional piece about a star. I took a ride with Paul Newman in his Volkswagen bug, which was equipped with a Porsche engine (he loved hurtling past Detroit's ponderous clunkers on the freeway). Steve McQueen explained to me how he was trying to become "grownup" and shed his bad boy reputation.

One week I decided to do a piece about a fellow New Yorker who had begun to cut a swath in Hollywood. Robert Evans had been introduced to me by a friend, a screenwriter named Abby Mann, and I liked his self-deprecating charm. Evans and his brother, sons of a New York dentist, had built a successful clothing company called Evan Picone, but his life had abruptly changed one day when Norma Shearer saw him lounging by the pool at the Beverly Hills Hotel. As she watched Evans, Shearer had an epiphany: In her eyes, he looked astonishingly like her late husband, Irving Thalberg, the fabled studio chief. A movie called *Man of a Thousand Faces* was about to shoot at Universal starring Jimmy Cagney, who was to play Lon Chaney, and the studio was looking for an actor to portray Thalberg.

Thalberg had been an attractive, slender, and rather fragile young man. Evans was handsome and more robust, but he fit Shearer's idealized memory of her husband, who had achieved mythic status as head of MGM.

To his amazement, Evans won the role, and in November 1956 the *Times* duly reported on the decision declaring that "the real and reel worlds of Hollywood had merged."

Within a year, however, Evans was destined to be "discovered" yet again. He was dancing with a girlfriend at a posh New York nightclub called El Morocco, when Darryl F. Zanuck, the feisty studio boss at Twentieth Century-Fox, summoned him to his table. Zanuck was looking for a young actor to play the bullfighter in his movie *The Sun Also Rises*, based on the

Ernest Hemingway novel, and, watching Evans's dance floor moves, he was convinced that he would be right for the role.

Evans had by then resigned himself to a return to the schmatta trade, as he called it—it paid better than his gig in Hollywood—but Zanuck's enthusiasm startled him. Here was a chance to play opposite Ava Gardner and Tyrone Power. Zanuck even offered to sign him to a five-year talent contract. Evans stammered a "yes."

The notion of a clothing executive playing a Spanish bull-fighter triggered skepticism in the gossip columns. When pressured to fire his protégé, the studio boss responded with his famous rant, "The kid stays in the picture." Evans's performance, though hammered by some critics, was praised by others. And so, having been doubly discovered by age twenty-seven, Evans decided on a sharp change in course. Considering that he had played Thalberg and been adopted by Zanuck, he now decided that he wanted to become a mixture of the two.

He wanted to run a studio.

He knew he had none of the necessary credentials and that he wasn't a member of the club that still ran Hollywood. But as Evans and I (and often Abby Mann) hung out together, I began to understand certain qualities about him that ultimately would defy the doubters. He was bonding with those power players of his generation—Richard Zanuck, son of Darryl, who was now the new studio chief at Fox, was one of his friends. Eager to master the dealmaking lexicon, Evans also was analyzing every contract he could get his hands on. He saw every movie that was opening and, over dinners, he would tear apart the performances and story structures.

As I got to know him better, I realized my new friend was smart and funny. He also had an insatiable appetite for beautiful women. He wanted to date them, photograph them, flatter them, and sleep with them, and his attentions were eagerly reciprocated. The girls were amused by him: He had money, he didn't do drugs (at the time), and there was a disarmingly old Hollywood quality to his romantic pursuit. The women understood that he'd be a one-night stand, and they seemed all right with that.

But Evans's reputation as an obsessive player further fueled the town's skepticism about him. It was understood in the community that Evans hungered to be a hot producer and to achieve power beyond that, but no one felt he would get there. Indeed, Abby Mann, who by now had won an Academy Award for his screenplay of *Judgment at Nuremberg*, took a certain amount of needling because of his friendship with Evans, as did I.

To further his producing ambitions, Evans soon hired a story scout in New York—a professional reader named George Wieser, who, for $175 a week, analyzed material coming into the publishing trade journals and talent agencies. Evans would forage through every novel and screenplay that was recommended to him. Wieser knew that Evans wasn't looking for great literature: he needed material to bait the studios.

The first book Evans submitted around town was a cheesy women's novel called "Valley of the Dolls" by Jacqueline Susann. With a certain naive excitement, Evans neglected to acquire film rights but simply offered the novel to Twentieth Century-Fox as a possible Evans production. The studio covered it and liked it but, when Evans inquired about a deal, he was abruptly told there wouldn't be any. A studio producer had been assigned to the project. Evans was shut out.

Angry but undaunted, Evans quickly settled on yet another potential property. It was a novel called *The Detective*, written by a onetime New York police officer named Roderick Thorp. This time Evans put down $5,000 for an option before he went back to Fox. Again, the studio agreed with his taste in material, this time offering him a meager deal as an associate producer. Even as the talks were still going back and forth, Evans assaulted the studio with yet another property—F. Lee Bailey's vivid account of the murder case involving Dr. Sam Sheppard. Evans persuaded a high-profile attorney named Greg Bautzer to plead his case at the studio, demanding an overall three-picture contract encompassing offices at the studio and a development fund.

This bold foray again met with rejection, but rather than being affronted, Evans seemed genuinely amused by the process. He knew he was earning a reputation as a major pain in the ass at the studios, but he didn't care.

I decided to write a short piece for the *Times* about Evans's relentless campaign to storm the fortress. Evans knew the town already put him down as the fringe actor who once played Thalberg. He was worried that a possible *Times* story would bring further ridicule down on him and did his best to talk me out of it, but I wrote it anyway.

My piece caused a minor stir in town. Why was the *Times* devoting space to an outsider who, at this moment, simply didn't matter?

What neither Evans nor I could know at the time was that the story had been avidly consumed by another outsider who had a yearning for Hollywood glitz. His name was Charles Bluhdorn.

I had never heard of Bluhdorn, nor had Evans. But a few days after my story appeared, a somewhat breathless Evans called to confide that he had received a surprise phone call from his attorney, Greg Bautzer. The gist of the call: Charles Bluhdorn had read about Evans and liked what he read. He wanted Evans to fly to New York for a meeting. And since Bluhdorn had just closed a deal to acquire control of Paramount Pictures, Bautzer thought it would be a damn good meeting. This was Paramount, after all—one of Hollywood's fabled studios, which had sprung to life some sixty years earlier under the name of Famous Players. The Famous Players had proved to be infamous in some cases, Bautzer reminded his friend, but the opportunity was real.

Evans was in shock. What was this meeting about? Bautzer's response was forceful: Bluhdorn wanted to be a player, he advised. "Pack your bags."

Some quick checking produced a few skimpy facts about this new player. Born somewhere in Central Europe, he'd come to the U.S. in 1942 and started work as a cotton broker and wannabe entrepreneur. He'd begun stringing together an odd mishmash of companies, starting with an auto parts company called Michigan Bumper, but his ambitions were far more glamorous. His acquisition of Paramount reflected not only a love of movies but also an urgent desire for social acceptance.

The individual that Evans met in New York was a coarse man with a guttural accent, a frenzied energy, and the instincts of a true gambler. He hurled question after question at Evans, starting another even before Evans had finished his response to the previous one. Evans had never met anyone quite like this, but he instinctively felt a chemistry. He was less impressed, however, by the person who hovered at Bluhdorn's side, a public relations man named Martin Davis, who had helped orchestrate the Paramount acquisition. Davis was like a Doberman, Evans later told me. He hovered, listened, rarely talked.

Evans admitted he was bewildered by the encounter, yet within weeks an astonishing offer came via Davis: Bluhdorn wanted to hire Evans to become his head of production in London. If he did a good job, he would be shifted to Los Angeles within a few months and become the production chief at the Paramount studio.

When Evans and I next sat down to dinner, I picked up on his mix of excitement and abject panic. I also realized there was a curious bond emerging between us. To a degree I had been responsible for this bizarre change in his life. It was my article that triggered the interest from Bluhdorn. This was becoming not only his adventure, but our adventure.

Typically, Evans was quick to acknowledge his own vulnerability. "I don't know how to be a head of production," he said. "I wasn't even convincing playing the part in a movie. I don't really know London. I think I've been there once. What am I getting into?"

I wanted to ask him the obvious question, but could not decide how to phrase it: Why did Charles Bluhdorn offer you this job? Why didn't he go after a member of "the club"—a Hollywood player with an established reputation?

There was no point asking, I decided, because I could tell Evans didn't have the remotest clue as to the answer. Indeed, it was months before I myself had any insight into this curious relationship.

Evans, I decided, personified a sort of dream fantasy version of Bluhdorn. He was an attractive, smooth-talking ladies' man; Bluhdorn was homely and abrasive and sexually repressed. Evans had an ingratiating boyishness and transparency. He wore his heart on his sleeve. Bluhdorn was devious, his appetites opaque. He was a European who had mastered the business mystique of his new country but none of its social subtext. He felt himself the foreigner, the outsider. Evans was the total insider.

Except he wasn't. Evans had figured out Hollywood's surface secrets, but had not really broken the code.

And over dinner, he urgently wanted to make a deal with me. He would be leaving for London shortly, and my responsibility as a friend was to watch his back in Los Angeles. More important, he wanted me to agree to read and give my opinion on a few scripts that he would send me.

He said he would arrange to pay me, but I told him emphatically that I would not accept any money. I had a great job at the *Times* and had no intention of compromising it. Besides, I had no experience as a script analyst. If he wanted to send something to me I would do my best to read it and tell him what I thought. It would be a personal favor, not a business one.

I told myself nothing would emerge from this conversation. I was wrong. Within days the scripts started arriving. I ignored most of them, but if the subject matter seemed interesting, or the author's name struck a bell, I started reading. Two or three times a week I would get a call from Evans in London asking, "What did you think of *The Italian Job?*" or some other title.

While I didn't really have much insight into screenplay writing, neither did Evans. At least I had time to read some of them, and clearly he did not. He was enmeshed in meetings with London movers and shakers and was relishing the experience. Suddenly he was no longer doing the pitching, people were pitching him! Talented young filmmakers were seeking him out. Plus an entirely fresh cast of beautiful women seemed to await him at every corner.

But Evans's exultant phone calls quickly began to take on a worried tone. The same hustlers who were now pitching Evans had previously found a patsy in Charles Bluhdorn who, in his first six months as owner of the studio, had committed to a bizarre array of what he considered surefire hits.

Bluhdorn had proved to be an easy target. A young performer named Tommy Steele had scored a success in London with a musical called *Half a Sixpence*, and Bluhdorn had committed to a movie version. The result was daunting: Here was a film, Evans told me, that could find no possible audience in the U.S. Another Bluhdorn acquisition based on the bestseller called *Is Paris Burning?* had just been screened in Paris—again, a film with no American appeal.

As the weeks went by, it became ever more obvious that London was not going well for Evans. A mini-bureaucracy had remained in place from the pre-Bluhdorn regime, and it was resisting Evans's efforts to connect with new ideas and new talent. London, too, had its "club," and Evans was not a welcome member. Before long, it seemed Evans's Paramount adventure would be over; he would be back in Hollywood putting together his production deals.

And that would certainly be fine by me. While I'd appreciated my basic education in script reading, I was never getting much feedback on my personal assessments. There was no indication that anything that I liked was actually getting attention.

My intuition was wrong again. Five months after Evans disappeared into the London fog, I received another urgent phone call. He was indeed coming back to Hollywood—not as a producer but as Paramount's chief of production. He would be replacing Howard W. Koch, one of the most respected executives in the movie industry. And he urgently wanted me to become his right-hand man.

Now it was my turn to be genuinely shocked. I had been playing a game, or what I thought was a game, and suddenly it wasn't a game anymore. It was one thing to chat about scripts with a friend, but now the stakes had been raised.

Much as I liked Evans and respected his native intelligence, I couldn't believe that Bluhdorn had decreed that he could be molded into a corporate executive. The reaction in the press to the Evans announcement matched my skepticism.

"Bluhdorn's folly," trumpeted one trade story. "Bluhdorn's blow job," said *Hollywood Close-up*, a gossip paper.

Arriving back in town, Evans made it very clear to me that his new job was real and so was mine, if I decided to take it. He had cleared my deal with Bluhdorn and his subordinates. There had been some resistance, but he'd won his point. "I told them I wasn't equipped for my new job, so I wanted someone at my side who was also not prepared," Evans said. That was such an absurd argument that I believed he'd actually made it. "This will be an adventure," Evans told me with a smile that was at once friendly and fatalistic. "What's the worst they can do to us? They won't kill us. What have we got to lose?"

I realized that was both the good and the bad news. Still only thirty-six, Evans had succeeded at everything he had tried. As a sort of playboy prince, he'd made his fuck-you money, earned a measure of celebrity, and had made it all seem like one grand party. Now along came Charles Bluhdorn to make the party even grander.

But what about me?

Pondering this "adventure," I found myself conflicted on several levels. Journalism was not a casual endeavor for me; I had been consumed with writing and reporting since boyhood. I'd been editor of my high school paper and of my college paper. When I walked into my first newsroom, I literally palpitated with excitement.

And my *Times* assignment in California had been a rewarding one; I had experienced the best and the worst. I had ducked behind cars in darkened streets as the bullets flew and cops sprawled next to me. I had also hung with the hippies at Haight-Ashbury and shared joints with them. And I had made a point of having lunch with those icons of the movie business who I felt deserved attention from the *Times*—Walt Disney, Jack Warner, Lew Wasserman, Sam Goldwyn, Alfred Hitchcock.

I appreciated what it was like to live in the *Times'* aura.

You could ask any question of any dignitary, and they felt compelled to answer. You were neither artisan nor celebrity, but you occupied your own unique space. You had amazing access but also unique responsibility: It was your job to get it right.

I knew I could never explain those things to Evans. He was in another orbit.

But I kept waking up in the middle of the night, realizing that the decision was not that easy. It wasn't just about the job, it was about the moment. The movie industry was in a state of collapse, studio regimes were tumbling. Paramount represented not so much a studio as a power vacuum. The place had ground to a halt.

And that's what was haunting me. Movies were either going to become anachronisms or there would be a rebirth, and maybe I could be a small part of it. Even a big part of it.

But the question remained, would our voices be heard over the din? Paramount itself was a maelstrom of competing agendas. We would be the new faces in production, and the old guard would resist the initiatives of newcomers. The writing and directing jobs were being recycled among the familiar faces, and they were not youthful faces.

So would I be able to change that? I solicited the advice of a few friends both in journalism and in the film business, and they all were dubious. I even sought out Howard Koch, the man Evans was replacing. A convivial and unpretentious man, Koch admitted he'd always been uncomfortable in his role as studio chief. As he explained it, "For every time you say 'yes' in this job, you say 'no' a hundred times, and I hate saying 'no.' I don't like disappointing people. Do you really want to do this job?"

I appreciated his candor. "But what would it be like if that rare 'yes' really made a difference?" I asked. "What if some smart, young people were given the chance to make smart pictures?"

Koch gave me a pained smile. "You realize, the only reason most guys want a job at a studio is girls or money."

"Evans has all the girls he needs," I said. "And I'm a happily married man."

"Then take the job, kid," he advised. "You and Evans—you're both so far off the charts, you may actually make things work for you."

I flew back to New York to tell my editors that I was leaving the *Times* but doing so regretfully. Claude Sitton was incredulous. "Please don't take this the wrong way, but I never figured you for the Hollywood type."

"I never did either," I said.

Clifton Daniel, who now held the title of executive editor, stared at me with the disdain of a father whose son had just told him he was dropping out of college. He said he wished me well, but he didn't really.

David Halberstam was blunt. "They'll chew you up and spit you out," he warned. "I never thought you'd go to the dark side."

Halberstam's words stung. Roughly a year later, Halberstam was to call me at Paramount to ask for a favor. It seems he was seeing a beautiful young wannabe actress and he wondered whether, in my new post at the studio, I could arrange for a screen test.

I told him I would be glad to do so.

It was a wrenching experience to leave the *Times*, but to my surprise there was not one moment in the coming months when I regretted it. I knew I was now on a theme park ride with freaks and demons, crooks and visionaries popping up all around me. Within weeks I became resigned to the fact that nothing would really make sense, and it was naive of me to expect as much.

I was no longer the earnest young journalist. I was a stranger in a strange land, and I savored it.

Within my first three or four weeks at Paramount, two realities became vividly clear. The first did not surprise me: my presence was not welcome on the lot. The Paramount studio, like every institution, was ruled by its resident bureaucrats, some of them second or even third generation. I was an alien invader and, as such, a threat to the established order. I was certainly not to be trusted and no special favors were to be accorded me.

The studio itself, I learned, had a feudal structure. Each fiefdom had its own leader who presided over his army of serfs. The art director had his constituency as did the head of physical production, the editing staff, and even the commissary. The various units operated with a high degree of autonomy, with everyone guarding their jobs warily.

It wasn't just about money. The chieftains who presided over the music department or casting or editing had great prestige among their peers because they controlled the budgets and the jobs. The head of music was influential in hiring composers and musicians and thus was accustomed to being fawned over. Even the head of the story department was revered for his influence in recommending scripts and hiring screenwriters for rewrite jobs.

As far as these folks were concerned, I had nothing to bring to this party, and their cool reception did not surprise me. What did surprise me, however, was my own reaction to the studio and its environs.

After a long and argumentative production meeting I

took a thirty-minute stroll around the lot and came to terms with my epiphany: I loved the place. I knew I did not belong here. I was not a student of studio lore. Unlike hard-core movie brats like Peter Bogdanovich, I did not know where Cecil B. DeMille's old office was located, nor on which soundstage Elvis Presley had just finished shooting.

Friends had warned me that I would be seduced by the studio glamour and power, but it was not glamour or power that was grabbing me now. The studio seemed like a wonderful old village that had grown shabby, but was still clinging zealously to its dignity. The paint was peeling from the faux tenements on the New York street; there were shingles missing on the dusty structures lining the Old West town, and it had clearly been a long time since the last scene had been shot there. In the screening rooms, the seats were worn, and a musty smell pervaded.

The studio was a land of shopworn make-believe, but its integrity was oddly intact. Every corridor, every room, bespoke its past. People had worked diligently to craft their scripts, hone their reels of film, or act out their fleeting bits of dialogue. Walking the studio streets, I heard their cumulative noise. And it was a welcome sound.

My office exuded the contradictions of my new environment. It was a big room, downright stately, with handsome paneling. Its furnishings, however, seemed like they'd been recycled from an old rooming house. The oak desk had served many masters, and the faded green sofa sagged morosely.

One day, after a production meeting, the erudite head of the story department, a self-described "failed novelist" named John Boswell, asked for a few private words in my office.

Boswell, it seemed, hadn't taken a vacation for two years because of his nervousness over the transitions at the studio, and he wanted to go away for a week. "Fine by me," I told him.

Boswell seemed relieved. "By the way," he confided, "this sofa I'm sitting on—it was in my office for five years before I asked for a replacement. It doesn't seem fair that you would end up with it."

"My whole office is strictly from Goodwill," I said. "Or maybe from the Salvation Army. I think the powers-that-be are delivering a message."

"You *are* the powers-that-be," Boswell replied. "I don't want to give away secrets, but have a look at the building behind Stage Twelve. It's the studio's furniture trove. It would satisfy a foreign monarch."

I thanked him for the tip and decided to take the action that I'd been putting off. As the chief of physical production, Frank Caffey controlled studio facilities and their furnishings. I phoned him and asked if he would drop by my office. "Be right over," he said.

Caffey was smartly attired in a dark brown suit and tie. With his regal bearing, his appearance matched his reputation—he was the studio's mayor.

"I am a journalist by training, so I am going to get right to what we call our lead," I said. "You and your colleagues are convinced that Evans and I are mere passersby. You are entitled to your opinion, but our attitude is that we are going to be here for a while. Hence, we want to be reasonably comfortable."

Caffey peered at me and then glanced around my office. "I take it you are referring to furniture, among other things," he said, not at all defensively.

"Let's just focus on the furniture," I said. "I don't want grandeur, but I don't want Goodwill, either. And I assume this is an issue that can be resolved by tomorrow morning."

Though my tone was respectful, my words caused him obvious disquiet. "I don't think the situation can be resolved that easily."

"I know they call you the Mayor," I said. "If I do not have new furniture by ten tomorrow morning, either your tenure or mine will end abruptly. Thanks for dropping by."

Frank Caffey nodded and departed. When I arrived at work the next morning my office had undergone a smart makeover—new desk, sofa, matching chairs, even a rather elegant painting to adorn the stark walls. There was a terse note from Caffey. It simply said, "I hope you have a long and successful stay."

Evans, too, was quickly rewarded with some new pieces, and he, too, was relishing his environs. To the press, however, the casting of Bob Evans as a studio chief was still less than credible. He was too young, too inexperienced, and too good looking. In their eyes, he remained an actor playing the part. Even as new deals were announced—*Goodbye, Columbus*; *The President's Analyst*; *The Odd Couple*—items also were regularly planted in columns and in *Variety* that the new Paramount regime was shaky.

I was regularly getting calls from journalist friends asking about my well-being and whether I had made contingency plans. I could detect their skepticism when I assured them that I was enjoying myself thoroughly.

While Evans was unnerved by the fusillade of bad press, I found it downright amusing. My journalistic experience had taught me that reporters habitually write their stories in advance. To them, the making and unmaking of Bob Evans was a hot story—one they were certain would reveal itself imminently. To my mind, they were anticipating it too greedily.

And my fall from grace would provide a delicious nugget too. I was keenly aware that my journalistic colleagues were either contemptuous or envious of my new position. My dismissal would affirm their view that writers should not stray. True to expectations, *Variety* ran a speculative story six months after my arrival at Paramount suggesting that my departure was expected hourly.

"Don't get used to the big paydays," Art Murphy of *Variety* warned me one day.

If journalistic friends were cool to my new responsibilities, more and more producers and filmmakers were displaying a sharply contrasting attitude. With each passing week, I was receiving more visitors who were looking for a receptive ear, or rather, for a sympathetic sensibility. The fact that I had been a newspaper reporter with the *New York Times* intrigued them. And they had interesting stories to tell.

Sure, they were looking for a deal—I was alert to that fact. I was a new buyer, but I was also a different type of buyer, and the folks who were coming in to see me were different types of sellers. They weren't the standard hustlers with shrewdly crafted packages. They were poets and songwriters and artists and novelists and even an occasional scientist. They were brilliant, creative people who normally would not have invaded the precincts of a Hollywood studio.

And I realized: They were here for the same reason I was here. There was a new adventure at hand. And a lot of free spirits wanted to be part of it.

CHAPTER 2

The Tenuous Team

Not long after joining Paramount, I was privy to a debate between two key executives of its corporate parent, Gulf & Western. One argued that Charles Bluhdorn had the soul of a romantic but the mind of a criminal. The other contended that he had the soul of a criminal but the mind of a romantic. Listening to them, I realized that the Führer, as he came to be called by some of his associates, was both inspired and crippled by these contradictory traits. As a wannabe Don Quixote, he desperately yearned to foster great movies, build a global business empire, teach the glories of capitalism to the leaders of the Dominican Republic and even Cuba, and transform himself into a modern Renaissance man.

Not only did Bluhdorn harbor the Big Dream, but it all but burned a hole in his consciousness. When I was in proximity to him, I sensed a curious heat—his mind was whirling too intensely, his heart beating too fast. The ideas came bursting out in a disorderly, unedited, uncensored clump—great ideas, terrible ideas, and vulgar ideas. But like a small child, he seemed incapable of assessing or prioritizing them, nor could he keep himself from impulsively putting them into action. Further, no moral compass was ever in evidence: a strategic objective was put on the table and its implementation became an instant imperative. Questions of ethics, or even efficacy, were not part of the equation. Anything was possible in the Bluhdorn universe. And any tactic, whatever its implications, was an open option.

If Charlie Bluhdorn was a man possessed, he never tried to disguise that fact. Michael Korda, the acerbic editor in chief of Simon & Schuster, a distinguished publishing house acquired by Bluhdorn, described him as a man who "had a wild look in his eyes and the red complexion of someone whose blood pressure was off the scale. Bluhdorn's teeth seemed either too big or too many, like those of a shark. Huge and glistening white, they filled his mouth like bathroom tiles."

The fact that Bluhdorn would end up owning a renowned book publisher was perplexing to Korda. Gulf & Western's array of scattered holdings included the New York Knickerbockers basketball team, Madison Square Garden, Dutch Masters Cigars, a zinc mine, vast sugar plantations in the Dominican Republic and in Florida, an auto parts business that comprised the original core of the Bluhdorn empire, and, of course, now Paramount Pictures.

Bluhdorn's buyout of Paramount was almost an inadvertency. He had been looking for other random industrial companies to scoop up when a search committee headed by an exhibitor named Sumner Redstone contacted him to see if he'd have any interest in a movie company. Despite its history, Paramount was floundering. It needed both money and initiative. Its head of publicity, a dour man named Martin Davis, was especially ardent in courting Bluhdorn because he had heard the financier loved Hollywood movies. Davis also intuited that if Bluhdorn got involved, it would mean a new career for Davis, too.

Bluhdorn was thrilled by the notion of owning an old Hollywood company. There's disagreement as to the true cost of his investment, but insiders said Bluhdorn paid only $100 million for the takeover.

Paramount, Korda knew, had come to represent an obsessive toy for Bluhdorn, but that obsession surely didn't extend to books. Indeed, shortly after gaining control of Simon & Schuster, the Gulf & Western chairman toured the company offices and complained to Korda that he saw too many employees reading at their desks. "When are these people going to get down to work?"

"They are editors and part of their job is to read," Korda responded patiently to his new boss, but Bluhdorn was dissatisfied with the explanation.

It didn't take long for Korda or the rest of us to realize that Gulf & Western was not a conventional corporation. Bluhdorn ran it like a personal fiefdom. He regularly took personal loans from the G & W treasury. When he traveled the world on his corporate jet (which he did almost constantly) he carried no personal money, but lavished millions of dollars on art for his personal collection in addition to buying the rights to movies. Upon his return he would hurl packets of receipts at his financial flunkies and they would duly record his expenses (an SEC investigator was stunned years later to come upon these records and learn that Bluhdorn had reimbursed the company for his personal purchases, including the art).

He spent much of his workday trading in securities including G & W stock. On several occasions when I visited his office, I would find him in a veritable trading frenzy, aides scurrying. He would often shout orders, as though he were actually on the floor of a commodities exchange.

His skills as a trader were formidable. Bluhdorn would shortly build up a portfolio approaching $850 million (worth several billion in today's dollars). These were Gulf & Western funds—his personal portfolio was of even greater value.

Though the Gulf & Western chairman was spending so much of his time trading, rather than managing, he had no concern about scrutiny from his board of directors because he saw to it that it was a "friendly" board.

Eight of his sixteen board members worked directly for G & W or its subsidiaries; three had formerly worked for Bluhdorn and remained large shareholders; two were lawyers whose firms drew large retainers from G & W; and two were large shareholders in companies acquired by G & W. That meant the only independent director was an obscure rumpled little man named Irwin Schloss, who claimed to be an investment banker but was a Bluhdorn sycophant.

Bluhdorn's operating philosophy was no secret to government regulators. During my years at Paramount there were constant rumors of SEC investigations and even speculation that the boss might end up in jail. One SEC probe focused on Bluhdorn's obsession with the old A & P chain of markets, a sprawling and badly run company which Bluhdorn felt symbolized capitalistic ineptitude. He was desperate to add it to his collection of holdings, and he played with its stock relentlessly. Contrary to SEC regulations, however, he steadfastly refused to publicly declare his takeover attempt. Under SEC pressure, Bluhdorn finally relented and sold his A & P shares, charging that the government had acted to protect the "business establishment" from the incursions of the new class of "Jewish money."

Bluhdorn's representations startled associates, since he

had always steadfastly denied any connection with a Jewish identity. "New money," he later explained to me, was always wrongly characterized as "Jewish money."

Clashes with government regulators also focused on another Bluhdorn favorite—the Dominican Republic. Everything about the island nation fascinated him—its climate, its politics, the paramilitary protection provided him on his visits, and, especially, its sugar crop. He purchased a vast beachfront estate on the island and regularly entertained present and prospective business associates.

On two occasions I found myself on the invitation list along with an exotic mix of corporate players, film producers, fashion designers, and mysterious Europeans who always identified themselves vaguely as "bankers," but didn't look like bankers. A few of the "bankers" at Bluhdorn parties would shortly end up in jail, as I was later to learn. But at the Dominican soirees, the food was sumptuous, the alcohol flowed freely, and guests seemed relaxed in the tropical heat.

Yet while the atmosphere on Bluhdorn's estate was hospitable, it was also vaguely threatening. If a guest wandered toward the periphery of the property, he encountered machine-gun-bearing security guards attired in paramilitary uniforms. The cadre of personal security men was buttressed by soldiers dispatched by the government.

As far as the Dominican government was concerned, Bluhdorn was not only an occasional tourist but a major benefactor, and the SEC knew the reasons. G & W was the sugar daddy to the regime, advancing aid on an as-needed basis. In one transaction, G & W advanced the Dominicans $40 million in sugar export money to help bolster the regime's balance of payments. In return for this convenient prepayment, the government "adjusted" G & W's foreign exchange rates to enhance the unrestricted profits the company could take out of the country. The SEC remained on full alert to Bluhdorn's Dominican dealings, at one point declaring that Gulf & Western failed to disclose the full scope of its profits from sugar revenues.

Eager to bolster his public image, Bluhdorn agreed to establish a $39 million economic and social development set up in the Dominican Republic. He also funded construction of an elaborate replica of a historic Italian village. Called Altos de Chavón, the faux sixteenth-century town, replete with amphitheater, was designed to be a major tourist attraction, but for some years remained in obscurity because of the financial and political intrigues associated with its construction.

To the Hollywood community, Charlie Bluhdorn was an outsider—indeed an intruder—and Bluhdorn knew it. Now he was determined to close a macho deal with mainstream talent and thus persuade the town that he was indeed a player. When he learned that Howard W. Koch, the outgoing production chief at the studio, had earlier optioned the rights to Neil Simon's hit play *The Odd Couple*, Bluhdorn saw his opportunity.

The Gulf & Western chairman flew to Hollywood, checked in to a suite at the Beverly Hills Hotel for a week's stay, and summoned Koch and his successor, Bob Evans, to a meeting. "*The Odd Couple* can be a big hit for us," he declared, building excitement as he spoke. "Who is going to star in this film?"

A wary man, Koch started to respond and then halted. He didn't want to upstage his youthful successor, Evans. "I've started talks with Frank Sinatra and Jackie Gleason," Koch stammered. "I haven't made any offers. No one is committed to anything."

Evans shook his head. The task of recruiting two such famously difficult actors would be painful, he pointed out, and so would the ultimate cost of the film. Art Carney and Walter

Matthau had starred in the Broadway play—perhaps that team would make more practical targets.

Bluhdorn had been taking a series of phone calls, listening to the discussion intermittently. Slamming down the phone now, he barked, "That was an agent from William Morris. Do you know a Hershman or Hirshan or something like that? He says he wants to come in tomorrow to talk about *The Odd Couple*. He wants to bring Jack Lemmon along with him."

"Tell him to come," advised a surprised Evans.

The next morning Leonard Hirshan and his client arrived promptly at the studio, and Bluhdorn was ebullient about meeting Lemmon, shaking his hand fervently, assuring him he was his favorite actor. The William Morris agent, a genial six-footer (an exception among the mostly short and stubby functionaries of that company), thanked Bluhdorn and said that he and his client were delighted to meet with the Paramount contingent over such an important project. "*The Odd Couple* is a great play," said Hirshan, "and my client is perfect for the role."

Jack Lemmon smiled uneasily, not knowing quite what he was supposed to say in this meeting. His agent had urged him to be there to underscore his passion for the show. From what he had heard about Bluhdorn, Hirshan knew there was a deal to be made and that the star's presence would impress the Paramount newcomer.

Bluhdorn got quickly to the point. "We all love Jack Lemmon," the chairman declared. "But what's his deal on this picture?"

Evans winced at Bluhdorn's impetuous question. It was an unwritten rule, they knew, not to discuss deals in front of "talent."

Neither Hirshan nor Lemmon seemed offended, however.

"Jack's deal is $1 million against 10 percent of the gross," Hirshan announced calmly, as though he were giving out a telephone number.

Again, Evans sucked in his breath. This was a very rich deal, and he wanted time to find out what Lemmon had received on his previous pictures, then construct a counteroffer, but Bluhdorn had no interest in a delay. "You've got a deal," he announced, placing his hand on Hirshan's shoulder.

Lemmon beamed, but there was more on Hirshan's agenda. "I think you all should understand that Walter Matthau is perfect for the role opposite Lemmon, and his price is $350,000 against 10 percent of the net," he said.

"I'm not giving Matthau any fucking points," Bluhdorn snapped.

"We need a moment," Evans broke in, grabbing Bluhdorn's arm and guiding him to the bedroom of his suite. "We've listened to their proposals," said Evans. "Now let's take a breath and come back to them with our counter. This is a very rich deal."

Bluhdorn's nostrils were flaring, however. He was a dealmaker by instinct, and there was a headline-grabbing deal to be made, with a star standing by to see it through.

"We've got to close this deal," he said. "And then we need to sign a director. Billy Wilder, maybe."

Bursting back into the room, Bluhdorn tossed out his suggestion about Wilder. Hirshan responded that he didn't represent the great filmmaker, but promised to do some investigating about interest and availability.

Thrilled, Bluhdorn clasped Lemmon and then extended his hand to Hirshan.

"You did good work here," Bluhdorn told Hirshan. "I want you to become my head of production in London." The William Morris agent stared down at Bluhdorn, startled. He did not reply. "Didn't you hear me?" Bluhdorn persisted. "London, production chief."

Hirshan saw Evans staring across the room at him, trying to figure out what his boss was offering. "I am a talent agent," Hirshan calmly explained to Bluhdorn. "That's what I'm good at. I intend to stay a talent agent."

"Think about my offer," the chairman persisted. "We'll talk more. Meanwhile let's get this movie going."

Hirshan nodded. "I'll work out the details with Bernie Donnenfeld," he said, referring to Paramount's chief of business affairs.

"You'll speak only with me. I make the deals," Bluhdorn replied sharply.

Later in the week, Hirshan saw Bluhdorn again to inform him that Billy Wilder wanted $1 million to direct *The Odd Couple*. When Bluhdorn became apoplectic at the price, Hirshan quickly changed the subject, advancing the name of his client Gene Saks, a stage director who he said would be acceptable to his other clients, Lemmon and Matthau.

One catch was that Bluhdorn wanted *The Odd Couple* to go into production in March and there was no screenplay. Further, Saks had committed to direct a play in London scheduled for June.

These seemed like serious obstacles to Evans, but not to Bluhdorn. Under prodding, Neil Simon agreed to adapt his play and prepare a script in eight weeks—for an incremental payment. And Saks agreed to compress his shooting schedule to free him for his London show.

Within one week, *The Odd Couple* had become a reality, but the details of the deal defied precedent. When Evans related the events to me, he was exasperated. "Bluhdorn's so hungry to be a player that he gave away the store," Evans said.

I tried to assuage his fears. "Lemmon's probably worth a million," I said. "And we need a comedy."

"It's not just the numbers," Evans said. "Gene Saks is going to rush the shoot to do his cockamamie play in London, and he can walk off the movie if he runs behind schedule. Besides, the agents in this town are going to laugh at us. We've just committed to a pay-or-play deal with two stars and a director and we don't even have a script."

"Who would finish the movie? And who edits it?" I put in.

"Welcome to Bluhdorn's Hollywood," Evans said.

The Odd Couple was completed on schedule, and Howard W. Koch, the producer, supervised the editing. The movie went on to become a major hit. And neither Bluhdorn nor anyone else ever brought up the topic of Leonard Hirshan becoming Paramount's head of production in London. Indeed, Hirshan was to remain at the William Morris office for three more decades before departing the agency to become Clint Eastwood's manager.

It didn't take me long after arriving at Paramount to realize that, while Charles Bluhdorn had a genius for trading, he had a blind spot when it came to judging people. Bluhdorn's personality was so dominant, his presence so overwhelming, that he all but suffocated those in his company. When Bluhdorn interviewed a prospective executive, he usually did all the talking. He would pose a thoughtful question, but then deliver his own answer.

Given these traits, Bluhdorn was incapable of assembling a management staff that could implement his strategic objectives and compensate for his own shortcomings. If anything, his executives exacerbated his problems rather than tempering them.

Bluhdorn's management issues were evident across his empire, but they were especially blatant at the film studio.

If Bluhdorn had set out to find an array of executives who were unfit to work together, he could not have done a better job. Members of the team didn't complement one another and didn't trust one another.

There were several common denominators in the Bluhdorn picks. None of the executives he hired had ever performed the responsibilities to which they were now assigned. None had the appropriate qualifications. Educational background did not figure in; most had never progressed beyond high school.

All were impulsive hires. They were at the right place at the right time. And they were recruited by a man who prided himself on taking chances.

Stanley Jaffe was a mere twenty-eight years old and had just finished producing his first feature film, *Goodbye, Columbus*, when Bluhdorn anointed him president of Paramount. His closest claim to executive experience stemmed from the fact that his father, Leo, had served as president of Columbia Pictures. Leo Jaffe was a short, soft-spoken accountant, whose rise to corporate power surprised others in the industry, including himself. His son, Stanley, was well read and thoughtful but, unlike his father, had a trigger temper.

Stanley had come of age in the sixties but was definitely not a sixties person. He was the product of an affluent and conservative Jewish background. A family man, he did not smoke pot or favor rock 'n' roll and did not sport long hair— in fact, he had almost no hair at all. His taste in movies was somewhat literary—thus he chose a Philip Roth novella, *Goodbye, Columbus*, as his first film project.

I had been the first at the studio to read the screenplay, written by Arnold Schulman, and got to know Jaffe pretty well

as he toiled on the picture. He was serious about his responsibilities, but was not either charismatic or imaginative. Indeed,
I found his personality rather rigid. He rarely smiled. The give-
and-take of a film set seemed to intimidate, not inspire him.
Bob Evans liked dealing with Stanley, as did I, but no special
personal link emerged. Evans was pleased, if surprised, when
Bluhdorn named him president. At least Jaffe was someone he
could deal with on a rational level. Or so it seemed.

Jaffe did not particularly like Martin Davis, who now held
the title of president of the parent company and was almost
always hovering at Bluhdorn's side. Davis was a gruff, flinty-
eyed man who always seemed to be muttering one-sentence
admonitions in his boss's ear. When Bluhdorn went on one of
his rants, leaving a roomful of executives in confusion or even
tears, Davis would try to clean up the mess, but his idea of
diplomacy was itself edgy and harsh. Davis did not approve of
most of the executives his boss was appointing and made no
effort to conceal his attitude. Once, when I told Bluhdorn that
I disagreed with one of his decrees, Davis murmured to me,
"Charlie never considered you management material."

While Davis now stood between Jaffe and Bluhdorn, it
quickly became apparent that Bluhdorn did not want Davis's
input when it came to movies. Bluhdorn looked to Jaffe to run
Paramount and to his sharp young general sales manager,
Frank Yablans, to move the goods. If Jaffe could keep Evans
and Bart under control, he reasoned, Yablans, a fiercely ambitious thirty-two-year-old, could run the distribution and marketing machine.

A bald, short, bullet of a man, Yablans knew how to ma-
nipulate exhibitors and stoke their appetites. Yablans also understood that the movie business was unique in that every new
film represented a start-up business—one that demanded its
own distribution and marketing.

Yablans had cultivated his reputation for corporate fe-rocity. Growing up poor in Brooklyn, his first job, at age twelve, was plucking chickens at a meat market. Rivals in the distribution business enjoyed relating the story of how Yablans had once called a theater owner in Washington, DC, who had just been released from intensive care following a heart attack and yelled expletives at him because he'd been selling tickets to a Paramount movie at a two-dollar discount.

Jaffe, refined and introverted, did not like Yablans's style. The sales manager liked to boast that he'd saved Paramount by demanding big advances for Bluhdorn's bombs like *Paint Your Wagon* and *Darling Lili*. He'd created "event pictures" out of films that were singular nonevents. In so doing, Yablans kept rising in the distribution pecking order. As sales manager, he'd integrated the clashing advertising and distribution struc-tures into a strong marketing unit and fired road-weary exec-utives who had formerly ruled those divisions.

While Jaffe understood Yablans's ambition, and distrusted his motives, he never considered Yablans a threat to become his replacement. Yablans didn't have the politesse to be pres-ident of a public company. Or so he thought.

For his part, Yablans did not feel Evans had the tact or dis-cipline to run a Hollywood studio, but he knew Charlie Bluh-dorn admired his style. Yablans was unattractive and arch, and whereas Bluhdorn addressed Yablans crudely, as though he were a waiter in a restaurant, he treated Evans like a naughty son. To Yablans, Evans was a snobbish rich kid whose tastes were too elitist for a business that fed off the pop culture.

In Bluhdorn's eyes, the team of Evans, Bart, Yablans, and Jaffe, though an odd mix of personalities, had the potential to pull Paramount out of its malaise. He knew his own instincts in picking movies were problematic, but now there would be a new plan, and his team was in place to implement it.

Jaffe was intensely nervous as he assumed his new presidential duties. Attired in a dark pinstripe suit, he greeted his staff with a cautious, respectful speech. This would be a new moment for Paramount. Better times were ahead.

But not immediately. On the fourth day at his new job, Bluhdorn summoned Jaffe to a screening of a first cut of *The Adventurers*, an adaptation of a Harold Robbins potboiler. The movie was both expensive and long (three hours). Bluhdorn had committed to the movie soon after buying the studio—who could resist a Robbins bestseller? he argued.

When the screening ended, the chairman faced his audience of twelve and demanded their opinions. First in line was his driver, an elegant and reserved black man named Owen. He said he loved the movie, then went quiet. Bluhdorn next called on the heads of advertising and foreign distribution, both of whom confirmed Owen's positive assessment.

It was now Jaffe's turn. This was his first week but already his moment of truth. Jaffe responded in a quiet and quavering voice: "The movie is terrible. It is un-releasable."

The chairman didn't blink. He continued around the room and all the other responses were positive. Jaffe anticipated a screaming denunciation behind closed doors, but none was forthcoming. The atmosphere was tense but restrained.

Upon its release, *The Adventurers* was uniformly panned by critics. One columnist wrote that "Bluhdorn's bombs" were still in evidence. Filmgoers stayed away in droves.

When Jaffe first visited us in Hollywood, he requested time for a leisurely "think session." He still seemed a bit shaken by his experience with *The Adventurers*. "I love Charlie," Jaffe told me. "He's a catalyst. But he can also be a catalyst for chaos."

Bluhdorn may not be able to fully restrain his dealmaking impulses, Jaffe said, but in any case our mandate was clear. Paramount should aim high. The studio must make quality movies. We should go after the big stories, not the big deal or the big name. We should make "people pictures."

The meeting ended on a positive note. Here we were, three young guys, somewhat miscast for our new roles, both excited and daunted by the power that had been put in our hands. Problems and pitfalls loomed all around us, but still the moment was ours.

The first potential movie from our new team already showed promise, at least on paper, and it was a project we all seemed to agree on. Stanley Jaffe's first movie, *Goodbye, Columbus*, had starred a young actress named Ali MacGraw, and she now was interested in a screenplay titled *Love Story*. Also circling it was Larry Peerce, who had directed *Goodbye, Columbus* and who was friendly with Jaffe.

I liked *Love Story*, despite its blatant sentimentality—or maybe because of it. In a sense it represented the culmination of our earlier discussion: it was a "people picture," eminently accessible to ordinary filmgoers.

It was hardly a reflection of a new cinematic sensibility, but for a new regime, indeed for a "new" company, it was a safe bet. Even its title seemed right—on-the-nose, but oddly appealing.

Love Story would be our big shot. But first, there would be some serious road hazards for the new team to survive.

CHAPTER 3

The Salon

It was a salon, albeit an idiosyncratic one. Bob Evans presided over it with baronial panache. Even though the estate was modest in size, it reflected, in his mind, an aura of grandeur and elegance. Evans worshipped the traditions of Old Hollywood, and his French Regency home was positioned within walking distance of the residences of movie stars of old like Jimmy Stewart and Fred Astaire, north of Sunset Boulevard in Beverly Hills. A loan from Paramount helped Evans acquire the spread for some $290,000 from James Pendleton, an elderly decorator, and he quickly set about to embellish the structure and grounds—it would turn out to be a $500,000 renovation. Evans liked the stately elegance of the main house and hired craftsmen to enhance its features. The small living room exuded a paneled formality. A dining room seated twelve. There were only two bedrooms, but adjoining the master bedroom was a dressing room of equal size. The requisite hot tub, enclosed by tall hedges, adjoined the master suite. Stand-alone structures containing an office suite and two guest bedrooms huddled at the south end of the grounds, all but hidden beneath the tall eucalyptus trees.

Though he greatly admired the property, Evans felt it had been ill-planned. His first stroke was to close the main entrance on traffic-heavy Beverly Drive, building a gated entrance off secluded Woodland Drive at his eastern boundary. This meant that visitors would drive along the full length of the grounds before pulling into a circular driveway at the front of the house. Along the way, they would journey past a tennis court, a screening room (also built with studio subsidy), and a swimming pool and lawn before finally arriving at the newly installed driveway. Hence, guests felt they were arriving at a vast estate rather than facing the usual facade of a garage tucked in behind the house.

Evans was in love with his circular driveway. At its center he installed a graceful fountain, with water spewing onto a large and regal copper cock. It was as though the cock announced the mood of the estate.

From the outset, Evans's manor conveyed mixed messages, and that was the way he liked it. Though most of his visitors were youthful, the house itself bespoke formality. A butler in suit-and-tie greeted visitors, and the staff of housekeepers were attired as in British upper-class tradition. The screening room, too, reflected disdain for the aggressively contemporary look of other Hollywood home theaters. Again, Evans's instinct was to emulate Old Hollywood rather than cater to the hippie impulses of the moment.

Once the house became operational, its mood fluctuated radically from one moment to the next. Filmmakers and dealmakers were ushered into the screening room, where they would sit around the elegant card table, re-arraying themselves on the theater seats to screen film tests. If Evans was courting a star—a Jack Nicholson or a Mia Farrow—these encounters would take place at his main house rather than his studio office, which was a mere twenty minutes away.

By early evening, the mood would shift. Tennis players might drop by the screening room or sip drinks at poolside. Young women would arrive to welcome guests. Evans would be on full alert greeting visitors, yet also fielding the unceasing blizzard of phone calls. The house would be at once all business yet all play.

During the occasional formal dinner parties, the guest list would encompass a mix of stars and power players, plus visiting royalty—a member of the Agnelli family or even a sheikh from the Middle East. Almost every evening would conclude with a screening, with regular attendees such as the agent Sue Mengers or Warren Beatty.

As the evening progressed, the mood and subtext of Evans's salon subtly changed. The phones stopped ringing, the dealmaking ended. The salon would now become a playpen.

The girls kept arriving. They were young and beautiful—aspiring actresses, party girls looking to hook up with a rich guy or movie star.

The ground rules were clear. In this particular playpen, everyone was expected to be on his or her best behavior. There was to be no overt hustling and no drugs were to be in evidence, except for an occasional joint. A girl might end the night with Jack Nicholson, Ted Kennedy, or Alain Delon. Often, one of the bedrooms at the south wing of the house might serve as a way station.

Evans himself liked to watch over the proceedings, always amused by the unfolding melodramas. If he witnessed what he felt was bad behavior, his intervention was prompt. He sharply rebuked his attorney, Greg Bautzer, when he saw him slapping around an actress, and told him to leave. A handsome, hard-drinking man, Bautzer never returned.

While Evans reveled in his role as the grand host, he was sensitive about the community's perception. When he learned that Freddie Fields, a top agent, had labeled him "the prince of all pimps," he was genuinely offended. To him, beautiful women were a sort of treasured resource to be cultivated and traded, and the act of introducing them to the rich and famous was an act of graciousness, not of commerce. After all, the girls were willing participants in the roundelay. They were ambitious and they knew what they were getting into.

Before his marriage to Ali MacGraw, Evans indulged his fantasies with energy and finesse. Usually his girls would stay the night. In admiring their beauty, he would often take photographs of the girls in uninhibited poses. On occasion, his friend Helmut Newton, the renowned German photographer, would shoot one of his favored beauties, always in the nude, always smiling.

Evans zealously collected these photos along with other remembrances. One of his prize possessions was a small porcelain jar containing samples of pubic hair from his favored partners. On rare occasions he would display his "pussy pot" to fellow players, like Warren Beatty or Jack Nicholson.

As a connoisseur of sex, Evans felt a sense of accomplishment in enhancing Henry Kissinger's range of acquaintances and those of other repressed friends. Evans also felt a kinship with other connoisseurs, like Beatty, but also a certain competitiveness. At the end of one production meeting, Evans and Beatty decided to compare their mastery at summoning up phone numbers. "276-8451," Evans would say, to which Beatty would respond, "Janice." Beatty would then say

"472-9867," to which Evans would say, "Melanie." The exchange of phone numbers continued for three or four minutes with neither combatant stumbling, until Evans finally drew a blank. "I made that one up," Beatty confessed with a grin.

Evans took pride in his salon, and he became resentful if he felt either his home or his services were being taken for granted. He grumbled to me on one occasion when Bluhdorn commandeered his screening room for a high-level corporate meeting to which Evans was not invited. Similarly Evans was infuriated when one of the girls provided for Bluhdorn was hospitalized after a prolonged evening of sexual activities with the chairman. "He's a savage," Evans snorted.

Evans was all the more disdainful of Bluhdorn's vulgarity because Evans had lifted himself from the rough-and-tumble of the "schmatta business." In dealing with Hollywood's brand of thugs, Evans felt he had graduated to a different social class. He was a studio chief, and like Irving Thalberg, the icon he had once portrayed, he was a gentleman studio chief. As such, Evans dressed impeccably in custom-made shirts and suits and usually wore a tie to work.

The tennis scene, too, was an important element in the Evans landscape, the games cast as carefully as his movies. Champions like Pancho Gonzales or Jimmy Connors would be on hand to boost the egos of celebrity players like Ted Kennedy or his brother Bobby. The drinks flowed and a movie would follow. To Evans, tennis was a mind game; his backhand was weak but his strategy astute. He would suddenly bet an opposing doubles team $1,000 a point, and then start lobbing balls to throw off their concentration. Evans usually lost money, but his guests relished the contests.

At its zenith, in 1969 to 1971, Evans's salon was the hottest scene in town. The turnout of guests was dazzling, the deal-making was incessant, and the undertone of sexual adventure was pervasive. Like the studio itself, it seemed a wonderland of limitless possibility. Everyone who happened by understood both its excitement and its evanescence.

Its moment would quickly pass.

CHAPTER 4

The Boss's Bombs

When Charles Bluhdorn stormed into London shortly after acquiring Paramount, one of the first producers who courted him was a shrewd young Brit named Michael Deeley. A business partner of the actor Stanley Baker, Deeley had heard from an agent friend that Bluhdorn had an avid appetite for deals, and the aptly named Deeley had an expertise in formulating them. Deeley was experiencing modest success with a low-budget film called *Robbery*, which Stanley Baker starred in, and hence thought it a good idea to pitch Bluhdorn on other projects that would offer low financial exposure.

No sooner had Deeley launched his presentation but Bluhdorn cut him off. Projects of this sort were of no interest to him, Bluhdorn barked, his hand gesturing dismissively. Bluhdorn had just completed a study of the film business which, he said, had demonstrated clearly that big-budget movies outgrossed low-budget ones throughout the history of the movie business. "You spend the most, you make the most," ranted the Gulf & Western chairman. "Research proves it, but Hollywood doesn't get the message. I'm going to run Paramount like a business," he said.

Deeley went away a bit intimidated. His own experience in the British film industry, limited though it was, had seemed to prove the opposite of Bluhdorn's theory. Respected filmmakers including Tony Richardson, Karel Reisz, and Lindsay Anderson had recently formed a company called Woodfall and had started to do well with movies like *Saturday Night and Sunday Morning*, *Look Back in Anger*, and even *Tom Jones* (the latter became a hit on a budget of only $1.2 million), but Bluhdorn discarded all this as a local British phenomenon.

He was intent on demonstrating the validity of his own theories on a worldwide stage.

In the coming months, Bluhdorn put his ideas into action as Deeley, along with many others in the industry, watched with a mixture of envy and astonishment. A lavish musical called *Paint Your Wagon* was launched by Paramount, starring Clint Eastwood and Lee Marvin. Yet another semimusical, *Darling Lili*, starring Julie Andrews and set against the background of World War I, was also given the green light. Sean Connery and Richard Harris got the go-ahead to make an expensive film called *The Molly Maguires*, which focused on a union dispute in the coal mines of Pennsylvania.

Deeley was impressed. Big bucks were being spent, as Bluhdorn had promised. But Deeley was nonetheless skeptical about the results. The subjects, he felt, seemed hopelessly old-fashioned and anachronistic. Yet, if Bluhdorn wanted and favored this sort of material, he and Stanley Baker owned a musty script called *Where's Jack?*, which might pass the Bluhdorn test.

Deeley, Baker, and his agent, Martin Baum, marched on Bluhdorn's office in New York to make their pitch. The chairman was impressed, as always, to meet a movie star. Baum, the high-powered agent, told Bluhdorn that *Where's Jack?* would be a "can't miss"—its director, James Clavell, had just completed a modest hit called *To Sir with Love*; its coproducers, Deeley and Baker, had just finished *Zulu*, also a success; and its star would be Tommy Steele.

The mention of Steele would have brought most Hollywood meetings to a close. A young musical star in London, Steele was very much a local celeb—and his appeal was very British. His newest movie, *Half a Sixpence*, was about to be released amid negative advance reports, but Bluhdorn was in a dealmaking mood, and he gave an exuberant "yes" to the pitch.

Martin Davis, Bluhdorn's number two, had sat in on the presentation, and he looked unhappy. Moving to his boss's desk, Davis said, "Charlie, we'd agreed not to commit to a deal until we'd read the script."

"I've read it mentally," Bluhdorn replied. "Goddamn it, Marty, it will be a smash. Now get out of here."

Deeley and Baker exchanged a befuddled glance. They'd managed to make a Paramount deal even without a star like Julie Andrews. Indeed, the only element of Bluhdorn's favored formula they could meet was the budget: the two Brits knew that *Where's Jack?* would cost far more than the typical British movie, and, indeed, far more than it deserved.

Even as *Where's Jack?* rolled into production, Deeley did a Bluhdorn runaround by quietly submitting a project to me called *The Italian Job*. Unlike *Where's Jack?*, this film had a very hip script, a tight budget, and starred a young actor who, unlike Tommy Steele, had true breakout potential. His name was Michael Caine. Neither Deeley nor I let Bluhdorn know about *The Italian Job* until it was well into preproduction. By that time, the reviews of *Where's Jack?* deemed it disastrous, and Bluhdorn's theory about megafilms already was proving self-destructive.

In retrospect, Bluhdorn's "research" on movie financing had a germ of validity. It presaged the blockbuster mentality that began to overtake Hollywood in the 1980s, when films like *Jaws* and *Star Wars* opened up a whole new audience to buy not only theater tickets but also videos of favorite films. By the year 2000, the studios were reserving a major portion of their development budgets for so-called tent-pole or franchise films—mostly sequels or prequels, many based on comic book characters or video games.

But to Bluhdorn, films like the Batman series or Steven Spielberg's science-fiction projects were far beyond his field of vision. A European by birth and an outsider by instinct, the chairman of Gulf & Western was a sucker for Hollywood glitz. To him, Hollywood musicals were box office gold, even though the studio that invented them, MGM, had effectively gone out of business by the time Bluhdorn bought Paramount. Having spent his years with businessmen who knew about automobile bumpers or zinc mining, he was hungry now to surround himself with the glamour that Hollywood represented to him.

Bob Evans did not share this obsession. As much as he himself reveled in the legends of Old Hollywood, Evans believed that musicals now represented an expensive anachronism. The mood of the audience was shifting, and while no one was smart enough to predict the direction of this shift, this was not a moment to try to re-create the past.

Four months after moving into his new job, however, Evans got a tip from an old friend, an agent named Charlie Feldman. Columbia Pictures was having trouble securing the financing for *Funny Girl*, a filmed version of the runaway Broadway hit. Its producer, the mercurial Ray Stark, had a brief window of time in which he could take the project to another studio. "This is your chance to steal a hot project," Feldman advised. Evans immediately snapped to attention: Securing

Funny Girl would give Bluhdorn the musical that he craved; at the same time, *Funny Girl*'s brash young star, Barbra Streisand, was the celebrity of the moment. Young audiences would respond to her.

Several problems confronted him, however. First, Evans would have to elicit Bluhdorn's green light, and there was only a forty-eight-hour window during which the project could be wrested from Columbia.

The other problem was Ray Stark, the producer who had discovered Streisand and was locked into *Funny Girl*. Charlie Bluhdorn felt Stark had suckered him into financing the disastrous venture *Is Paris Burning?* Hollywood had laughed at him for impulsively funding a movie no one else wanted. Stark had exploited Charlie's virginity in the film world.

Evans knew he had to play his hand carefully with his boss, to choose the right moment, stressing the musical angle first then sliding into the Stark problem. On a project of this size, he would need not only Bluhdorn's acquiescence but also his enthusiasm.

"Charlie takes a bath every Sunday afternoon—that's the only time he turns off the phones," Evans told me. "I have got to nail him just before his bath so he can think about it in a relaxed setting."

"Or maybe he'll drown himself," I put in.

I was present at Evans's house that Sunday as he placed his call. He talked for several minutes, spelling out the various elements. When he put down the receiver, he drew a deep breath.

"OK, I think it went well," Evans told me. "Charlie was talking in his Sunday voice. He wasn't yelling. I think he will go for it. He said he wanted the afternoon to think it over."

What neither of us knew was that Bluhdorn decided to forgo his ritual bath that afternoon. Having been criticized for acting hastily on *Is Paris Burning?*, the chairman opted to do some crash homework. One by one, he started phoning Paramount offices around the world—subdistributors and marketing specialists—soliciting their opinions on a Streisand musical. The "troops" were startled to hear from him.

Later that evening, Bluhdorn called Evans back with the upshot of his impromptu survey. "They don't like her," Bluhdorn announced. "They don't like her in London or Johannesburg or Hong Kong or Rio. Maybe with Shirley MacLaine, they would like *Funny Girl*, but not with the Jewess."

The word "Jewess" did not resonate pleasantly with Evans, especially given Bluhdorn's guttural German accent, but he was not going to get drawn into a fight over ethnicity. A bigger principle was at stake. Paramount's distributors, he felt, had hardly distinguished themselves in selling the studio's pictures around the world. Would they now be given a veto over future movies?

The argument raged for roughly twenty minutes over the telephone before Bluhdorn angrily brought it to a close. "You've been in your job for four months, not four years," he shouted. "I'm not going to go against the advice of all my distributors. They don't want a Streisand movie and that's the end of it."

Evans understood that he had lost that battle, but what he could not know was the ultimate price the studio would pay. Ray Stark would soon manage to put his financing back together and get his musical into production at Columbia, where it would become a major hit. Its success left Bluhdorn feeling frustrated and out-maneuvered. He had lost his chance for a hit musical, but that only re-doubled his determination. "The audience wants musicals," he reiterated to me during one of his visits to the studio. "I know what the audience wants."

Determined to sign a musical star who was bigger than Streisand, Bluhdorn was an easy target when a well-known filmmaker named Blake Edwards flew to New York to pitch his movie titled *Darling Lili*. It was a romantic comedy set during the Great War, and Edwards admitted the screenplay was still a work-in-progress. But his wife, Julie Andrews, would star in it, several songs would be added, and it would, he promised, become a worldwide hit.

What Edwards chose not to mention was that the script had already been seen by several studios, including ours. To my taste, the script was neither funny nor romantic. I didn't get it and had told Edwards's agent my opinion.

Then there was also the matter of the budget. A final estimate, Edwards said, would await completion of a rewrite and the addition of the songs. Ireland would be an ideal location—its prices were reasonable and it was far removed from distractions, he added.

When Charlie Bluhdorn laid out the project to Evans and me he did so in near ecstatic terms, and was visibly exasperated by our cool response. To him, the equation for success was self-evident. Julie Andrews meant *Mary Poppins* and *The Sound of Music*. Blake Edwards was the man who gave us *Breakfast at Tiffany's*. And Edwards and Julie had recently been married; this movie represented their first time working together. It was a sort of wedding present to his wife. How could it go wrong?

Much later, Charlie Bluhdorn gave me a more personal insight as to why he was drawn to *Darling Lili*. "Yvette told me her big ambition was to have dinner with Julie Andrews," he confided. Bluhdorn's rather stately and steely French-born wife, Yvette, was not a movie buff and normally kept her distance from her husband's frenzied business activities, but she venerated Andrews's work on the stage. To both Bluhdorns, Julie Andrews represented the ultimate superstar, and Yvette's demands would have to be honored.

As things turned out, Paramount's flirtation with Julie

Andrews and her husband would turn out to be a costly one. And Yvette never even got to have dinner with Julie. Almost immediately after getting into business together, Charlie Bluhdorn and Blake Edwards were at each other's throat.

As I traveled between Paramount's New York and Hollywood offices during the weeks when *Darling Lili* was coming together, I felt that I was working for two completely different companies. Bluhdorn had mesmerized the troops in New York into believing that the studio had finally found a superstar vehicle that would bring revenues and celebrity to the company. The marketing and distribution teams had apparently bought into it.

The attitude toward *Darling Lili* at the studio was the mirror opposite. "Evans won't even listen when I raise the subject of cost. He walks out of the room. And the room is his own office," complained Jack Ballard, who had recently become Paramount's head of physical production.

As Ballard started reeling off his list of "hot buttons" on the project, I sensed that this tough, dome-headed production executive was close to desperation. This was a movie with complex song-and-dance numbers that would be staged on location in Europe. There would also be aerial dogfights featuring vintage aircraft. And it all would take place during World War I, which meant period wardrobe for vast numbers of extras.

And if shooting began to lag, what controls could the studio exercise? With a husband directing his wife, the studio would have no points of leverage, Ballard pointed out. And the couple had even chosen their own producer—another relative—so there would be no ranking studio representative on the picture.

When Edwards's team finally submitted a budget, it totaled a mere $12 million, well below studio estimates, Ballard said. (In point of fact, the final budget would total three times Edwards's estimate.)

I understood Ballard's anxiety. No matter what warnings he would send forth, he'd still take the heat when the cost overruns starting coming in. If *Darling Lili* became a mess, it would ultimately be Ballard's mess. Those were the studio ground rules—he understood them all too well.

While I empathized with Ballard's panic, my problems with *Darling Lili* went beyond its production issues. Even when I described the story to my staff, I had trouble keeping a straight face.

Julie Andrews would play a German spy whose assigned mission was to seduce an American squadron commander. And the perfect actor for this role, Edwards had decided, was none other than Rock Hudson.

I found myself gasping over his casting epiphany. Where was the chemistry? Julie Andrews had been superbly effective as a governess in *Mary Poppins*, but her on-screen efforts at romance had never clicked. As an accomplished stage actress, she always seemed to keep a distance between her and the audience.

As for Rock Hudson, there were suspicions about his sexuality even in the late sixties. He never denied that he was gay, but he also went along with the official studio propaganda that he was dating various young actresses. I once found myself sitting next to him on a Pacific Southwest Airlines flight to San Francisco, and he cheerfully confided that he was going to "the baths." At the time, I wasn't even sure what "the baths" connoted. But, again, while Hudson was a friendly and scrupulously polite man, his "sex scenes" on camera registered zero on the passion index.

Within the first two weeks of principal photography, the predictable production problems began to loom. Edwards and Andrews arrived in Paris to shoot an elaborate scene at a railway station only to discover the city ablaze in rioting. Paris, like many U.S. cities, was caught up in sixties antiwar insurrection. The company quietly shifted to Brussels, where the scenes were shot at double the cost.

The next move was supposed to be to Ireland, but because of a production mix-up, no accommodations for director and star had been prearranged. Edwards's producer charged that the Paramount production team was getting in their way. The Paramount folks responded that no one was running the show on Edwards's side. Edwards himself was technically the producer, but his uncle, a gentle white-maned man named Owen Crump, was supposed to fulfill these duties. He in turn looked to a neophyte thirty-year-old associate producer named Ken Wales to hammer out the production details.

Wales knew he owed his career to his boss, Edwards, a man with expensive tastes. Panicked that no accommodations had been negotiated, he leased a thousand-acre estate that had long been the residence of one of Ireland's wealthiest families. The sumptuous mansion was so vast it had a pipe organ in its grand salon.

When Julie Andrews saw it, she was ecstatic. There were even horses available for her to ride over the vast rolling acreage, and there were myriad rooms for guests.

Though the accommodations were felicitous, production delays continued to mount. A small theater in Dublin had been booked for the dance numbers, but its stage was too small to hold Edwards's grand numbers. The initial scenes of an aerial dogfight went well, but suddenly the sun came out, the clouds disappeared, and Edwards and his cameraman, Russell Harlan, were cursing that they were stuck with a placid Southern California sky that didn't match the first setups.

Then there was the inevitable Julie-and-Rock problem. The script called for an avid Julie Andrews to arouse passion in the stolid, dedicated American squadron leader, but, despite repeated takes and varied camera angles, the relationship between the two performers remained tepid.

Bob Evans was so irritated by the movie that after the first couple of days he abjured the ritual of dailies completely, and the rest of the executive staff followed suit. One day Jack Ballard joined me in the screening room, and he burst out laughing in the midst of a love scene. "I may never make love again," Ballard blurted.

I found myself in Evans's office later that day and, while I knew he hated *Darling Lili* stories, I could not restrain myself. "I was at a party last night when naked people were spilling out of the hot tub," I said. "Everyone in this town seems to be fucking everyone else, and we're making maybe the unsexiest movie in the history of Hollywood."

"Rock's a faggot," Evans snapped. "What idiot would sign a faggot to shoot love scenes?"

The other individual in our company who was not watching dailies was Charlie Bluhdorn, but he had been briefed about the production delays, and his famous temper was steadily rising. Two or three times a day he would call Evans or Ballard to vent his frustration. "If you think you can control Blake Edwards, why don't you go see him in person?" Evans finally demanded one day. He knew Bluhdorn hated confronting artists; but one morning Evans got a call from his boss in mid-flight, headed for Rome. On impulse Bluhdorn had diverted to Ireland. The time had come for a confrontation.

When Ken Wales got the call, he all but dropped the phone. This would be the worst possible moment for a Bluhdorn visit. Edwards had shot almost nothing for four days waiting for the clouds to return. The crew was playing soccer on the front lawn. Edwards's daughter had broken her collarbone after falling from a horse, and Edwards was spending time with her while Julie was riding in the countryside with friends.

Wales phoned me in panic. "You've got to call him off," he burbled, referring to Bluhdorn. "This would be a disastrous time."

"He'll be landing in a couple of hours," I told Wales. "It's out of my hands."

"Then fly over yourself," he urged. "Maybe if you were here . . ."

I'd actually been planning a visit to the set in Ireland. I knew Bluhdorn's visit would last only a few hours, but perhaps if I were on hand the following day I could comfort the survivors.

It was midafternoon when Charlie Bluhdorn arrived on the set of *Darling Lili* outside Dublin. He saw the crew kicking around a soccer ball. He saw the cameras standing idle. He saw no sign of his director—indeed no one was at hand except a stumbling Wales, trying to make excuses.

Sensing a major confrontation, Bluhdorn phoned his assistant in New York, instructing her to book a suite at the best hotel in Dublin she could find. She came back on the line to report that *Darling Lili* had booked every room and, further, that Rock Hudson had reserved the grand ballroom that evening for a major party.

Bluhdorn jumped back into his limousine and demanded to be taken to the Blake-and-Julie estate. When he approached the baronial spread, his anger became a full-fledged tantrum. Emerging from his limo, Bluhdorn encountered Owen Crump, and he didn't stop to shake hands. "Why the fuck is everyone standing around?" he roared. "Why are you living in the fanciest castle in Ireland when you are causing my company to go BROKE?"

His tirade went on for fifteen minutes and continued as

Blake Edwards joined them. There were no questions asked. Bluhdorn was not interested in hearing any apologies or explanations. His message was clear and bellicose: start shooting some scenes or the movie gets shut down.

When I arrived on the set a day later, Edwards and his wife were shuttered in their mansion. Crump and Wales were still in shock, seeking sympathy and reassurance, neither of which I could offer them.

"Bluhdorn can't fire Blake—Julie would walk," Crump said. "And he can't shut down the movie because too many millions have already been spent."

The two men were not being defiant, I realized, but merely helpless. They were employees of a star director and his superstar wife. Bluhdorn might now be outraged at his impotence, but he had approved a deal in which the studio had no controls. My sympathy was more with them than with Bluhdorn.

We had a very alcoholic dinner together. Toward the end, Edwards himself materialized, looking pale and agonized, and started explaining his dilemma. "I've got a movie here that I don't know how to shoot," he said. "The goddamn sky—it doesn't match. I could move the company to South Africa. The clouds are great there and dependable."

"That's a big move . . ." Wales offered meekly.

"We never intended to spend the rest of our life in Ireland," Edwards said.

When I next encountered Charlie Bluhdorn in New York, he seemed uncharacteristically subdued. He'd taken a beating from his board of directors. Gulf & Western shares were foundering, but there were ways of "finessing" the *Darling Lili* numbers, Bluhdorn assured me. He did not go into details. It was only a couple of years later that I learned of Bluhdorn's scheme of shifting the rights—and hence the losses—from

Gulf & Western to phantom companies. Suddenly they were not Paramount mistakes; they were the problems of another corporate entity entirely.

These were dangerous financial maneuvers, and Bluhdorn knew it, but he was desperate to save his Paramount investment not only from the fiasco of *Darling Lili* but also from the looming nightmare presented by his other would-be blockbuster, *Paint Your Wagon*.

Even as editing teams were still struggling to cut *Lili* into a coherent movie, yet another Paramount mammoth musical—one I had known virtually nothing about—was being unveiled to bewildered audiences on October 15, 1969. *Paint Your Wagon* had been an early Bluhdorn pet project—one he had been protecting like a mother hen. I had seen its title on the production sheets, but knew little about it.

All I did know was that its timing could not have been more disturbing.

Across town, Twentieth Century-Fox had just capsized because of its own musical calamities, thus abruptly ending the rule of the Zanuck dynasty at that studio. A close friend of Evans, Dick Zanuck, had inherited the studio from his fabled father, Darryl, and had turned out a series of worthy films such as *Butch Cassidy and the Sundance Kid* and *Patton*. All was going well for the young Zanuck until he, too, came under the spell of the musical. In quick succession his company produced bombs like *Doctor Dolittle*, *Star*, and *Hello, Dolly*, resulting in giant losses that threatened the very life of the company.

Dick Zanuck's firing cast a pall over Evans. If the scion of the Zanuck dynasty could be abruptly dismissed, surely Evans, too, was headed for the guillotine, even though he had opposed the musicals that now enshrouded the studio.

Paint Your Wagon, like *Darling Lili*, grew out of an early Bluhdorn infatuation. Julie Andrews radiated stardom to Bluhdorn, and Alan Jay Lerner belonged in the same constellation. He was the impresario who seemed to own Broadway and who would surely have the same impact in Hollywood.

Bluhdorn had met Lerner a couple of times, and Evans had dated Karen Gunderson, the attractive young actress who was about to become Lerner's fifth wife. A small, fidgety, hyperactive man, Lerner had been born into money thanks to his parents' chain of low-end clothing stores. At forty-nine, he was determined to build his career in show business beyond Broadway. His partner, Fritz Loewe, at sixty-three, was a genteel European who pined for semiretirement.

Both had been frustrated by their earlier experiences in the movie business. The screen adaptations of *Brigadoon* and *My Fair Lady* had seemed tasteless and cheesy in their view. Lerner, a control freak, felt an urgent need to prove himself and to bring the same mastery to cinema that he had evidenced on Broadway.

Hence, Lerner was highly susceptible to Bluhdorn's exuberant courtship. Not only would both *Paint Your Wagon* and *On a Clear Day You Can See Forever* be made, but Lerner would exercise creative control, and receive producer credit. To further sweeten the deal, Paramount offered to put up $2.5 million to develop yet another Lerner-Loewe musical called *Coco*, based on the life of the French couturier Coco Chanel. The show had allegedly attracted the interest of Katharine Hepburn.

The deal seemed too good to be true, and Charlie Bluhdorn even assured them that he would consent to Barbra Streisand starring in *Clear Day*—his admission that his disparagement of *Funny Girl* had been a mistake.

An aura of desperation seemed to surround *Paint Your Wagon* from its moment of inception. No one seemed to believe it would be a success. The sheer mention of the title evoked apprehension, even denial. *Paint Your Wagon* was like a virus, and everyone around it seemed eager to distance himself.

From the moment I learned of the project, my own attitude was one of disbelief. I vaguely remembered seeing the show, which had been launched during the 1951–52 Broadway season. I think I nodded off even then when an actor started to sing "I Talk to the Trees." And I never understood why the wind was named Mariah.

On Broadway, the show got mixed reviews; critics found the plot about the 1849 California gold rush to be an odd setting for a musical. The book was weak and there was no runaway hit song. After a decent run, the show ended up with a modest $95,000 deficit.

Nonetheless, the team of Lerner and Loewe had already established an aura of invincibility. *Paint Your Wagon* seemed clunky, but there were hints of momentous things to come—*My Fair Lady*, of course, in 1956, was to transform Lerner and Loewe into theater royalty, as was *Gigi*, in 1958, and *Camelot*, in 1960.

The notion of a *Paint Your Wagon* movie musical had been dismissed by one studio after another since the show's opening. The consensus in Hollywood was that the basic plotline of a drunken old prospector who finds love with a Mexican outcast was intrinsically unappealing.

Paramount had flirted with it as a possible Bing Crosby vehicle, but Crosby had rejected it. The MGM hierarchs considered it for Spencer Tracy and Kathryn Grayson, but that went nowhere. Louis B. Mayer optioned it as he was departing as boss of MGM, and he'd talked to Clark Gable as a possible lead (Gable couldn't sing). Finally, Eddie Fisher, the crooner, optioned the show as a possible role for himself, but that, too, could not find a backer.

When I first learned that Paramount had acquired *Paint*

Your Wagon, I told Evans: "This show is beyond creaky—it's comatose."

"Bluhdorn loves it," Evans said defensively. "Alan understands the problem with the book. We're hiring the best writer in the business to fix it, Paddy Chayefsky."

"Paddy Chayefsky writes movies like *Network* or *Hospital*, I said. "He writes great satire, but this is a period musical—"

"It's Charlie's passion," Evans said. "We've got a fighting chance with Chayefsky."

As it turned out, Chayefsky's take on the musical was bizarre. Instead of sticking with the original narrative, he created a bawdy tale of a town called No Name City, which was occupied by French hookers and grumpy prospectors. The principal characters were two partners who apparently shared a wife and who hung out in saloons and bawdy houses.

My suspicion was that Chayefsky, who was rumored to have writer's block, had simply decided to earn a quick payday. Still Lerner, to my surprise, said he liked the draft and was going to do some further work on it. He also was bringing aboard André Previn to create two fresh numbers to be titled "Gold Fever" and "The Best Things in Life Are Dirty" (Lerner's old partner, Fritz Loewe, had quietly dropped out of the adventure).

Since the "new" *Paint Your Wagon* was even stranger than the original one, I felt that the studio would never find a director willing to tackle the project. Lerner had earlier approached Blake Edwards, who'd turned it down (unfortunately, one reason he passed was that he was about to spring *Darling Lili* on the studio). Don Siegel, another Hollywood veteran, also passed.

But Lerner had his own secret weapon in reserve—the veteran Broadway director of *South Pacific* and *Mister Roberts* named Josh Logan. Lerner went to Bluhdorn with the proposal to go with Logan, and the studio officially agreed. This was now a "go" picture, Evans informed me. "Grin and bear it."

The subtext of what he was saying was clear: This was going to be a surreal exercise and all we could do was watch. How bad could it be?

Truly bad, as we were to find out. And each step in the process was, to use Evans's word, increasingly surreal.

The Josh Logan–Alan Jay Lerner favorite to play the lead was James Cagney, who had no intention of coming out of retirement. Their backup was Lee Marvin, who, like Clark Gable, Louis B. Mayer's choice, couldn't sing. Marvin, a famously heavy drinker, needed a job.

His movie sidekick would be another apparent non-singer, Clint Eastwood. Having made his name in the *Rawhide* TV series and in Sergio Leone westerns (*The Good, the Bad and the Ugly*, for one), Eastwood felt it would be a kick to sing in a Hollywood movie.

Though few in Hollywood knew about it, Eastwood had once made an album in which he sang country-and-western songs—numbers that sounded as though they'd fallen out of a vintage Hollywood western. The album didn't generate any excitement, but Eastwood was proud of it nonetheless.

As his final casting inspiration, Logan settled on Jean Seberg to play the wife of the Mormon traveler who is auctioned off to the Marvin and Eastwood characters. Again, this marked a sharp departure; the actress had played the title role in *Saint Joan* and then appeared in *Bonjour, Tristesse*.

The one decision on *Paint Your Wagon* I favored was the choice of location. By building a huge set in a remote section of northeast Oregon, forty-five miles from the town of Baker, Lerner and Logan guaranteed that few would bother visiting the set. The show would be isolated, as though it were a crazed relative. And starting in late spring of 1968, that is how it was regarded.

The shoot was troubled from the outset. Arriving on location, Eastwood was indignant over Lerner's extensive rewrites of Chayefsky's screenplay. He felt the story had been conventionalized. Marvin started drinking heavily and was late to the set most mornings. Lerner and Logan soon started quarreling over performance and even camera angles, with Lerner criticizing his director in front of the company.

Not surprisingly, the show was soon drifting behind schedule with Logan losing control of his set. Though the shoot was hermetically sealed from the outside world, word of trouble was now seeping out. One gossip column quoted Tom Shaw, the line producer, as saying, "We're in one helluva fucking mess up here." Eastwood summoned his agent to fly up for a meeting, and Lee Marvin was asked to join them. Marvin, having been drinking, promptly fell asleep at the table even as the salad was served.

An alarmed Lerner started a furtive conversation with Richard Brooks, the veteran director of *The Professionals* and *In Cold Blood*, asking him to take over the reins from Logan. Brooks rejected the idea, but the approach nonetheless made a column item in the *Los Angeles Times*, thus causing Logan to fall further into panic.

Evans flew to Oregon to reassure him. "Josh has been on lithium since preproduction," Evans told me. "Now even the lithium isn't enough to get him working."

Seberg and Eastwood, bored with the slumberous pace, had started a blatant affair. When Seberg's husband, the French novelist Romain Gary, unexpectedly arrived on the set, he challenged Eastwood to a duel. Lee Marvin started disappearing regularly. The budget had almost doubled to roughly

$100 million in current dollars. And Lerner, impotent as a producer, kept biting his fingernails so ferociously that the white gloves he habitually wore were bloody at the fingertips.

Finally, production didn't so much end as simply expire, its principals exhausted. The actors later grudgingly returned to rerecord their songs, Marvin's in a low growl, Eastwood's in a reedy tenor. Seberg's songs were a total loss—another singer was summoned to record them. Lerner and Logan, meanwhile, kept quarreling, reediting each other's work. One unexpected editing problem: Paramount wanted the film to be rated for family audiences, like most musicals, but its ad line announced: "Ben and Pardner shared everything—even their wife." The motion picture code demanded an M tag, putting *Paint Your Wagon* in the rare position among musicals of earning a "mature audiences" admonition.

Upon the film's opening on October 15, 1969, the critics picked up on the off-center plot. Vincent Canby of the *New York Times* acknowledged his pique over "the rather peculiar psychological implications in the plot"—namely the bonding of the two leading males. Writing in *Holiday*, Rex Reed dismissed it as "a monument of unparalleled incompetence."

In one magazine interview, Logan described Lerner as having been "pieced together by the great, great-grandson of Dr. Frankenstein from a lot of disparate spare parts." The director described the movie as "the most flagrant throwing away of money I've ever seen." To be sure, he'd presided over the excesses.

After the movie's release, Marvin promised never to sing again. Eastwood vowed he would henceforth commit only to films made on a disciplined budget. Josh Logan never again directed a movie. Jean Seberg's career all but disappeared.

Lerner and Loewe would live to regret their exuberance over their Paramount connection. Despite Lerner's creative control, or perhaps because of it, both *Paint Your Wagon* and *Clear Day* would be major failures at the box office, both critically and commercially. *Coco* never opened on Broadway. Instead, an original film for the screen called *The Little Prince* would go into production and it, too, would be a dismal failure. A version also failed on Broadway.

Alan Jay Lerner in particular became embittered by his Paramount experience. It utterly confounded him that his films would seem to reflect, if not exaggerate, his weaknesses—extravagance and an absence of discipline—rather than give voice to his soaring imagination. To compound his frustration, Lerner was to see Paramount's fortunes climb from the moment that he left the studio. It was as though the studio suffered from a Lerner curse.

Bluhdorn was bitterly disappointed over *Paint Your Wagon*.

He was now aware that while his ferocious willpower could reshape financial deals, it could not reshape a motion picture. Egos like Alan Jay Lerner's and Blake Edwards's were simply immune to the Bluhdorn bluster. He could rage and fume, but films would still fall relentlessly behind schedule. He could promise blockbusters to theater owners, but now they became keenly aware that he was delivering bombs.

But, Bluhdorn was not ready to give up on the movie business. And even as he raged at Bob Evans, and tried to blame him for his own shortcomings, he knew that Evans in fact represented his only hope.

Surrendering any measure of control was terrifying to Charlie Bluhdorn, but reality was beginning to sink in.

CHAPTER 5

Lovers

It was an hour into the screening when I sensed something was amiss. A fidgety audience usually spells trouble, but this crowd was definitely unfidgety; in fact, it seemed eerily quiet. No one was whispering, no one was heading to the bathroom. Indeed, no one seemed to be breathing.

Now there was a new sound in the theater, the sound of people sniffling. I stared through the flickering darkness. The hankies had come out and folks throughout the audience were dabbing at their cheeks or blowing their noses, men as well as women. One woman's audible sob caused a nervous titter in the theater.

Seated in the last row, I, too, found myself dabbing away my tears—tears of relief. I elbowed Robert Evans, seated next to me. His expression seemed dazed. Together, we were experiencing for the first time the curious alchemy of our movie, *Love Story*. This was its initial public screening, and the audience reaction confounded us. We had been told repeatedly that this movie—this old-fashioned "weepy"—couldn't work.

The times were too hip, the audiences too edgy. The people out there wanted *Midnight Cowboy* or *Easy Rider.*

They were wrong, of course. Within days the entire community seemed to be uttering those signature words, "Love means never having to say you're sorry." I never really understood the meaning of that sentence, but it sold the movie. For some unfathomable reason, filmgoers wanted to accept that murky message and to indulge in its sentiment. The ultimate "date movie" was born.

In the following weeks and months, hundreds of thousands of young couples would shed tears over Ali MacGraw's cinematic send-off, would hold hands and comfort one another, and, from all reports, would go on to have comforting sex. Young men all over the world would testify to the qualities of the film as Hollywood's supreme aphrodisiac. I remember running into one nineteen-year-old outside a Los Angeles theater telling me with great sincerity, "See it and score, man." He loved the movie and had seen it three times with three different girls.

Three weeks after the test screening I would be riding in a limousine on a dark Saturday night in December 1969, in the company of Charles Bluhdorn, the manic chairman. Bluhdorn wanted to tour the movie theaters in Manhattan to discover who (if anyone) would turn up to see what he'd labeled "this fucking tearjerker." He had heard that the film had done well in its first screening, but was nonetheless skeptical. He had been there before—glowing reports had been delivered on other Paramount films and they had turned out to be turkeys. They'd been pricey failures at that—all of them Bluhdorn's personal picks. Bluhdorn tensed as we saw the line outside the Loew's State Theater on Broadway. It was already snaking its way around the corner. He stared at the marquee in excitement—*Love Story* was heralded in giant letters.

At Bluhdorn's command, the driver pulled to the curb. A harried-looking man who seemed to be the theater manager was out front trying to shepherd the line. He, too, looked astonished by the size of the crowd.

Bluhdorn now bolted from the limo. I saw him charging the theater manager. "Don't just stand there," Bluhdorn screamed at the startled man. "Look at this line! Do something! Raise the fucking prices!"

It was a preposterous proposal, of course—one which the theater manager ignored—but it was pure Bluhdorn. And it told me that *Love Story* would change everything. The studio would never be the same, nor would my job. This little movie that no one wanted to make would, in its own way, become one of the truly transformative hits of the moment—the movie that would save Paramount.

Love Story was effectively the first film that I had gone out on a limb for.

Bob Evans had liked it, too, but in his job as production chief, he was consumed by corporate intrigues and fiscal shortfalls. It was my role to tee up new projects, and I decided to keep persevering on *Love Story*. Every time it fell apart I found an excuse to keep putting it back on the table. It became a standing joke between Evans and me—I was supposedly the overeducated literary type who kept salvaging this sentimental sob story.

Its instant success made me both smile and wince: smile because we had defied the doubters, but wince because we knew that *Love Story* was at once as bogus as it was effective. As its advocate, I had also become a coconspirator. I knew that its story was absurdly manipulative, its characters wafer thin. The man who created the story would lie about its origins. The man who directed it took the job only to earn a quick buck and ended up with the biggest payday of his career. The man who starred in it opposite Ali MacGraw was persuaded by everyone around him that the movie would be career suicide for him, that he'd be forever labeled as the TV soap actor who went on to make a movie soap.

And the final irony: *Love Story* would generate one of the major tabloid "love stories" of its time—one that would turn out to be as fragile as the plot of the movie. And costarring, in that brief melodrama, would be my friend, Bob Evans, whose entreaties had brought me to the studio to begin with, and Ali MacGraw, his bride-to-be.

What had drawn me to *Love Story* to begin with? It was a question I asked myself many times that year, and since. The story was too square, too predictable.

Perversely, that was why I liked it. Something in the back of my head kept saying, be counterintuitive, don't scramble after the trend of the moment.

Besides, there were effective elements in *Love Story*. The rich boy–poor girl theme had always worked in movies, as had father-son conflicts. I also liked the academic aura: Jenny Cavalleri really knew her Mozart and Oliver Barrett was a third-generation Harvard student as well as a hockey jock. At least there was a slender core of intelligence to the piece.

Despite all this, and despite the fact that the screenplay was slickly written, I was surprised by the total disdain that other studios had displayed. An agent turned producer named Howard Minsky had patiently plodded all over town submitting it and re-submitting it only to confront a stone wall of rejection.

Indeed, when talent agents learned that Paramount had optioned the script and was trying to cast it, they, too, made it clear that it was "tired goods." Too many submissions, too many rejections. Minsky, a sharp salesman, seemed beaten down.

The project had been written by a young classics professor at Yale. His name was Erich Segal and he himself was a bundle of mixed messages. At our first meeting, Segal played the part of the serious academic. As I got to know him better, I realized that this young professor was also something of a hustler. In explaining why he'd written *Love Story*, he'd hinted that it was his story, that Jenny had been his doomed girlfriend. Yet Segal was in fact a thin, gawky guy from Brooklyn—the opposite end of the spectrum from Oliver Barrett III.

Segal also seemed very conflicted about the impact *Love Story* would have on his academic career. This issue surfaced when I broached the idea of a novelization. The studio would pay him $15,000 if he would recraft his script into the structure of a novel.

The idea seemed to alarm him. What would his fellow professors think about a pop novel? He'd kept his script a secret, but a novel was a different, more public, exercise.

On the other hand, there was the money. Segal took the deal and churned out a novel in less than a month—one that was as slickly written as his screenplay. When I again raised the issue of the story's origins, he changed the subject. The story was pure fiction, he seemed to be saying.

But months later, celebrating publication day on the *Today* show, Erich Segal was once again tearfully relating the Jenny-and-Oliver story as though it were his own. And the audience bought it. By nightfall, *Love Story* had become a top-of-the-list bestseller.

Segal, it turned out, loved the sudden adventure of celebritydom. After he appeared on Johnny Carson's *Tonight Show* and told some good stories, he was promptly invited back. He phoned to say that he was, despite his apprehensions, "a hero at Yale," with some undergraduates comparing him to F. Scott Fitzgerald. In an interview with *Time* magazine, he admitted, "Before I finished writing the ending I cried and cried for forty-five minutes. Then I washed my face and finished writing the book."

A slender 212 pages, *Love Story* was to go through twenty-one hardcover printings within twelve months. Its first paperback run totaled 4.5 million copies, a record for the time. The hardcover hovered for over a year on the *New York Times* bestseller list and evoked almost universal scorn from the critics. A *Newsweek* review said "The banality of 'Love Story' makes 'Peyton Place' look like 'Swann's Way.'" Nora Ephron, writing in *Esquire*, wrote that the book's massive popularity remained "something of a mystery." Early in 1971 the novel was submitted for consideration for a National Book Award, and the entire fiction jury threatened to resign as a body unless it was removed from contention.

Soon Erich Segal's concerns about his academic career proved to be justified. He was denied tenure at Yale, ultimately moving to London where he continued writing pop fiction and movies. He later cowrote the screenplay for the Beatles movie *Yellow Submarine* and ground out such novels as *Oliver's Story* and *The Class*, as well as academic tomes such as *The Death of Comedy* and *Roman Laughter: The Comedy of Plautus*. In one retrospective article, he acknowledged that the success of *Love Story* had unleashed within him "egotism bordering on megalomania."

But Segal took his writing seriously and was appalled that the *Love Story* legend stirred so much satiric scorn. In the 1972 comedy *What's Up, Doc?* starring Barbra Streisand, her character repeats the "love means never having to say you're sorry" line, and Ryan O'Neal's character responds, "That's the dumbest thing I ever heard." Segal was not above reminding people that the precise line in the novel was "love means not ever having to say you're sorry."

If Erich Segal sent forth mixed messages, so, too, did Ali MacGraw. The Segal script had been given to the young actress by Minsky, and she was enticed by it. She understood that Paramount was interested in it but no deal had yet been made.

Ali had been a Wellesley girl; she felt she understood Jenny, a Radcliffe girl. She also understood her own limitations as an actress—her first movie had reminded her of that—but Jenny was a role she felt she could play.

Ali's passion for *Love Story* surprised me. After the success of *Goodbye, Columbus*, many projects had been tossed her way and she had turned them all down, making it clear that she distrusted Hollywood and its emissaries. Indeed, an odd tension existed between her and Bob Evans. Ali told me that, in her view, Evans embodied the prototypical shifty Hollywood operator. Evans, meanwhile, was equally impatient with Ali's dismissive attitude. "She thinks she's a fucking flower child," he told me. "She thinks Hollywood is beneath her."

When *Goodbye, Columbus* enveloped her, she was neither flower nor child. At age thirty, her life seemed unfocused. She'd toyed with several possible careers, but had not committed to any of them. She'd had several brief relationships with men from sharply contrasting backgrounds, but none had proved enduring.

Ali had been working as a stylist at a modeling agency when a young agent named Martin Davidson first contacted her. Though not a model, she had posed in one ad which had caught Davidson's eye. Davidson immediately responded to what he described as "her crooked-tooth smile." As he later put it, "She was beautiful, but not a beauty. She was too natural to be an actress."

Six months later, Davidson got a call from Ali. Her latest relationship had ended and she was now eager to pursue an acting career. Coincidentally, another client, a young director named Larry Peerce, had just become attached to a project called *Goodbye, Columbus*, based on the Philip Roth novella, and was trying to cast it. Impulsively, Davidson introduced Peerce to Ali, and he liked her.

Two screen tests ensued with mixed results. Ali did not come across as an accomplished actress, and, for that very reason, she appealed to Peerce. His producing partner, Stanley Jaffe, loudly dissented; he pointed out that *Goodbye, Columbus* was a movie about a Jewish family and that "this shiksa" didn't register as Jewish (no one knew at the time that she was, in fact, part Jewish on her mother's side).

Now a fresh set of eyes saw the test—those belonging to Bob Evans. Worried that Peerce, too, lacked experience, he had originally wanted an accomplished actress for the part, but now he liked Ali, even though, as he admitted, "I can't figure her out."

Goodbye, Columbus proved to be a modest hit, and Ali MacGraw suddenly had a career—one that both excited and troubled her. Hollywood scared her, she acknowledged. "If I'm going to be an actress, I want to do sophisticated movies like *The Great Gatsby*," she told me. "I don't want to be manipulated into doing crap, and the only studio people I meet are manipulative."

But she coveted the script to *Love Story*. Jenny and Oliver were smart and they were in love. If only a director of taste and talent could be lured to the project, she said.

The only director Ali really knew, however, was Larry Peerce. *Columbus* had worked, she said. Why not reassemble the team?

While this made sense to Ali, it didn't to Peerce. The son of the opera star Jan Peerce, he, like Ali, was frightened of Hollywood power. He, too, wanted to make "serious" pictures, not studio pictures, and *Love Story* didn't fit that description.

Peerce had become enamored of a densely constructed, rather cerebral thriller titled *The Sporting Club*. When I met with him, ostensibly to discuss a start date for *Love Story*, I could sense his interest was waning. If he were to do *Love Story*, he said, the character of Oliver would have to be rewritten. Perhaps he could be a wounded Vietnam vet who was caught up in the political anger of the moment.

"We have an opportunity here to make a statement about the times and we're blowing it," Peerce told me.

"Larry, face it, this is *Love Story*. It is about two lovers, not Vietnam. It's by Erich Segal, not Philip Roth," I responded.

Larry was a good-natured man. We shared a good laugh about our dilemma. But he clearly wanted out.

A new list of potential directors was prepared by Stanley Jaffe, and Ali, too, had some suggestions. They were the hot directors of the moment—filmmakers who I knew would pass on the script, if they hadn't done so already. It was clear that Evans and I needed a reality check.

As we drove to work one morning, our focus was firmly on *Love Story*. The previous night Bluhdorn had shouted on the phone that the studio was developing too many projects, but nothing was yet in production. "Make a fucking picture already," the boss had screamed.

Grasping at straws, Evans pointed to *Love Story* and said Larry Peerce would be directing Ali MacGraw and that the *Columbus* team would have another hit.

"Good. Make it for $2 million. If it goes over budget, it comes out of your pocket," Bluhdorn retorted.

Now Evans was clearly troubled as we sped through traffic. "You know . . . it's not happening with Peerce," I said quietly.

"We've got to make the movie," Evans said.

"I've been talking to Arthur Hiller," I said. "He has a slot open. Everyone's talking about 'arty' directors like Anthony Harvey, but this is a commercial movie. I like Hiller for it."

"Hiller will be OK," Evans replied. "I've always liked Hiller. Bluhdorn will never remember. Peerce, Hiller . . . he wants movies."

"There's an Ali problem," I said. "She'll say Hiller is Hollywood commercial."

"She thinks she's Audrey Hepburn," Evans said. "She also needs a job."

A few quick phone calls reinforced my apprehensions. When Martin Davidson told his client about Hiller, she immediately had a tantrum. "How dare Paramount assign a director I've never heard of and without my approval!" she raged.

"Talk her down," I told Davidson. "Tell her if he's good enough to do a Jack Lemmon picture (he'd just wrapped *The Out-of-Towners*) then he's good enough for Ali MacGraw."

A compromise was quickly reached. MacGraw agreed to see a cut of *The Out-of-Towners*, which was still in postproduction. A screening for MacGraw would require a trip to Los Angeles. And it would have to be a furtive trip—if Hiller or his agent, Phil Gersh, learned that Hiller was being "auditioned" for Ali MacGraw, they'd likely have tantrums of their own.

Marty Davidson had been a champion of *Love Story* for some time. Marty also understood that Evans and MacGraw knew each other superficially—their relationship had consisted of a few random encounters in New York.

"If I can talk Ali into going to LA, where would she screen the movie?" Marty asked me.

"Probably Evans's screening room at his house; it's got to be off the lot so Hiller won't find out."

There was a pause at the other end of the line. "What happens if Evans makes some moves?" Davidson asked. "She has plans to marry a young actor, Robin Clark."

"Evans needs this movie to go forward," I told Davidson. "He's obsessed."

The events moved forward with a certain clumsy inevitability. Ali got on a plane. She was met by a limo which took her to Evans's house. She saw *The Out-of-Towners*. She said she liked it. She and Evans then shared a few glasses of champagne, after which she stripped and jumped into Evans's swimming pool.

I never received a detailed report of the postscreening activities. The official word was that Ali MacGraw had decided to stay over for a day or so at the Beverly Hills Hotel. She wasn't meeting with anyone because she had suddenly contracted a bad cold.

And not surprisingly, Arthur Hiller was approved by her. A short, stolid Canadian, Arthur Hiller was a no-nonsense filmmaker who liked to keep working. While other self-styled "auteurs" spent years in development, Hiller moved quickly from movie to movie.

Hiller liked *Love Story*, but for him it was a job. He'd finished shooting his Neil Simon comedy, *The Out-of-Towners*, and was scheduled to shoot yet another, *Plaza Suite*, but that had been delayed. Hiller didn't like the slim upfront money offered on *Love Story* (a mere $250,000), but he liked the 25 percent of the net that was added as an inducement. His "yes" to the deal would turn out to be the smartest business decision of his career, ultimately netting in north of $5 million.

During preproduction meetings, Hiller didn't present any ideas for a rewrite. *Love Story* was a script that he felt he could shoot, and that's what he knew how to do—shoot.

Similarly, he was not intimidated by the list of actors who had turned down the role of Oliver. The list was daunting; it included Michael Douglas, Michael York, Michael Sarrazin, Jon Voight, Jeff Bridges, Peter Fonda, and Keith Carradine. One actor who'd been vaguely receptive was Ryan O'Neal, but Hiller balked. *Love Story*'s problem had always been that it was too much like a soap, and O'Neal had just concluded a five-year stint on *Peyton Place*—the ultimate TV soap.

After making an eleventh-hour pitch to test some unknowns, Hiller finally capitulated. A start date was staring him in the face and it was clearly Ryan or no deal.

"Ryan's a good pro," Hiller said. "He'll be a reinforcement for Ali, but we'll need rehearsals—at least a week, maybe two."

Love Story was at last on track. The budget had been approved, the Boston locations nailed down. After the first couple of days of rehearsals, Hiller checked in with a positive report. The chemistry between Ali and Ryan was strong, he said. "Almost too strong." There was something in his voice that set off an alarm.

Ali had only recently become Mrs. Evans. I assumed, therefore, that her relationship with Ryan would remain on a professional level, and Hiller clearly wanted me to assume that as well. The important thing, he said, changing the subject, was that Ryan was a good enough actor to sell himself as a Harvard student even though he had, in fact, never cracked a book, let alone pulled all-nighters in the study hall.

Hiller was delighted, too, that he'd succeeded in persuading Ray Milland to play Oliver Barrett's father. Milland had even agreed to play the part without his usual toupee. To Hiller, this would enhance Milland's credibility as a Boston Brahmin.

John Marley, another fine character actor, signed on to play Ali MacGraw's father. Tommy Lee Jones, an actual Harvard man who was later to become a star in his own right, was signed to play Hank, Oliver Barrett's friend.

With work finally going well on *Love Story*, my interest shifted to other intrigues. Some promising projects were coming together—many of them volatile. They ranged from *Harold and Maude* to *The Godfather*, from *Rosemary's Baby* to *The Longest Yard*. Yet each movie in development seemed to have its own self-destruct button—a writer with a drug problem, a director with a divorce problem. The danger was always there, as well as the promise.

Evans, meanwhile, had still more urgent issues to confront. Charlie Bluhdorn had lost the confidence of his board of directors at Gulf & Western. The directors admired their chairman's gift for buying new companies, but they wanted industrial companies—not movie studios. Their demand was now quite specific: Sell Paramount and get out of the movie business.

Bluhdorn clearly did not want to leave the movie business. He loved the action, and the women. His married status did not deter him from dating an array of beauties around the world. He remembered all too well his pre-Paramount days. Several top restaurants had once barred him for his boisterous behavior and foul language. Now those same places eagerly courted him. Socialites who once turned their back on him were now his best friends.

Now he needed ammunition to fend off his board, and Evans was ready to supply it. He'd once played Thalberg in a film; now he thought, what would Thalberg have done in this sort of situation?

The only way to save a movie studio was to make a movie, Evans decided. Pulling together writer and director and crew, Evans devised a fifteen-minute film in which he would passionately talk about the new day coming to his studio. The centerpiece would be *Love Story*, a movie not yet finished, but a "surefire hit," by his testimony.

Evans and I prepared the script for his short film. He would wear a sharp sport jacket and black slacks. He wanted to look young, but savvy, hungry but knowledgeable. He knew his limitations as an actor, but this was one performance he could bring off.

The cameras rolled: "*Love Story* will be the start of a new trend in movies," Evans intoned. "A trend toward the romantic, toward love, toward people, toward telling a story about how it feels, rather than where it's at."

Evans went on to explain that his production team had adopted austerity measures to cut costs. "The money we spend is not going to be on extravagances. It's going to be on the screen," he declared.

He then showed some very brief excerpts from *Harold and Maude*, *A New Leaf*, *Plaza Suite*, and *The Conformist*—a dizzying mix of films. He talked about the hot new novel *The Godfather*.

His final pitch: "We at Paramount look at ourselves not as passive backers of films, but as a creative force unto ourselves. I promise you Christmas '70 will be very special throughout the world. Paramount's gift, *Love Story*, will make it that. It's what life and love and Christmas is all about."

After the screen went black, Bluhdorn told Evans to wait outside for further instructions. Within a few minutes, Bluhdorn and Martin Davis burst from the boardroom. They congratulated Evans effusively and said the directors had reversed their decision. Davis gave Evans a quick hug and whispered: "You're even a bigger fraud than I thought."

Evans called me with the good news. He was exultant.

"We bought some time, kid," Evans said.

"And we're way out on a limb for a movie neither of us has seen," I said.

"It's all we got," Evans replied.

A week later, Arthur Hiller called to say he was ready to show a first cut of his film. He warned that the cut was rough; there was much work to be done.

The screening was a disaster. The movie was deadly. Key scenes between Ali and Ryan simply didn't work, and Ali's performance was the problem. Her eyes fluttered, her voice quavered; her performance was self-conscious. Ryan's timing, too, was suffering.

Evans was distraught. "Where's my movie?" he demanded. "Where's the emotion? The key love scenes are flat."

His stolid director stayed calm. "It just needs more work," Hiller said in his usual taciturn manner. "Just needs more time. Needs more cutaways."

"The scenes are flat . . ." Evans was almost in tears.

Hiller was glacial. "When I took this job I knew I would not just be shooting Ali, but I'd also be shooting around Ali. It will come together just fine. Even the key love scene." In the next cut, he said, the two lovers wouldn't even be seen; the camera would be focused on Harvard Yard or the exterior of the dorm, and we'd hear the voices of Ali and Ryan.

Hiller clearly knew he needed his bag of tricks. Evans was worried whether the bag was big enough. "You need to shoot more footage!" he said.

"I could use more," said Hiller. "With another couple of shooting days . . ."

That was all Evans needed to hear. A week's additional work on location in Boston was promptly authorized. Further, the forecast was for snow. Some romantic scenes with the lovers frolicking and tossing snowballs in Harvard Yard would be perfect.

Then there was the issue of the ending. While a hint of Jenny's fate would be dropped at the outset, the doctor's final verdict would be saved for the ending. That was the way Arthur Hiller wanted it, but that was not the way Erich Segal had written it. In Hiller's mind, the final Ali-Ryan scene in which Oliver hugs the bedridden Jenny would melt the audience. At least, that was the hope.

But it would only work if the music was right, and that was yet another topic under dispute. Hiller's suggestions were predictable—the solid Hollywood composers. Evans had a brainstorm.

"I want Jimmy Webb," he insisted. "And I want a sound like . . . like Bach."

This one floored me. I knew Evans well and I respected his instincts, but I knew he wasn't a Bach aficionado.

Webb went off and wrote a theme for *Love Story*. It was the closest he could come to Bach. Evans hated it, but he now had a better idea. He had just seen the Claude Lelouch film *A Man and a Woman*, and had fallen in love with the theme by Francis Lai. The problem: Lai was neither available nor interested. And since he spoke no English, he wasn't interested in discussing it.

But Evans had a good friend in France who spoke English and Evans begged him to intercede. Alain Delon, at the time Europe's biggest star, made a few phone calls. Lai agreed to come aboard.

Billy Wilder once explained to me that once a film is finished and the cut is locked, an inevitable "soufflé effect" sets in. For reasons no one can explain, it either rises or it sinks.

In the case of *Love Story*, it rose, and a media fever took hold. *Time* magazine did a cover story on Ali. Ed Sullivan invited Ali to read Christmas poetry, and every columnist demanded a story. The book soared to number one on the bestseller list.

The sheer noise level of the promotion baffled and amazed me. As a former creature of the media, I had never seen anyone massage the press with the skill of Evans. The premiere at Loew's State Theater on December 16, 1970, was pure red carpet theater. It was followed by a Royal Command Performance for the Queen Mother in London, then a gala in Paris for Madame Pompidou.

Evans somehow had turned this wisp of a film, made on the cheap with a cast of nonstars and a director with little cachet, into *Gone with the Wind*. It was suddenly being ballyhooed as a seminal filmmaking event, a product of, in *Time*'s worshipful words, "The New Hollywood."

It wasn't "New Hollywood" at all, of course, but rather a throwback.

During the buildup to *Love Story*, Ali and Bob, even as they argued over the script and over its director, also had been quietly conducting their own love story. When Evans intimated to me that marriage was imminent, I thought he was joking. He simply was not a marrying man. He'd tried it twice before with dire results. But on October 24, 1969, he and Ali impulsively drove to the town hall in Riverside for their license and then got married before a judge in Palm Springs. The witnesses were his housekeeper, Tollie Mae, his butler, David Gilruth, his brother, Charles, and a friend of Ali's from New York, Peggy Morrison.

Their honeymoon lasted two days before she flew to the location in Boston to begin shooting and Evans flew to Europe on business.

CHAPTER 6

Modus Sexualis

Several weeks after joining the studio, I was walking toward my car after a difficult day when I spied someone leaning against its trunk. I quickly recognized her. She was a lissome young actress who had aspirations to become a producer. A few days earlier an agent had introduced her to me in the corridor after she had been in to see Evans.

Now here she was waiting by my car, and she looked downright stunning in the fading June sunlight. Her jeans clung to her like a second skin and her blouse provided maximum cleavage. She was holding a screenplay.

"I was just leaving the lot and thought I'd check whether you'd gotten my script," she explained, flashing a smile that was at once winsome and sexually inviting.

OK, she had a script, and she knew which car was my car. "Didn't you see Evans the other day?" I asked, trying to figure out the setup.

"You know Bob. He's a honey, but he doesn't read. That's why I thought you and I should get to know one another."

"Look, it's late and . . ."

She took a step forward. ". . . and that's why I'm going to buy you a drink and not just thrust my script on you."

It didn't take great insight for me to realize the actress was pitching more than a script. It was more like a package deal, and she was part of the package. "It's been a long day. I've got to get home," I said lamely.

The actress was peering at me. "My movie is really interesting."

I had to smile. Her lines were too on-the-nose. "You're beautiful and I'm probably a fucking idiot, but I'm going to go home."

With car key in hand, I started moving past her, but she tapped my elbow. "You and Evans . . . what a team," she said, and she, too, was grinning. "The only reason guys go to work at a studio is to get laid—is that news to you?"

"Like I said, I'm an idiot," I replied, as I started my car.

The incident stuck in my mind because the girl surely had a point. Hollywood's dream factories have projected an aphrodisiacal aura from their inception. The business is all about marketing romance and sexual fantasy, and the frumpy old guys who ran the business in Old Hollywood were eager to exploit their fringe benefits.

Given this atmosphere, the sexual revolution of the late sixties and early seventies hit Hollywood with a special forcefulness. Virtually every encounter between a man and a woman, even if it was a straightforward negotiation about a deal, carried a sexual subtext. Suddenly the casting couch seemed like a pathetic anachronism. You didn't need to pretend to be casting a movie to justify an advance. It seemed as though society as a whole was going through a midlife crisis.

The manifestations were everywhere. The uniform of the day, even in Hollywood's executive offices, was jeans (preferably old, scruffy, and skintight) and hippie-style shirts and maybe some love beads. If you had hair, you wore it long and maybe affected a ponytail. The mandate was to look hip and talk hip; even the straightest of attorneys called you "man" and told you what they were smoking and what music they were listening to.

It was a few months into my Paramount gig when I succumbed to the inevitable: I decided that I needed a makeover. I looked like a stereotypical New York journalist, replete with dated sport jackets and baggy tan trousers.

I dropped into Carroll & Company, the prestigious Beverly Hills clothier of the moment, to seek sartorial advice. The salesman quickly assessed my wardrobe and suggested I try on one of their new line of blue blazers. I told myself I was heading in the wrong direction.

My mind flashed on a hot clothing store I'd been passing on the Sunset Strip. The place looked trendy—intimidatingly trendy—and I noticed it was open late into the evening. That night after work I decided to mobilize my courage with a quick vodka and stroll into the store, hoping that no other customers were present at that hour.

I was greeted by a very beautiful black woman swathed in red who looked about six foot five, but probably was shorter. The place was empty. I took a breath. "I've got a new job, I'm working with a lot of hip people and I look like someone's loser accountant," I said, the words clotted together so that they doubtless were marginally incomprehensible.

The tall lady looked down on me with what I felt was a mixture of amusement and pity. "You looking for a new wardrobe, boy?" she said.

"I need a wardrobe. I need a look."

"Where you say you're working?"

"A movie studio. For real."

"You come to the right place," she said. "My name is Rita, you get your ass into that dressing room and strip."

I felt a tug of abject panic. "Strip?"

"Down to your little jockeys," she commanded.

For the next forty-five minutes I stood shivering in Rita's dressing room as she and yet another very tall black woman paraded in and out with trousers, jackets, and shirts, all of them very trendy and also very tight. They carefully inspected me, gave their assessments, and kept coming. The tab kept mounting, but, looking in the mirror, I began to feel like I was getting geared up for my new life.

I bought a lot of clothes that evening, and Rita and I developed a healthy rapport. As she accepted my credit card, she jotted down the names of a barber and eyeglass store, which she urged me to patronize, and also tossed in, free of charge, several pairs of brightly colored socks and underpants. "The hair has to grow, and lose the glasses and the jockeys," she admonished.

I left the store feeling oddly liberated. I had no desire to become another Bob Evans, but it was time to acclimate to my new surroundings. Molting season had arrived.

To be sure, Evans and I were destined to remain the odd couple—that much I accepted. Even though he was intently focused on his new responsibilities, a corner of Evans's brain, or some other organ, kept scrupulous watch over his sex life. There was a girl almost every night, and there was scant time for repeat business. Evans needed women; that had been his way of life since adolescence. And the affection, if that's what it was, was reciprocal. In all the time I spent with him, whether evening or morning, I never overheard a scene, with a girl screaming about a betrayal or a forgotten commitment, but I did witness fond farewells. It was almost as though there was an understanding within Evans's pulchritudinous inventory that these were to be one-night stands and that all emotions expressed therein were perforce evanescent.

I understood Evans's modus sexualis, was grateful that it did not interfere with the work, and I had no intention of emulating it. Given the massive neuroses confronting me each day, my marriage and my two small children seemed all the more important as anchors of reality. I also observed the risks of entrapment. I knew several executives at other studios whose lives had been entangled in sexual favors or who had been caught in blatant "setups." And the industry had its own folklore of top executives, like Jim Aubrey of CBS, whose careers had been undermined by scandal.

I knew that my behavior probably was regarded as prudish. I felt like a teenager who'd been invited to an orgy but was too timorous to partake. And the temptations were abundant. Virtually every party, and they were almost nightly, had their standard offerings—lines of cocaine and piles of joints. And it was customary to strip down after dinner and climb into the hot tub. As a completely nonaddictive personality, I smoked the joints and welcomed an occasional cocaine high after an arduous day, and the hot tubs became habitual, as did the subsurface wandering hands. I was having a very good time and was keenly aware that I seemed to be perpetually surrounded by uncommonly attractive people.

But an incipient lunacy seemed baked into the lifestyle. People who should have known better were betraying their loved ones and destroying their careers. Parties were ending in screaming fits of domestic betrayal. Movies were being abandoned by filmmakers who were ODing on drugs they knew nothing about. Lurking beneath the atmosphere of prurience and play was a chasm of self-destruction.

By the early seventies, I could already foresee both the promise of the period and the seeds of its destruction. Some brilliant work was emerging from the playpen that was seventies Hollywood, but the achievements would be ephemeral.

If social Hollywood was consumed with sexuality, so too was the studio. Everyone seemed to be balling everyone else. Bluhdorn was being serviced on his travels as a matter of course, with executives routinely organizing his assignations. Even the gruffly impersonal president, Martin Davis, was engaged in an affair with the vivacious young head of casting, Andrea Eastman. After an especially unpleasant meeting with Bluhdorn and Jaffe, one of their secretaries matter-of-factly asked me if I shared her interest in oral sex and would like to participate that evening. Even as she plugged in another call, she told me casually, "I give great blow jobs."

One morning I'd had an intense negotiation at the Beverly Hills Hotel with an attractive female literary agent on rights to a hot novel. I'd been so stubborn over the deal points that, over a final sip of coffee, I said, "I feel bad—you didn't get much out of this breakfast."

"That problem can be solved," she said, gingerly plunking her room key in front of me. "I have forty-five minutes if you do."

For Evans himself, the lexicon of sex was as routine as the lexicon of filmmaking. His frustration, however, was that he was not able to find the connective energy between his two favorite domains. "The audience doesn't want to see actors fucking," he would say to me. "The smart director understands what to show and what to cover up."

On the other hand, movies about sex fascinated him. "Ellen Burstyn picks lice out of her pussy, but other than that the movie is a goddamn bore," he announced to me one morning as he climbed into my car for our morning drive to work.

"What the hell are you talking about, Bob?"

"I made a deal for Paramount to release *Tropic of Cancer*," he explained. "I didn't tell you about it. I forgot. I knew it was a stupid deal so I didn't say anything."

"You're talking about Henry Miller's *Tropic of Cancer*," I said in disbelief. "How can you make a movie of a Henry Miller novel?"

"You can't," Evans replied. He explained that he had a long-standing friendship with Miller, the sexual rebel whose work had been labeled obscene by the defenders of morality. Another Evans friend, Joseph Strick, had raised the money to shoot the movie, provided he could direct it, and now Paramount would have the privilege of distributing it. Except the studio wouldn't, because it was lifeless. I screened *Tropic* the next day and agreed with Evans's dire assessment; I couldn't even find interest in the Burstyn scene.

Evans said he'd learned his lesson about sex movies. Shortly thereafter he returned from Paris, however, with a new passion project. He had seen a rough cut of *Last Tango in Paris* starring Maria Schneider and Marlon Brando, and was convinced the movie would find a big audience in the United States. "Brando fucks her on the floor. He fucks her in the ass. The movie is amazing," Evans rhapsodized.

Directed by Bernardo Bertolucci, *Last Tango* stirred both alarm and fascination in the international film community. To Hollywood's young filmmakers, Bertolucci had managed to merge art with porn. It was an act of singular cinematic defiance. Further, he had hired one of the mythic stars of the movie world, Brando, and had told him to break all the rules.

In Hollywood's sacrosanct celebrity screening rooms, *Last Tango* was the hottest picture since *Gone with the Wind*. But in New York's corporate boardrooms, the movie sent up red flags. The official mantra: America's shareholders didn't want to be in the porn business.

"To the New York bankers, Hollywood has gone over the

edge," Martin Davis lectured me during a trip to New York. "The money men are only comfortable backing a company that makes family pictures. *Mary Poppins* is a product they're comfortable with. That's where the money is."

I stared at Davis for a moment. It was as though he knew what I was going to say, and almost dared me to go there. "Marty, we both know that there's only one movie in release with lines around the block. And it's not *Mary Poppins*."

Davis paused. "Gulf & Western isn't in the porn business," he snapped, and walked away.

What had prompted my remark was simply this: I had heard that Davis himself had been seen in line a week earlier to see *Deep Throat*. I'd wondered whether the Gulf & Western COO had worn his usual navy blue uniform or had tried to blend in with the great unwashed. But the fact that Davis had been impelled to see the new porn epic underscored the ambivalence of the corporate players toward the booming porn industry. At this moment in 1972, *Deep Throat* was generating more heat than any movie Hollywood had produced in years. And with the nation sliding into a recession, the revenues from porn were delicious to behold.

To the movie industry, *Deep Throat* was confounding for several reasons. At a time when Hollywood was still throwing big budgets at brash musicals, *Deep Throat* looked like what it was—a home movie made on a dime. It had no stars; its principals were not even professional actors. Neither Linda Lovelace nor Harry Reems even professed to be proficient at oral sex, according to their interviews.

To Hollywood CEOs, however, the biggest frustration stemmed from the revelation that the Mafia essentially owned *Deep Throat*. Gangsters had not only succeeded in buying up the lion's share of the rights, but were craftily managing its release. In market after market, the pattern was the same: *Deep Throat* would open in a single theater and the cops, who'd been tipped off beforehand, would promptly shut it down. The local newspapers would herald the censorship fight and within a week or so the local authorities would invariably retreat from the free speech advocates. When *Deep Throat* reopened, long lines would form outside the theater thanks to all the free publicity.

The Mafia understood a prime rule of marketing: that the surefire way to lure an audience is to announce that the "authorities" don't want them to see something. In one town after another across the U.S., the censors played into the hands of the Mafia.

The reaction of the Hollywood studios to all this was similar to that of the audiences. Porn both scared and enticed them. They had all subscribed to the traditional view that mainstream filmgoers coveted romance and happy endings, but not the types of "happy endings" that now played out on the big screens. They did not want to see penises entering mouths, vaginas, or other human orifices.

Or did they? In *Deep Throat*, *Behind the Green Door* (also released that year), and a sudden parade of other porn films, explicit sex scenes were not only splayed across the wide screen, but the box office returns were downright exultant. Porn was suddenly serious competition.

And though Bluhdorn and Davis officially parroted the industry position on porn, Paramount nonetheless had quietly become part of the porn world. Within weeks after the shady Italian financiers of Immobilière acquired a principal stake in the Paramount back lot on Melrose Boulevard, its mammoth soundstages were being rented out to porn producers. On the same soundstage where Roman Polanski had labored with Mia Farrow on *Rosemary's Baby*, pornmeisters were shooting hardcore scenes.

By this time, the Paramount production staff—a much

slimmed down team—had moved off the lot to a compact little building on North Canon Drive in Beverly Hills. Once the lot had been sold, it seemed like an excellent opportunity to streamline costs and move to smaller quarters. Initially, I was troubled by the move. I loved strolling the studio's faux neighborhoods, but most of the stages were now empty and so were most of the dressing rooms. I was on the lot one day when I came upon an argument between a director and an actress outside a dressing room. The director, a sleazy looking guy wearing a Hawaiian shirt, was unhappy with his buxom blonde star because she'd apparently been late for her morning call. "Professionals are never late," he ranted. "We got only four days to shoot this fucking thing." I quickened my stride; I didn't want to know about four-day porn shoots on a Paramount soundstage.

All this underscored for me the value of the move to Beverly Hills. We were beginning a new chapter in the bumpy history of the studio. And while the mandate had been set forth that the studio would not be in the porn business, our new array of films still registered a rather fervid sexual temperature. Shortly after moving into my tidy new office on Canon Drive, I found myself entangled in a fight over the sex scenes in a thriller called *Don't Look Now*.

Based on a deliciously creepy short story by Daphne du Maurier, *Don't Look Now*, was about a married couple who, having lost a child through a drowning accident, take refuge in Venice to recover their bearings. Three financing entities had agreed to fund the picture, which was directed by Nicolas Roeg and starred Julie Christie and Donald Sutherland.

When I visited the set in Venice, I had no idea that this would turn out to be an auspicious day—one that would foreshadow future controversy. I was greeted by Roeg, a gracious if artistically demanding former cinematographer who had codirected *Performance* with Mick Jagger. It was the middle of the afternoon and Roeg explained that they were about to shoot an important love scene.

"Good day to come by," Roeg remarked, and as he spoke, I could tell that, consistent with his reputation, he had fortified himself with a cocktail or two. "The scene is supposed to be semierotic, and we've rehearsed it so everybody's fine with it," Roeg said. "Fortunately, Julie and Donald are getting on quite well. There's nothing worse than a love scene involving two actors who hate each other."

I told Roeg about my experience watching the flaccid Julie Andrews–Rock Hudson love scenes and, amused, he assured me that this one would definitely not be a repetition. As "action" was called, I retreated behind the camera as the two actors arrayed themselves with a cool professionalism, their expressions purposeful. Now suddenly they were into their characters, registering passion, if not lust. They were clearly naked, which surprised me. I had assumed that the usual skin-colored panties would cover their privates.

As the scene progressed, my mind drifted. I had a plane to Paris to catch; and as I peeked at my watch I also glanced at the open script, which was perched on the script supervisor's desk. The scene was about action, not dialogue, and the action was now continuing, unabated for several minutes. I stared at Roeg, who was looking on passively. My gaze shifted to the actors, and I was riveted.

"Nic," I whispered to the director. "Don't they expect you to say 'cut'?"

"I just want to be sure I have the coverage," he mumbled.

"Cut," said Roeg. The actors did not seem to hear him, or simply didn't care. I decided to make a run for my plane.

Several months later, back in Beverly Hills, my assistant told me that Warren Beatty was unexpectedly in the reception room and wanted to see me urgently. Beatty was not one to turn up on a whim; I had gotten to know him pretty well when we worked on *The Parallax View*, months earlier.

Beatty was all business. "I am here to protect Julie," he explained, referring to his then girlfriend, Julie Christie.

"Protect her from what?" I asked.

"Nic Roeg exploited her in *Don't Look Now*," Beatty said darkly.

"I haven't seen the cut yet," I replied.

"Then you will see what I mean," Beatty said ominously.

"I'm afraid I'm a little dense about this," I protested. "What's the issue here?"

Beatty sucked in his breath. He was clearly an angry man. "The love scenes. You can see her pussy."

It all started clicking for me. I now remembered the love scene, which had gotten out of control, and apparently Nic Roeg had not cut it judiciously. "Look, Warren, I appreciate your concerns. You are being the protective boyfriend, and I get that. I promise you that I will talk to the editor and we will deal with the problem."

Beatty's gaze was intense. "Not good enough," he retorted. "I want to run the scene with you on the Moviola."

As he spat out his words with great intensity, I could not suppress a smile. This was a bizarre conversation at best, but it was now becoming surreal. "With great respect, Warren, I don't do 'pussy hair' cuts. Why haven't you brought this up with Evans?"

"Evans likes the cut," Beatty said. "He thinks it's sexy. Evans has no taste."

"Look, you guys are pals; I don't want to get in the middle. Besides, the code will not approve the scene as you describe it without pinning an X rating on it, and that would be our excuse to make further cuts."

Beatty shook his head again. "I'm not leaving this to the censors; I want to cut the movie with you."

"OK," I cut in, "we will do that, I promise you. I'll take out the offending footage. But first I'm going to run the movie alone tomorrow and then give you a call."

"I'll be waiting," Beatty said.

The following day I ran the cut and was delighted to see that Roeg had delivered a brilliant, if overlong, movie. Roeg's scary creations, such as the mysterious dwarf who reappeared menacingly, all helped sell the disturbing atmospherics.

But Beatty was right. The love scene was very convincing—too convincing.

Two days later I sat at a Moviola editing machine with Warren Beatty, and together we cut Julie's scene. It was a quick editing job, but it seemed to represent a triumph for Beatty. I did not understand why this was a matter of such high principle to him—according to the gossipmongers, he and Christie had just broken up anyway—but Beatty felt he had triumphed over studio evils.

Don't Look Now did fairly well at the box office, and survived as a minor cult classic. And while many film buffs remember Julie Christie's memorable performance, the sex scene was otherwise a routine blur at a moment in time when flaunting one's sexuality was no longer an option, but rather a mandate.

CHAPTER 7

The Bad Guys

He was a tall, silver-haired man, square-jawed with a military bearing, always impeccably attired in a dark blue suit. It was only a few weeks into my Paramount job when I came to understand that Sidney Korshak would be part of my new corporate family, even though he did not work for Paramount. His visits were a daily occurrence, but he did not linger or chat with anyone other than Bob Evans, nor did anyone on staff ever refer to him or acknowledge his visits. Korshak was the ghost who was always there but never there.

Evans had talked earlier about him once or twice, always in a manner that betrayed not only respect but near-reverence. Sidney Korshak was not so much his personal attorney (he never paid him) or even his mentor as he was his consigliere. And when Korshak arrived for an Evans audience, all other plans would be set aside. Whoever happened to be in the reception room would have to wait until the big man had come and gone from Evans's sanctum sanctorum. And this procedure was replicated by other power players at other offices in town, as I was to learn.

Sidney Korshak, it seemed to me, was the man who knew everything—the big corporate deals as well as the personal peccadilloes. It was some time before I also realized that Korshak was the man who knew too much.

It was Korshak's role in life to dwell simultaneously in two separate and distinct worlds which, in his grand design, would remain hermetically sealed against each other. There was his celebrity world—he liked to drop names like Kirk Douglas or Dinah Shore or Debbie Reynolds, or to casually mention that he'd just had dinner with Sinatra in Las Vegas, or with Nancy and Ronnie Reagan in Beverly Hills.

But he would never mention his other friends, like Tony Accardo or Sam Giancanna from the Chicago mob or Jimmy Hoffa from the Teamsters or Moe Dalitz from Vegas.

Korshak would allude to the corporate deals he made on behalf of Lew Wasserman or Howard Hughes, but he never confided what he knew about Bugsy Siegel's murder or Hoffa's disappearance.

Korshak's life was built around a web of secrecy, and he was convinced that he would always be able to move effortlessly from one world to the next. It was only later in his life that he, too, found himself trapped. As the dangers in his nether life became more ominous, Korshak was unable to extricate himself from his underworld bonds. The celebrities would continue to decorate his life, like glitzy toys, but the bad boys would always be hovering out there with their furtive demands and threats.

Over the years my relationship with Korshak remained distanced but cordial. He never directly asked anything from me nor subjected me to his power games. When his son, Harry, began to produce movies at Paramount—I never figured out precisely how this deal came about—Korshak told me he would "appreciate it" if I were to "look out" for Harry and provide advice if he began to stray. But when young Harry's career did not go well, Korshak was the first to inform his son that he would do well to pursue other career possibilities.

In observing Korshak's superbly surreptitious maneuverings over time, I began to accept a reality none of us wanted to openly address. Sidney Korshak was a gangster, albeit a very civil and well-groomed gangster. The bad boys had achieved major clout in the entertainment industry, and Korshak, despite all his secrecy, represented the embodiment of that clout.

Ironically, while Korshak yearned for the trappings of "respectability," his pals in Hollywood venerated him, not for his cool or his great wardrobe or even for his lawyering skills, but rather for his fabled underworld ties. Bob Evans, for one, had always romanticized the lore of the gangster—hence his lifelong ambition to make the movie about the mythic, mobster-owned Cotton Club, which ultimately came to haunt him. Charlie Bluhdorn had a long-standing flirtation with the shadow world of fringe financiers in Europe and ended up doing deals that resulted in prison sentences for his partners and almost for himself. Frank Yablans subscribed to mobster mythology to such a degree that he even agreed to play the role of an underworld thug in a movie titled *Mikey and Nicky*. He was in rehearsal on the film before an apoplectic Bluhdorn vetoed his participation (even the often reckless Bluhdorn realized the potential jeopardy to his corporate image).

The Bluhdorn-Korshak romance was shaken badly in the early seventies by two developments. First, Korshak went to the chairman's office in New York to demand a substantial pay raise for Evans, telling Bluhdorn that he had not properly rewarded his production chief for his success (Evans's base pay never exceeded $350,000). Bluhdorn summarily rejected these demands and all but threw Korshak out of his office. (Bluhdorn later thought better of it and submitted to Korshak's pressure.)

In 1976, as the media was turning on Bluhdorn because of his freewheeling stock manipulations, the *New York Times* ran a multipart series on Korshak that exposed his underworld ties. Written by Seymour Hersh, the *Times'* respected investigative reporter, the lengthy series analyzed how Korshak had bolstered the fortunes of his "respectable" corporate clients through his connections with shady figures in Las Vegas and with the labor unions, but the story failed to produce concrete evidence that would lead to an indictment.

The story also alleged that millions in Paramount's corporate profits remained hidden from stockholders and that organized-crime figures were linked to Paramount and to its subsidiary, Madison Square Garden. Still later stories revealed that Joel Dolkart, Bluhdorn's onetime corporate attorney, who now faced embezzlement charges, stood ready to document these allegations in order to avoid a long prison sentence.

Shocked by the negative publicity, Bluhdorn, like other Korshak clients, backed away from his relationship with all his "shady" friends—even "the fixer." Korshak's presence suddenly represented a threat, not a benefit. Korshak himself had too much to hide, and so did Bluhdorn.

If Bluhdorn, Lew Wasserman, Evans, and their friends felt a kinship for Korshak, they were in effect carrying on a tradition that dated back to the early days of Hollywood.

The studio founders were themselves tough guys— immigrants from Eastern Europe who had to con and connive their way to money and power. Early on they gravitated toward businesses like exhibition and vaudeville, where a little cash and a lot of push could bring results and where they often interfaced with the mob. In the big cities local gangsters muscled into unions representing stagehands. Barney Balaban, who later ran Paramount, started paying off mob-run unions as early as the 1920s and kept raising the ante, covering even projectionists and ushers. Exhibitors had to pay Al Capone to keep their theaters operating, and by the 1930s a hood named Willie Bioff was even taking a "commission" for providing the studios with film stock.

As the union war chests kept building, the wannabe movie tycoons, having contributed to these funds, inevitably started tapping into them. A well-connected hood named Johnny Roselli arranged for a $500,000 loan to facilitate Harry Cohn's takeover of Columbia Pictures. The link was a natural one: Cohn's mannerisms mirrored those of the mobsters more than the bankers he also had to deal with. Louis B. Mayer, who was to become the mandarin of MGM, also had financial dealings with fringe figures from the mob like Frank Orsatti, and his inner circle of aides included some thuggish characters (the exception was Irving Thalberg, his studio chief, who displayed a self-conscious courtliness).

As the studios became big businesses, the mob's cut of the action also expanded. The same hoods who shook down stagehands—Tommy Malloy and Frank Nitti were among the most aggressive—also moved in on the IATSE, representing blue-collar workers like grips and gaffers, demanding ever higher kickbacks from studios. By the mid-1920s, the studio chiefs, brought together by Nicholas Schenck, president of Loew's, offered union leaders a onetime payoff of $150,000 if they agreed to a no-strike clause for a period of seven years. It was a good deal, but by the midthirties the payoff demands increased steeply to mollify representatives from the Chicago mob. Mobsters like Lucky Luciano and Sam Giancanna became regular visitors to the studios. In 1939 the emissaries from Chicago even made a bold bid to take over the Screen

Actors Guild, but stars like Robert Montgomery and James Cagney went public in opposing the incursion.

Given its links to gangsters, it was inevitable that Hollywood would also develop a propensity for gangster movies. In 1930 Howard Hughes bought the rights to a novel called *Scarface*, which focused on two brothers, one a mobster and one a cop. He hired Howard Hawks to direct it and signed a former dancer named George Raft to play a character modeled after Al Capone's enforcer.

As he emulated this performance throughout his career, Raft interfaced with the likes of Luciano, Meyer Lansky, and Joe Adonis. ("They were like gods to me," Raft later told his biographer.)

Mindful that elite members of the mob were fascinated by his movie, Hawks made no effort to hide the production—indeed, he even invited Capone to see dailies.

The ever-prissy Hays Office—the industry's censorship enforcer—was disturbed by Hawks's inclusive attitude and by the finished product, which it deemed excessively violent. To quell this anxiety, Hawks tacked on a subtitle, "The Shame of the Nation," and even mandated a pedestrian "crime does not pay" speech near the end of the movie. The film nonetheless was a hit when it opened in 1932.

The studios kept revisiting the gangster genre with profitable results through the days of *The Godfather* in 1972, *Bugsy* in 1991, and *Public Enemies* in 2009. All the while, various mob kingpins maintained their ties to Hollywood luminaries. Mickey Cohen professed to hang with Robert Mitchum and Errol Flynn. Sam Giancanna had links to Judy Campbell, who was John F. Kennedy's occasional "date." Mobsters liked to hover around the fabled Rat Pack, led by Frank Sinatra, especially in the "secure" environs of Las Vegas. The tabloids for months lived off the murder of Johnny Stompanato by Lana

Turner's daughter, Cheryl Crane—Stompanato had worked for Mickey Cohen, but, under the name of John Steele, had been a fringe player at the studios and had dated Turner.

A great body of folklore flowed from these random relationships. Did Frank Sinatra get his role as Private Maggio in *From Here to Eternity* because of the clout of his friend Johnny Roselli? Roselli supposedly reminded Harry Cohn that Columbia still owed money to the mob. Did Frank Costello mandate the murder of Sammy Davis Jr. because of his affair with Kim Novak?

To a degree, much of the mythology was propagated by the Kefauver hearings of 1950. Led by the geeky Tennessee senator Estes Kefauver, the televised hearings promised to reveal the links of organized crime to top figures in politics and entertainment. The committee let it be known that it had obtained photographs showing Sinatra conferring with Luciano and would offer other presumably sexy evidence. The testimony of Sidney Korshak, it was promised, would be a high point of the probe.

The publicity-shy Korshak, however, had no intention of blowing his cover. Arranging a private meeting with Kefauver at a Chicago hotel before his scheduled appearance, Korshak produced photographs showing the senator in a hotel room in the company of two underage girls. Upon glancing at the photos, Kefauver canceled Korshak's appearance.

Kefauver's probe didn't succeed in turning up the evidence it had advertised. Had it taken place twenty years later, its findings would have been more rewarding. The release of *Deep Throat* in 1972 would come to represent the most significant incursion of mob-owned product into the entertainment marketplace. Gerard Damiano Productions, which made the movie, allegedly included members of the Colombo crime family.

Given the appropriate calculations and adjustments, *Deep Throat* represented, by all estimates, the highest-grossing movie in the history of the industry. And given its success, the bad boys were encouraged to pump funding into other movies. Lou Peraino, one of *Deep Throat*'s producers, established his own distribution company, Bryanston, in 1973, and his releases included *The Texas Chain Saw Massacre* and a Bruce Lee film, *Enter the Dragon*. Under pressure from a cadre of investigators, Bryanston proved to be a short-lived venture.

But Charlie Bluhdorn's decision in 1970 to sell a 50 percent interest in the Paramount lot to a shady group of European financiers soon focused attention yet again on possible ties to "funny money." The deal had been engineered by Michele Sindona, a money launderer with close ties to the Gambino family as well as the Vatican bank. By 1980 Sindona had been convicted on sixty-five counts of fraud and perjury: he was shortly extradited to Italy and died in his jail cell from cyanide poisoning, a favorite mob medicine.

In the same period, the copresident of Warner Communications, Jay Emmett, became a major stockholder in an ill-starred venture in Westchester County called the Westchester Premier Theater. Again, the government alleged that "respectable" industry money had been mixed with Mafia seed money and that the Warner executives were in effect laundering the Gambino family's investment. Several indictments ensued.

To Sidney Korshak, the idea that "respectable" corporate money could end up being directly traced to a Mafia front was sloppy and unthinkable. In his world the two domains remained separate and distinct. He had been imbued with this modus operandi since his childhood in Chicago when he and his brother Marshall observed that two regimes ruled the city, existing side by side, separate but equal. There was the official government of Chicago, which ultimately became the province of the Daley dynasty, and then there was the "organization" run by Jake Arvey, a shrewd political operator whose reign was propped up by the Chicago mob.

Upon graduating from law school, Korshak was informed that Jews were not allowed to take the state bar exam and that his best career path resided in servicing the "shadow government." As it turned out, the Pritzker family, the emerging powers in the hotel industry, needed a young attorney who could negotiate with the powerful mob-infiltrated Chicago labor unions, and Korshak seemed to be that man. Meanwhile, the power players from the mob like Murray "The Hump" Humphreys and Tony Accardo needed to mobilize legal minds to ward off the increasingly aggressive "Feds." The murder of Alex Greenberg, a Jewish accountant who was the main financial strategist for the Chicago mob, dramatized not only the brain drain that the mob was facing, but also the perils of the job.

In addition to his Chicago clients, Korshak picked up a client who seemed, on the surface, to be a perfect match. Howard Hughes, like Korshak, was pathologically secretive and was eager to rid himself of RKO Studios, which generated more publicity than profits. Korshak managed to piece together a syndicate of Chicago operatives, some of whom had dicey reputations, but Hughes became squeamish when he examined the cast of characters. At the last moment, he torpedoed the deal.

Korshak was devastated: he had imagined himself running RKO and thus escaping the control of his Chicago mentors. Seeking new pastures, Korshak decided to focus on the casino business in Las Vegas. His initial mission was to build an alliance between the Chicago and the Cleveland families who were competing for control of the Riviera and the Desert

Inn. A key ally was to become Jimmy Hoffa, who by now had pieced together some twenty-two separate pension funds into one mighty Teamsters Central States Pension Fund. Together Korshak and Hoffa constructed a "family ownership" scheme that ran a cooperative skim operation at the key Vegas casinos. To be sure, members of rival families resented Hoffa's growing financial power, but that only strengthened Korshak's hand, given his link to the Teamsters' boss.

In Vegas and Chicago, Korshak was both respected and denigrated as "Mr. Silk Stockings" because of his celebrity contacts and fastidious attire. His blue-collar mob friends remained suspicious of him. They felt that his overriding ambition was to penetrate the inner circle of Hollywood.

Their intuition was valid. Korshak's principal entrée to Hollywood power was Lew Wasserman, the boss of MCA and Universal. The two had met before World War II when Wasserman was still an aspiring young agent. Having represented music acts playing the mob-controlled club circuit, young Wasserman respected Korshak's cool in dealing with the bad boys. Soon Korshak was meeting other Hollywood players who needed to capitalize on his Chicago pedigree. When Columbia's Harry Cohn died, in 1958, his investors from the mob were alarmed about possible public disclosure. Conveniently, Cohn's widow, Joan, hired Korshak to circumvent probate and negotiate a furtive resolution. A year later, Joan Cohn was remarried at a ceremony in Korshak's house.

Wasserman was later to seek Korshak's help in structuring a health and pension fund for members of the Screen Actors Guild—one containing a sweetheart deal for Wasserman's company. Wasserman knew that actors ultimately would demand residuals from their TV shows and surely would win their case. Under the Korshak-Wasserman strategy, Universal-MCA would agree to help endow a pension fund provided the guild would drop its demand for any pre-1960 residuals. Subsequently, when the actors went on strike over the issue (a six-week stoppage) Wasserman's company was conveniently exempt from the labor action.

The SAG president, the actor Ronald Reagan, was accused by some of his colleagues of being complicit with Wasserman—many SAG members for years labeled it "the great giveaway." The acting fraternity knew it was Korshak, not Wasserman, who had the true bond with Reagan.

By the early 1960s, Korshak was presiding over his shadow empire from his corner table at the Bistro restaurant in Beverly Hills, holding court for friends and allies at this citadel of celebrity power. He was influential in paving the way for the Dodgers to move to Los Angeles and averted an opening day disaster by resolving a strike at the parking concession. And, of course, he was regularly visiting with Bob Evans both in his office and at Evans's home, which was to become the ultimate Hollywood playpen.

It was in that period that Korshak's son also magically materialized as a Paramount appendage.

A film titled *Sheila Levine Is Dead and Living in New York* appeared on the studio production charts one day. Since it was my job to tee up our new studio projects, I was supposed to know about every new film and thus asked Evans about *Sheila*'s origins.

"It's something that came in the other day," he responded vaguely. "Low budget."

"And Harry Korshak? Does he have experience as a producer? Is his dad involved?"

Evans didn't want to engage on this subject. "Harry's a good kid," was the extent of his response.

Ultimately Harry called for an appointment. A slender,

self-effacing young man in his late twenties, he was as scrupulously polite as his father, but made no effort to emulate his
aura of power. He said he wanted to learn about producing—
about scripts and budgets—but was by no means committed
to it as a career. Indeed, I had the feeling that his father had
urged him to try his hand at the movie business and that he
himself remained unconvinced.

The issue that was never raised in our early talks was the
one that most obsessed other producers—whether *Sheila* would
get a green light to move forward into production. Though
other projects got stalled along the way because of cost or cast,
there was never a question about *Sheila Levine*—it was definitely
going to happen. Sidney, however, was never going to mention
it to me or refer to it even obliquely. *Sheila* was a fait accompli.
Shortly, another Harry project, ironically titled *Hit*, also appeared on Paramount's schedule and marched forward with
equal dispatch.

Finally I sat down with Evans to relate my discomfort
with the Korshak connection. "You and I are essentially responsible for movies made and released by Paramount, and
I'm troubled by the idea of contracting out some of these projects to the Korshak family," I explained.

Evans seemed unfazed: Harry Korshak's productions were
subject to the same rules and constraints as other projects, he
said calmly. I pressed onward: "As far as I can tell, Harry and
his father can produce whatever they want on whatever budgets they want."

Again, Evans patiently disagreed. He was personally supervising Harry's films, he said, which was news to me. It was
rare that Evans assumed hands-on responsibilities of this sort.

"Harry seems like a perfectly responsible young guy," I
said. "But folks in our community are beginning to notice the
Korshak connection at the studio. I know you're friendly with

Sidney, but we're talking about a guy who once represented Al Capone."

Evans gave me a blank look and took a call. "I've got a doctor's appointment," he said, terminating our discussion. Not long thereafter, I learned that Harry had decided to set aside his interest in filmmaking and that he was moving to London to focus on a new passion—painting.

Sidney Korshak's own Hollywood activities would not be curtailed, however. In October 1973, Bluhdorn, Lew Wasserman, and Kirk Kerkorian held a secret meeting in Evans's projection room to hatch a new venture that was at once collusive and creative. Presiding over the meeting was Sidney Korshak.

The purpose of the meeting was to instantly create an important new player in the international film industry. The new entity, Cinema International Corp., a joint venture of MCA and Gulf & Western, would buy MGM's major circuit of theaters overseas as well as acquiring rights to its library of films and TV shows.

It had taken a lot of patient perseverance on Korshak's part to bring the three titans together, but the negotiations on the $100 million deal were still not proceeding smoothly. Kerkorian distrusted both Wasserman and Bluhdorn; he was a loner who was accustomed to crafting his own deals. But he also was experiencing a financial pinch at MGM, which meant that the CIC deal was important to him.

On two crucial occasions during the projection room discussions, Kerkorian simply got to his feet and marched out of the room. It was Korshak who followed him and persuaded him to keep talking. Late in the evening the deal was closed.

Korshak's fee for his evening's work was $250,000. When a bill for Bluhdorn's share of the fee arrived on his desk, the Gulf & Western chairman called Wasserman to question him in indignation. "There's no detail on the bill—no hourly fees, no explanation, nothing," Bluhdorn protested.

Wasserman's reply was succinct: "Pay it, Charles." Bluhdorn promptly authorized a check.

To Wasserman, keeping Korshak happy was important for two key reasons. Not only did Korshak play a key role in deals like CIC but his savvy also helped keep Charlie Bluhdorn out of trouble with federal regulators—that is, if Bluhdorn could be persuaded to listen to him. The Universal boss was worried that if Bluhdorn drew intense scrutiny from the Feds, then that scrutiny would spread to other studios.

Not only did Bluhdorn's Dominican dealings make Wasserman uncomfortable, but so did his practice of "liquidating" troubled assets from the Gulf & Western books. Wasserman and Korshak both were keenly aware of Bluhdorns's tactic in assuming a $12 million stake in an obscure shell company called Commonwealth United, and then donating to that company the rights to its Julie Andrews clunker *Darling Lili*. In return for this largesse, Commonwealth United delivered stock and warrants with a face value of $30 million. When Bluhdorn sold off his Commonwealth United holdings, the value of which quickly disintegrated, the SEC was left with the untenable task of figuring out the tax implications. Meanwhile, Paramount's books were clean of the *Darling Lili* stigma. The loss had disappeared, just as losses on *Paint Your Wagon* would also disappear.

A year later Bluhdorn once again acquired debentures in Commonwealth United in an even more bizarre deal involving the aforementioned Italian financier Michele Sindona. The debentures were then delivered to Sindona in partial payment for some 15 million shares in Société Générale Immobilière, a construction and real estate company in which Sindona was a major shareholder. Immobilière then turned around and purchased a 50 percent interest in Paramount's back lot in Hollywood and some of its surrounding acreage. The transaction effectively doubled the value of the lot—Paramount had carried it on its books for half the amount Sindona had advanced. (Commonwealth United debentures also figured in a later Bluhdorn real estate purchase in Florida.)

The Immobilière deal sent a shock wave through Hollywood. Deputations of Italians were soon wandering the lot arguing about the disposition of the property. Sindona, it seemed, had not been aware of the severe zoning restrictions that would sharply inhibit development and rule out high-rise structures. Further, many of the soundstages were not in use—a problem Sindona resolved by leasing stages to a producer of porn movies.

The SEC, meanwhile, found itself saddled with so many Bluhdorn investigations that its limited staff was having a difficult time deciding priorities. The Sindona connection conveniently came off its books when Italian authorities arrested the financier on charges that he had embezzled $225 million from an Italian bank. The case drew wide attention in Italy because Sindona was also linked to yet another important financial institution—the Vatican bank.

The embezzlement charges brought an abrupt end to the Bluhdorn-Sindona friendship. Not long thereafter, the Italian dealmaker was found dead in his jail cell in Sicily.

Except for a small inner circle, Bluhdorn's key executives knew nothing of the Sindona negotiations. Sidney Korshak, who keenly understood the dealings, and their dangers, shrewdly kept Bob Evans distanced from them. Korshak knew the price of dealing with those "on the dark side," and felt that someone in Bluhdorn's exposed position should be more discriminating in choosing business partners.

Knowing Bluhdorn's proclivities, Korshak had also avoided

involvement in *The Godfather*, and its intrigues. He'd been approached by major producer-stars like Burt Lancaster and Kirk Douglas who had hoped that Korshak could pressure Bluhdorn into selling the rights, but he knew this was never going to happen. Korshak knew also that Evans was getting battered in the casting controversies over *The Godfather*—Bluhdorn had told him Brando was a terrible idea and Al Pacino was too young to play Michael.

Given all this, Korshak was shocked by a message from Evans urgently soliciting help on the Pacino issue. The studio had finally caved to Coppola—Pacino would get the role. The problem was that the arguments over casting had consumed so much time that Pacino had now accepted a role in another film, *The Gang That Couldn't Shoot Straight*, which was about to start production at MGM. Evans pleaded with his consigliere to carry a persuasive message to Kirk Kerkorian, who owned MGM—release Pacino from his commitment so he could star in *The Godfather*.

When I ran into Korshak as he was leaving Evans's office, the big man seemed genuinely surprised. As he described his new mission, he flashed a pained smile—a memorable sighting in view of the fact that I had never seen Korshak smile. "No one in town even knows who this kid is," he said, referring to Pacino. "Suddenly two studios are fighting over a nobody."

"The director feels he's right for the role," I put in.

"And that makes this nobody kid the hottest actor in town?"

"He's a talented young actor, and I'm sure Kirk Kerkorian has never heard of him either."

The pained smile disappeared. It was Korshak, not me, who would have to twist Kerkorian's arm. It was not a mission I would want to undertake. Korshak shrugged and headed for the door.

Korshak knew he had leverage with Kerkorian. The tough Armenian was trying to complete construction of the MGM Grand in Las Vegas. He was stretched thin and could not abide any delays from his unions, and he knew Korshak could do some mischief.

Pacino instantly became available. His role in *Gang* was assumed by another relatively unknown young actor—Bobby De Niro. And Al Pacino's destined future as a star was now in place.

Insiders in town were fascinated at the Korshak power play, but one Korshak friend, Frank Sinatra, was not amused. Sinatra resented *The Godfather* because he felt that the character of Johnny Fontane represented a nasty caricature of him. Ever since *Rosemary's Baby*, Sinatra had hated Bob Evans and me as well. That film, in his mind, had fractured his marriage to Mia Farrow. Now Paramount was inflicting still further wounds.

One evening at Chasen's restaurant, Sinatra's antagonism surfaced abruptly. I was dining with a producer, and Sinatra was three or four tables away with some friends. Suddenly Mario Puzo loomed over my table. The bulky writer had had a few drinks and was enjoying his first moments of celebrity. Puzo told me that he was going over to Sinatra's table to introduce himself.

My response was instantaneous. "Don't do it," I told Puzo.

"But I owe Frank a greeting," Puzo replied. "I know he had feelings about the Johnny Fontane character."

"Sinatra is not the sort of person you say 'hello' to," I warned. "He's a miserable prick."

But Puzo was feeling no pain. He went off to introduce himself to the star and, even before he'd reached the table, I could see that my warning had been valid. "You miserable son of a bitch, get out of my fucking sight," Sinatra was yelling, as soon as he saw Puzo.

"I just wanted to—" was all Puzo got to say.

"I'll tear your fucking head off," Sinatra was shouting, and Puzo already was beating a retreat.

The next day Puzo was on the phone to me. "Did you see the gossip columns this morning? They reported the whole incident. It's embarrassing."

"You're the star now, Mario. That's what matters in this town," I said.

"You're a journalist. I hope you're keeping notes on all this," Puzo said.

I had to smile. "Not exactly. I once had a visit from Korshak," I said. "It was in the middle of some complicated stuff. He offered me some advice."

"Like . . . ?"

"Korshak said, 'I hope you're not keeping notes. I learned long ago that keeping notes can be dangerous to your health.'"

"You took his advice?" Puzo asked.

"Damned right I did."

CHAPTER 8

Breaking the Mold

Early in 1970 I placed a small device atop my desk at my Paramount office. The device consisted of a narrow steel pole about two feet high. Atop the pole sat a little wooden woodpecker which, when I poked its tail, would slowly work his way down, making pinging sounds as he descended. The downward trek took just under three minutes.

I decided to make use of my faux woodpecker during pitch meetings. I found myself getting impatient during these sessions, since the stories often took too long in the telling and the storytellers were usually less than riveting. Hence when someone insisted he had a story to tell, I started my woodpecker on its journey and advised my visitor that he had three minutes to complete his narrative. The pings were so distracting that the stories often were abandoned well before the finish time, with the visitor saying, "I'll send it to you and you can read it yourself," which is what I wanted to hear.

It took only a couple of weeks for me to realize that my woodpecker was becoming infamous. "Some of my clients complain you're rude to them," an elegant, silver-haired agent named Evarts Ziegler told me. "You can't assign time limits. Besides, the fucking bird is distracting." Ziegler, who represented an important list of writers, had taken a fatherly interest in me.

"I don't like to listen to pitches," I protested. "I prefer reading them."

Ziegler wasn't buying that. "You're striking people as an angry guy," he said, peering at me analytically. "You're new at this and doing well so far. Why are you angry?"

Feeling defensive, I told Ziegler that I wasn't angry. In fact I really liked my job. But before going home that night, I placed my woodpecker in the closet and determined to retire it from play.

Driving home, I realized that Ziegler was right. I was indeed feeling a simmering anger, but it wasn't directed at story pitchers or their agents. I was angry at myself, or at least at the person I felt I was becoming.

I had gone to Paramount with Bob Evans carrying idealistic hopes of changing the game. I was not going to follow studio rules or become seduced by the Hollywood club.

Yet most of the submissions of projects that came before me were still emanating from the club. And often, when I happened upon material I liked, I found myself taking that material to clubbies rather than to the sort of creative young people I was hoping to lure into my web.

All this was brought home to me when I found myself dealing with one of the ultimate insiders, Hal Wallis, a gruff, curmudgeonly producer who was ensconced in a long-term producing deal at Paramount. Wallis had built a storied career as chief of production at Warner Bros., where his producing credits included *Casablanca*, but now he was relegated to turning out Elvis Presley vehicles. Since he had a deal with

Paramount, however, I felt obligated to pay him diplomatic visits and even to run material past him now and then.

When I stepped into Wallis's office, I found it jam-packed with memorabilia of all description, including an Oscar—I assumed it was the statuette for *Casablanca*, which Wallis had famously wrestled from the hands of Jack Warner at the Academy Awards show in 1942. Photos of Wallis with stars like John Wayne, James Stewart, Henry Fonda, Bogart, Bacall, and, of course, Elvis, filled every inch of wall space.

Wallis did not get up from his chair to greet me. This would be a "what-do-you-want-kid?" sort of meeting, I concluded.

Abandoning pleasantries, I told Wallis tersely that I had read the galleys of a new novel that I believed could provide the basis of a John Wayne movie. "It's a western," I explained. "But there's a great role for an older character. Its called *True Grit*, and I'm bringing it up because I know you have known Wayne for many—"

"Duke doesn't want to play older characters," Wallis cut in, using Wayne's nickname to emphasize his intimacy.

I plunked the galleys on his desk anyway. "I think he'd go for this," I said.

"I'll have it covered," Wallis replied, turning away.

I was out of there, regretting immediately that I had given Wallis the book. John Wayne now and then lunched at the Paramount commissary and I had exchanged friendly words with him on several occasions. I could have given him the book directly, but one of my responsibilities was to find deals to bury some of Wallis's overhead.

I did not hear from Wallis for three weeks. Worried that I would lose the book, I sent him a memo inquiring if he was planning to do anything with it. I received an immediate response from Wallis's assistant informing me that the producer had given *True Grit* to John Wayne, who urgently wanted to do it. Wallis was now looking for a director. There was no "thank you" or even a "let me know if you find something else."

So much for building a relationship with Hal Wallis. Our total give-and-take, I realized, would consist of Wallis supervising a script and submitting his budget. We would then say "yes" or "no"—that would be the extent of our input.

Still, I was gratified that I'd found a picture for John Wayne—as it turned out, it was a damned good picture. Still my role had been defined as that of a studio functionary, servicing the filmmaking establishment, or at least that sector of the establishment that was based at Paramount.

As I drove to the studio with Evans one morning, I blurted out my frustration. "I don't want to spend my life with the likes of Alan Jay Lerner, Hal Wallis, or Blake Edwards," I complained. "They're voices of the past, and if we don't do something radical about it, they'll become our voice."

Evans flashed a pained smile, but remained silent. I knew he agreed with me, but I also knew that he relished the attention of Lerner, Wallis, Edwards, and others of Hollywood's ruling class.

"What do you want to do about it?" Evans asked finally.

"I want to go out on a limb," I told him. "I want to find the unexpected. I want to beat the odds."

My friend looked at me quizzically. "What kind of unexpected . . . ?"

"Beats me."

Evans was obviously bemused. "Go for it," he mumbled.

The next weekend I read a script that perfectly fit my mood. It was utterly bizarre in terms of character and narrative. Its theme was one of rebellion if not downright nihilism. I had never heard of its author—a kid named Colin Higgins who had recently graduated from UCLA film school and was cleaning swimming pools to support himself. One of the pools belonged to a producer named Edward Lewis to whom Higgins had given his script, hoping for words of encouragement.

A tough, grizzled producer, Lewis knew the script—it was titled *Harold and Maude*—was off-the-wall. Apparently he'd decided that, of all the studio execs in town, I might be the least likely to reject it. "This may not be for you," Lewis told me as he handed me a copy. "This may be an acquired taste."

When I phoned Lewis that following Monday morning, my instinct was to express my unbridled enthusiasm, but I knew that was not the way business was done at studios. If you liked something too much in Hollywood, the price went up. The best attitude, I had learned, was one of mild disinterest.

"The script is different," I told Lewis warily. "But it's . . . well, out there."

Edward Lewis was known to be a stalwart liberal who had produced *Spartacus* and was one of the first to hire blacklisted writers. "But, do you personally like it?" he asked.

I was determined to be cagey. "The script has its own sensibility, I'll give you that, but how the hell do you translate that sensibility to the screen?"

"I'll give you the bad news," Lewis said. "The kid who wrote it—the Higgins kid—insists on directing it. That's the way it lays out."

The "Higgins kid," of course, had no credentials as a director except for his UCLA student film. "You know as well as I that you'll never get the picture made on those terms," I told Lewis. I was fencing. He knew it.

What I'd wanted to say was, "This is an amazing fucking script and I'll bust my butt to get it made." But first there were questions to be resolved. Was there interest in the script elsewhere? How cheaply could the movie be budgeted? Would

Colin Higgins agree to a test of some sort—a director's audition—to determine his capabilities?

There was another question as well. Would Bob Evans
think I was losing it when he read the script?

The next morning I went to Evans's office with *Harold
and Maude*. "I told you I was looking for some break-the-rules
material," I said. "So I've got *numero uno*. It's a love story
between an eighteen-year-old boy and an eighty-year-old
woman."

Evans shot me a look. "And I suppose there's a hot sex
scene between them. It's *Deep Throat* in a retirement home."

I drew a breath. "They have sex, but, this movie could be
. . . well, game changing. Please read it and tell me I'm crazy."

"You are *serious*?" Evans exclaimed.

I didn't answer.

"I'll show you what I'm going to do," Evans said. He disappeared into his bathroom. I heard the lock click. I retreated
to my office. Forty minutes later, he buzzed me on the inter-
com. "I love it. But you're going to get me fired, you prick."

This was a project that had to be semisurreptitious: that
much we both understood. We could not expose the script
to Bluhdorn or Davis or even to the head of marketing. It
would never survive the encounter. *Harold and Maude* would
have to be protected from the pack. It would not even be
given to the story department for the usual coverage by its
"readers."

Problem one, of course, was to zero in on a director.
Since the deal specified Higgins would get his shot, he was
given a check for $7,000 and told to shoot a test. My own
feeling, spending time with Higgins, was that he was not up
to the challenge. A bright and friendly guy from Australia, he
explained that he had written his script visualizing Elsa Lanchester as Maude and a young actor named John Rubinstein

as Harold. Neither seemed especially attractive to me in those roles.

Two weeks later, Higgins presented his filmed audition: it was not especially impressive—a fact that he acknowledged. I knew I had to spring quickly into action to find another director. A friend had told me about a newly completed movie called *The Landlord*, which was produced by Norman Jewison and directed by his former editor, Hal Ashby. When I saw the film and asked Jewison about its director, he was unstinting in his recommendation. "Ashby is brilliant," said Jewison, whose own work included *The Russians Are Coming*. "He's got the touch. He's a quirky guy—he may not be your cup of tea."

I dispatched a copy of *Harold and Maude* to Ashby with a note expressing my enthusiasm for the material.

When Ashby turned up in my office a few days later, I understood Jewison's message. Rail-thin and wearing tinted "granny" glasses, his straw hair splayed across his shoulders, mustache and beard fighting each other for space on his rumpled face, Ashby looked like a homeless person. Checking his background, I learned that he was from Ogden, Utah, the rebellious product of the Mormon culture, but was not himself a Mormon. When Hal was twelve years old, his father had shot himself, and Hal had left home shortly afterward.

Ashby had been married and divorced in his early twenties and floated around the West until he lucked into a job running a mimeograph machine at Universal studio. He befriended a young assistant editor and found himself developing an affinity for the Moviola editing machine. By this time, he had also acquired the nickname "Hashby" because of his fondness for marijuana and related substances.

Chatting in my office now, Ashby seemed diffident about our prospective project. "The writer, Higgins, he wants to direct his script," he said. "Why not let him do it?"

"We let him do a test," I said. "He's not ready."

"Let me talk with him," Ashby said. I remembered Jewison's warning. Ashby was indeed "quirky," if not funky.

Over the next few weeks, Ashby went through a sort of dance—one I'd ultimately become familiar with. He talked with Higgins, and apparently they liked each other. Higgins reiterated his interest in directing, but said that if Ashby wanted to take it over, that was OK with him.

Ashby's appetite for *Harold and Maude* seemed expansive one week, only to fade the next. In rereading the script, he'd decided that music had become an essential ingredient to telling the story—but what music?

He sent the script to Elton John, who reacted enthusiastically to it, and even talked about trying out for the role of Harold. His handlers reminded him that his career as a performer was just starting to take off. This was no time for an acting hiatus.

And then there was Cat Stevens. Ashby loved the funky ballads in Cat's album *Tea for the Tillerman.* The songs told a story that could be integrated into the *Harold and Maude* story.

Ashby would never get around to specifically saying, "I want to direct this movie." Direct communication of that sort wasn't in his repertoire, I concluded. So one day I told Evans that we shouldn't have any more meetings, we should simply start putting together our crew and cast.

Hence, in typically cool seventies style, *Harold and Maude* drifted into reality. There was no ceremonial green light, and no one at the corporate level asked about it when the title appeared on the production charts. It would simply become a "happening."

As he started reworking the script, Ashby's conceit was that Harold was a rebellious rich kid who was ambivalent about virtually everything except for two issues: He hated his mother and he wanted to stay out of the draft. Maude was a hippie empress whose background was either one of privilege or poverty, depending on which story she wished to spin (Harold even spied concentration camp numbers on her arm, but that was never discussed). Harold and Maude shared a fondness for funerals. He was enamored of her panache but appalled by her tendency to steal cars and defy the law. And somewhere along the way, Maude decided that, though she was nearing her eightieth birthday, she would make a man of him—and shortly thereafter, commit suicide.

One day Ashby called to say, "There are six guys I'd like to test for the part of Harold but I don't really know what to expect. In fact, I don't have a clue."

The actors were a study in contrast: John Rubinstein had a boyish charm, Bob Balaban was intelligent but nerdy, and Bud Cort was delicate and sexually ambiguous.

Of all the actors, only Cort had heat. He had recently starred in Robert Altman's picture *Brewster McCloud*, and he was now pursuing the role of Harold with a self-confidence the other young actors couldn't mobilize. He even promised Ashby that he would personally recruit Greta Garbo to play Maude. (Garbo at the time had long since retired.) Cort said he loved the script but warned he would do a lot of improvising—a suggestion that offended Colin Higgins but seemed to excite Ashby.

Cort got the gig. Ashby dismissed his Garbo idea, proposing Ruth Gordon for Maude—a notion that jarred Higgins. He felt Gordon would play Maude as too aggressive and surly a character. Ashby had earlier considered the gentler Dame Edith Evans, who had starred in *The Whisperers*, but after spending time with Gordon, he told his producer, Charles (Chuck) Mulvehill, "Let's go for the comedy—and that's Gordon."

Bob Evans concurred with this choice. He'd just seen Ruth

Gordon in a very broad comedy called *Where's Poppa?*, and also admired her work in *Rosemary's Baby* two years earlier.

"I want laughs," Ashby responded. "*Harold and Maude* won't work without big laughs and Ruth Gordon is funny. She also has a gentler side."

Though I'd resolutely avoided arguments about casting, I decided to join the Ruth Gordon cause this time. "You've seen her crass side in *Where's Poppa?* but, trust me, Ruth Gordon in person is a thoughtful, soft-spoken individual," I told Evans. "She's even a friend of my mother on Martha's Vineyard. She presides over a literary salon."

Ashby was similarly unpredictable in favoring a British TV actress with the unlikely name of Vivian Pickles to play Mrs. Chasen, Harold's mother. Again, he'd interviewed more serious and famous actresses like Gladys Cooper and Dame Edith Evans, but opted for a performer who would deliver laughs.

Ashby had taken a lot of time in choosing his cast, and Mulvehill, his young producer, learned that his director would be similarly deliberate in picking his locations. "I love Hal, but he's indecisive," Mulvehill complained. "Whenever he faces a tough decision, his instinct is to light up a joint and walk off by himself.

"Hal's life is all about dope," Mulvehill observed. "If he lights a joint, he feels he'll get a better idea." Be prepared, Mulvehill seemed to be warning; shooting *Harold and Maude* will be a hallucinogenic experience. "Hal doesn't even want to rehearse his actors," Mulvehill said. "He feels it takes away the spontaneity."

Mulvehill's foreboding was justified. By the third week of principal photography, it became evident that Ashby's indecisiveness was costing him, and also the studio. With every passing day, he was managing to accomplish only half a day's work. And when Evans phoned him to register his concern, Ashby refused to take his phone calls.

When I spoke with Mulvehill about these issues, the young producer was, as usual, candid. "Hal seems to be struggling to find the voice of the picture. It's that music issue we talked about at the start."

Ashby, it seemed, had been playing Cat Stevens songs over and over on the set. He even decided to ask Cat Stevens and his manager to fly to San Francisco to watch the dailies and perhaps compose some songs that could integrate the scenes. Uncertain about the flow of the narrative, Ashby hoped the young Brit could not only devise a score but also become a partner in creating the story.

Stevens was thrilled by the opportunity. He had never visited San Francisco; indeed, he had never flown first-class. And he liked both the script and its director. "Hal isn't like the predictable Hollywood director," Stevens told me. "He always seems to be high." And he wasn't talking about mood.

The experiment seemed to work. Cat recorded two of his songs, and then the editors cut them into scenes, and Ashby was excited by the result. Now *Harold and Maude* was emerging as a comedy with music.

But it was still emerging too slowly. As its principal advocate, I was the obvious candidate to visit the set and forcefully inform the filmmaker and producer of the studio's growing alarm. *Harold and Maude* was a delicious adventure at $1.4 million. At $2 million or beyond, it could become an embarrassment to the new production regime.

Mindful that Ashby was habitually noncommunicative, I flew to San Francisco and walked onto the set one morning. Mulvehill was the first to spot me, and his look was one of panic. Ashby pretended to ignore me at first, but when I started in his direction he advanced to meet me.

"Didn't expect you," he said, not offering his hand.

"Look, Hal, you and I know how this conversation between us will play out, so let's make it simple. You have to go faster. Much faster." My voice was calm but firm.

"Faster is not better," he replied.

"Faster is better for me and that makes it better for you," I replied. I then handed him an airline ticket.

"Why are you giving me a ticket?"

"It will be your ticket home to LA if you don't maintain your shooting schedule," I said.

Ashby's pallid face turned pink. He nervously adjusted his granny glasses. "I'll try," Ashby said, and turned away. "No promises."

"The ticket is a promise," I told him.

It was not a warm-and-fuzzy meeting, but studio executives rarely have warm-and-fuzzy meetings with directors. This one apparently served its purpose. Ashby stepped up his shooting pace. He smoked a little less and shot a little more and the Cat Stevens songs were playing constantly and seemed to give him heart.

As I watched the dailies, Harold's ceremonial suicides were hilarious. His dialogues with Maude were poignant. Though he required myriad takes, Bud Cort's reaction shots were inspired—his wistful contentment upon his sexual initiation with Maude was classic. And the bits from the character actors were consistently on target.

My colleagues in the screening room broke up when Eric Christmas, cast as Harold's priest, delivered his reaction to the news of Harold and Maude's imminent marriage. "The commingling of withered flesh, sagging breasts . . ." represented his imagining of the Harold and Maude wedding night, and it somehow epitomized the opaque love story.

Once the final scene had been shot and Ashby had a

chance to return to his natural habitat—the editing room—the expectation at the studio was that a tidy first cut would soon be delivered. By this time, however, I had already learned that expectations of any kind were dangerous at a studio. In fact, Ashby soon found himself stymied. The first act of the film, embracing Harold's faux suicides, his "auditions" of the girls recruited by his mother, and the initial encounters with Maude all fell deftly into place. Ashby cut together forty minutes, replete with Cat Stevens music, to show us, and our reactions were exuberant.

At the same time he was struggling with several key scenes toward the end of the movie, which had been desperately overwritten. From the time Maude announced her intention to end her life through the hospital sequences, the movie simply died. Scenes were talky; emotions were announced, not dramatized.

In desperation, Ashby played repeatedly with montage and with music, but the first full cut came in at three hours, and Mulvehill told him, "This movie is fucking awful." Reacting to one Ruth Gordon scene, Mulvehill blurted to his director, "If this fucking broad says one more wiseass word I'm gonna smack her."

That scene was cut. In the end, after much anguish and many joints, Ashby turned in a streamlined cut of ninety minutes. Evans and I loved it and arranged for a test screening before what we thought would be a sympathetic audience in Palo Alto, adjacent to the Stanford University campus. The young audience seemed stunned by the movie at first then started laughing and even applauding. At the end the audience was on its feet.

Evans and I were delighted. The time had finally come, we agreed, to show this film to the Paramount marketing and distribution executives.

Alas, the Stanford reaction would not be replicated. A few

professed to like the film, but I could sense the furtive dismissal. Frank Yablans, the newly anointed president, did not "get" *Harold and Maude*. He labeled it "an art house picture" and proposed a limited Christmas release, designed as counter-programming to the rival studios' would-be blockbusters. The marketing team meanwhile struck out again and again in their effort to design a campaign. Their final effort was a sort of tombstone ad that simply showed a background of type.

A reason the key Christmas dates were suddenly available, of course, stemmed from our studio's *Godfather* problem. Intended to be the big holiday blockbuster, *The Godfather* would not hit its dates because of substantial re-editing. Suddenly prime theaters like the Village in Westwood had become available, but *Harold and Maude* was not suited for "big barns." It needed to be nurtured in select art theaters where it could be "discovered" by discriminating filmgoers. This was especially true since the studio had failed to come up with a distinctive ad campaign—indeed any ad campaign.

Frantic, Ashby broke his usual zone of silence to call Yablans in protest. The way to sell *Harold and Maude*, he argued, was simply to explain what it was—namely a comedic love story between an eighteen-year-old boy and an eighty-year-old woman. Yablans didn't want to listen.

The opening reviews didn't help. The first was written by *Variety*'s Art Murphy, a conservative Catholic who was at war with what he felt to be the corrupt values of the youth culture. To Murphy, *Harold and Maude* "had all the fun and gaiety of a burning orphanage." The film, he wrote, "joins the inventory of contemporary comedies, witless efforts which make one feel embarrassed for those involved." Several favorable reviews emerged from the big city critics, but they were all but drowned out by the publicity accorded the big Christmas movies like *A Clockwork Orange* from Stanley Kubrick, *Dirty*

Harry, starring Clint Eastwood, and Paddy Chayefsky's *The Hospital*.

Audiences in most major cities simply didn't show up. Once again, Ashby was on the phone to point out that in those markets where the film was strongest, exhibitors had thrown out the Paramount ads and were vamping on their own. In Baltimore, for example, the local theater owner had substituted his own simple campaign emphasizing the Harold and Maude love story. And it was working.

My own sense of frustration easily matched that of Ashby. The Palo Alto screening had convinced me that there was an audience out there for *Harold and Maude*. When I screened it for friends in Los Angeles, they embraced it too.

With earlier films like *Goodbye, Columbus* and *Rosemary's Baby*, I had surreptitiously hired Stephen Frankfurt, the star of the Young & Rubicam ad agency, who had come up with brilliantly innovative campaigns, but my initiatives caused utter rage within the studio. Now with Frank Yablans, a self-proclaimed marketing wiz, I had been warned not to reach outside the company again.

Yablans, though gruff by nature, tried to be sympathetic. "I know this is a passion project for you," he told me, "but give it up. Let it go away. A year from now no one will remember it ever got made."

I listened to him, but I was not prepared to forget this movie. On the other hand, I never would have suspected its immortality.

Harold and Maude was a momentary failure, but it would live forever as a cult classic. Some theaters played the movie for over a year, while others revived it once a year. And over time, scores of people have told me where they were when they first saw *Harold and Maude*, who they were with, and what happened as a result.

Hal Ashby would go on to make several more distin-guished films, like *Shampoo* and *Coming Home*. Years later we were to work together once again on *Being There*—yet another film that achieved its own special immortality.

A month before he died, in 2001, Hal paid me a visit, and even then, gravely ill, he peered at me, adjusted his granny glasses and said, "I'll never understand why *Harold and Maude* failed. It deserved a better fate, didn't it?"

"It didn't fail, Hal. It will live forever."

CHAPTER 9

Hard Lessons

At some moment during my first few months at Paramount, two facts crystallized for me: First, that Evans and I (indeed, the studio as a whole) were being all but suffocated by the onrush of projects already in the pipeline. And second, that the only way we could inject our own movies into the studio bloodstream was by stubborn advocacy, bordering on corporate demagoguery.

I felt a growing urgency to act on this conclusion. Every weekend Evans and I would watch one or two movies that we had inherited and that theoretically were now ready for distribution, and Evans finally turned to me at the end of one screening and asked, "Would you pay to see any of these movies?"

My response was instinctual: "I'd pay to avoid seeing them."

But we had to see them—we were being paid to do so. They were an odd mix: Some consisted of European films that Bluhdorn or other colleagues overseas had impulsively acquired for

U.S. distribution. They ranged from *The Stranger*, directed by Luchino Visconti, an opaque adaptation of the classic Albert Camus novel, to *Fraulein Doktor*, a clunky spy movie from director Alberto Lattuada. Though they ranged widely in ambition and quality, the one element these pickups had in common, as we were to learn, was that American audiences had no interest whatsoever in them.

By and large, Paramount seemed to be missing out on the truly transformative films emanating from Fellini or Truffaut while it was locked into a second and third tier of semi-exploitational fare.

This phenomenon became all the more alarming when several new and very expensive overseas epics, also Bluhdorn deals, began to arrive with a series of loud thuds. *Waterloo*, a $100 million broad-canvas Italian-Russian-British coproduction starring Rod Steiger as a blustery Napoléon, was a total flop. Another Euro epic, *The Red Tent*, starring Sean Connery and Peter Finch, which dramatized a 1928 dirigible disaster in the Arctic with extravagant effects, also found no audience in the U.S.

There were two exceptions to this chain of disasters: One was a French gangster film, *Borsolino*, starring Alain Delon and Jean-Paul Belmondo, which played like a vivid homage to Hollywood's Cagney-Bogart genre movies. The second was Franco Zeffirelli's English-language lyric imagining of *Romeo and Juliet*, which succeeded in winning a young audience back to Shakespeare.

If the work of the foreign filmmakers was proving difficult to introduce, the response to the U.S. films commissioned by the previous studio regime proved equally dismaying. For reasons I will never understand, Paramount had decided to make an expensive deal with the famously dictatorial German-born director Otto Preminger, giving him total autonomy over the choice and casting of his pictures.

The results were appalling. The humorless Preminger ground out two numb comedies called *Skidoo* and *Tell Me That You Love Me, Junie Moon*. The latter's principal characters were a gay cripple, an epileptic, and a girl with a disfigured face, all of whom left a hospital to start a new life together. Preminger's effort at melodrama consisted of *Hurry Sundown*, a lifeless racial drama starring Jane Fonda and Michael Caine.

After the initial screening of *Junie Moon*, Preminger threw a lavish dinner party at his Bel Air home, serving pounds of the finest caviar wrapped in potato skins and adorned with sour cream and onions. I had never savored such fine caviar and I was enjoying the evening until the director suddenly confronted me. "Were you not moved by these amazing characters?" he demanded, taking on the demeanor of a German officer confronting a junior aide.

Not knowing how to reply, I inadvertently dropped my potato skin on his shoe. It landed with a splat. Preminger wheeled and stalked away.

Between Preminger's misbegotten efforts and the steady flow of films from overseas, the Paramount distribution pipeline was all but groaning, and so were Evans and I. One morning when I picked Evans up on the way to the office, he started humming softly. Usually, the Evans hum—it's a low and slightly ominous monotone—portends trouble.

"What's bugging you, Bob?" I asked.

Evans kept humming for a few beats. Finally: "Two more Paramount pictures are opening this weekend," he said. "They're both unwatchable."

It was too good an opening. "If we don't want to see them, who will?"

Evans started humming again and I was getting a headache. "Look, Bob, we've got to start jamming our own movies into the goddamn pipeline," I said. "Even if some are misfires, at least they won't be Otto Preminger's."

Evans remained silent the rest of the trip. He didn't even hum.

That week I started making offers—different kinds of offers. Instead of buying finished films for distribution, we started buying the rights to screenplays, novels, and plays, and suddenly, literary agents who had been ignoring Paramount were lining up with their submissions. The studio was in business again. But it was an entirely different style of business.

The timing was propitious. By 1967 it had become vividly clear that filmgoers were buying tickets again, but their tastes were difficult to chart. Paramount, like every studio, had its dogmatic marketing gurus who claimed they could analyze which movies were commercial and which were not, but even these folks were shaken by the obvious changes in the pop culture. Sure, Elvis Presley movies still had their loyalists and *The Sound of Music* was registering record business around the world, but the five films nominated for Oscars in February 1968 were *Bonnie and Clyde*, *Doctor Dolittle*, *The Graduate*, *Guess Who's Coming to Dinner*, and *In the Heat of the Night*—a group representing a mind-boggling spectrum of generational sensibilities.

The studio system was clearly in a state of confusion and, perched at its nerve center, I quickly determined to use that confusion to my advantage. The secret to getting a movie made at Paramount, I had found, was simply to keep putting it back on the table time after time. If protests emerged from distribution or elsewhere that the budget was too high, the star wattage too low, or the subject matter too arcane, I'd simply pull it, make a few adjustments, perhaps change the title, then put it back in contention. And since the flood of submissions had become so formidable, no one, I discovered, was carefully tracking them.

A degree of arrogance was intrinsic to this process, I realized, and that disturbed me. I was a journalist who was toying with the careers and passions of accomplished professionals in what was still an alien field. On the other hand, what was driving me was a sense of rebellion against the creaky studio mechanisms at Paramount and other companies when the wrong movies were being made for the wrong reasons.

With the support and encouragement of Evans, I felt I could help instill a modus operandi that was more responsive to the energies and passions of the moment. Movies had instantly become the most vital mode of expression for young artists. Rock 'n' rollers wanted to make movies, painters wanted to shoot film, poets were pitching scripts. Suddenly, Hollywood was becoming a sort of pop culture mecca, or at least aspiring to be that.

As I began to assemble my cadre of new talents, my motivations were at once pure and self-serving. I wanted to find myself in the company of smart people. I didn't want to deal with members of the club who merely wanted big paydays. I sensed that the top agents both distrusted and disdained me—I was the enemy who would likely be inhospitable to their packages and packaging fees. My name was noticeably absent from the lists of hot parties hosted by established producers in the community.

But amid all this I was beginning to have fun. An array of interesting projects was being paraded before me and I was trying to get my arms around them and also their potential traps.

The traps were abundant. I was the new boy in town and the old pros were eager to teach me a few lessons.

They didn't have to wait long.

Lesson one was a project called *Blue*, which turned into a case study in the pitfalls of studio management. I sensed *Blue* was a problem from the start, but I allowed myself to be sucked into its vortex.

I came upon *Blue* through my casual friendship with a young producer named Judd Bernard. Judd was all the things a producer was expected to be: He was hyper, funny, and, like every gifted sociopath, had a habit of telling you what you wanted to hear. He knew my impatience with my studio's attitudes, and confided that he was assembling a "hot" but counterintuitive package.

Robert Redford, who had just made a name for himself in *Barefoot in the Park*, wanted to star in a western. The director would be Silvio Narizzano, whose unexpected hit *Georgy Girl*, an urban comedy, had just been released. Bernard himself had just produced a successful thriller titled *Point Blank* starring Lee Marvin.

All the players in *Blue* were coming into their own. Moreover, the movie wasn't mired in the usual cowboys-and-Indians formula but was a complex story about a young American who, having been raised by Mexican bandits, tries to settle down as a Texas farmer. *Blue* was attracting interest at other studios, Bernard told me. Paramount was not first in line.

I bit. Even though the script needed embellishing and Narizzano, a Canadian living in London, had never directed a western, I rationalized away these reservations and became an advocate.

Blue quickly ran into opposition from my colleagues. The "no" votes were emphatic, but I kept putting it back on the table. At a cost of slightly under $3 million, *Blue* didn't represent much of a gamble, I argued. In due course, the deal was closed. *Blue* would start shooting in two months in Moab, Utah. Judd Bernard had become my best friend.

Then I began getting the dire signals. Redford, it seemed,

had met with Bernard in New York and had expressed second thoughts about the screenplay. His character lacked nuance, the actor said. The dialogue was on the nose.

"Don't worry," Bernard told me reassuringly. "It's just actor insecurity."

Narizzano, meanwhile, remained home in London accepting accolades for *Georgy Girl*. He was a hot ticket in town and wasn't eager to come to the U.S. to scout locations. Again, a "don't worry" from the producer.

But I was getting worried. Worry turned into outright alarm when Bernard called to say Redford had abruptly withdrawn from the movie. The actor did not seek a meeting to put forth his problems with the script. He did not express his regrets (this was true to form, I was to learn). He simply walked.

My first instinct was to absorb my losses and run, but Judd Bernard was not ready to accept quick defeat. Since I was no longer an advocate, he decided to go over my head and march directly into the office of the ubiquitous Charlie Bluhdorn.

"I have exciting news about *Blue*," he told Bluhdorn. A hot young actor, Terence Stamp, had committed to his project.

"But Redford . . . ?" Bluhdorn protested.

"Not needed anymore," Bernard assured him. Stamp was coming out of a terrific movie called *Billy Budd*. He was a better "name."

Bluhdorn considered Stamp to be a rising star in Europe. The fact that Stamp was a Brit who had never tried to master an American accent did not seem to worry him.

I summoned Bernard to a meeting at the studio to berate him for his tactics, but he was brimming with confidence. Terence Stamp would be perfect in *Blue*, he insisted. Indeed, he now wanted to present yet another great idea. Even as *Blue* was being shot, Bernard planned to produce a simultaneous movie to be called *Fade In*. This, too, would be set in Moab, Utah, and would be a touching love story involving an attractive film editor who was working on the movie and fell for a local rancher. Bernard had already elicited commitments from a promising young actress, Barbara Loden, and a young actor named Burt Reynolds, to play the leads.

"Think of the publicity buzz," effused Bernard, who had started as a publicist. "This will be the first time in movie history that two intertwined films would be shot simultaneously. Audiences for the first time will understand what it's like to be caught up in the tensions of creating a movie on location."

In presenting his brainstorm to Evans, Bernard shrewdly described the first scene in his movie—Bob Evans, the glamorous studio chief, stepping off his private plane to visit the location and welcome his stars. It would be a great scene for Evans and, obviously, he would play himself.

A draft of *Fade In* was already being written by Mart Crowley, said Bernard, and Jud Taylor, a sharp young television director, was also interested. Everything was ready to go, and Bernard was even prepared to foot the bill if Paramount demurred.

Evans and I had the identical reaction. Judd Bernard registered a 10 on the index of sheer brashness. Instead of being on the defensive for losing his star (Redford) he was doubling his (and our) bet by pitching yet another speculative movie to shoot alongside his first one.

Still, for $800,000 no one seemed willing to say no to *Fade In*. With Bluhdorn's blessing, *Blue* was rolling ahead into preproduction. To kill *Fade In* seemed like more trouble than it was worth.

As principal photography drew closer, I felt a growing dread about these two adventures. I had stupidly started the ball rolling, and thus I should have done more to stop it. And as the dailies began to arrive my apprehensions grew into a quiet terror.

Silvio Narizzano's solution to the problem of Stamp's Brit accent was to eliminate almost all his dialogue. The English actor stood around, looking self-conscious and occasionally grunting. The lines enunciated by other actors sounded as though they had been translated from the Spanish. "No, my brothers," one bandit said. "We only play games, the games of children or of madmen."

The movie wasn't playing. Neither was *Fade In*. The Loden-Reynolds romance, too, seemed stilted. Judd Bernard was creating the perfect nightmare: zero for two!

Months later, several of us gathered at the old Plaza Theater in Westwood for the test screening of *Fade In*. The theater was packed with filmgoers who had just paid to see another film and were now getting a "bonus." By the time *Fade In* had been running for thirty minutes, half the theater was empty. By the close, only ten or fifteen filmgoers remained.

Four weeks later, the first screenings of "Blue" were even more disastrous. "These debacles are my damned fault," I told Evans. "I should have shut them down."

Evans changed the subject. Not long thereafter, I had the same conversation with Bluhdorn. I told him that I had messed up and was willing to take the fall. But the normally combustible chairman absolutely refused to play the blame game. That was not his style. "*Blue* is history," he declared with fierce finality.

While I appreciated Bluhdorn's refusal to be judgmental, I was disturbed by his unwillingness, and that of my colleagues, to face up to our mistakes and analyze the causes. It was as though any form of self-criticism was utterly alien. The sheer onrush of events provided the perfect cover for all of us. There was simply no time for looking back and seeking perspective.

In reaction, I began to keep a careful log on the projects I was most closely involved in, charting the good, the bad, and the ugly decisions along the way. Over the course of the ensuing months and years it would, I hoped, become clear to me where my instincts proved valid and where I went drastically wrong.

The lessons that I logged in were roughly as follows.

LESSON: Politics and movies are a disastrous mix.

Haskell Wexler's phone calls were always cryptic, if not abrupt, but his taut tone at the other end of the line this time put me on alert. "I am going to make a proposal," he said. "I don't want to back you against the wall, so I'm going to pose it this way: If you approve of my proposal, do not say anything. Just hang up. I'll understand and will move forward. If the answer is 'no,' just tell me now and I will stop."

Over the next five minutes Wexler told me his proposal for the movie. I listened to him carefully, and when he was done, I promptly hung up. As far as I was concerned, it was a done deal.

A brilliant young cinematographer (he'd shot such films as *Who's Afraid of Virginia Woolf?* and *In the Heat of the Night*) and a committed social activist, Wexler had made a deal with Paramount to shoot a movie called *The Concrete Wilderness* about a kid growing up in the slums of Chicago. I had liked the novel and felt Wexler represented exactly the sort of savvy and dedicated filmmaker I'd been trying to recruit. Under his stewardship, *Concrete* could be a tough, street-smart urban thriller.

Only now Wexler had a better idea. Even as he was in preproduction in Chicago, the Democratic Party was gathering for its 1968 political convention and the chaos was already building. The cops were beating back demonstrators, waves of tear gas wafted through the streets, and there were rumors of intervention by the National Guard.

Wexler had originally intended to shoot his story with a sort of guerrilla film unit, but now he and his crew were pinned down, caught between the warring factions that were poised for revolution on Chicago's streets. Hence his phone call: Though he was in preproduction on *Concrete Wilderness*, he felt driven to shoot another story entirely—a movie about the events swirling around him. He would concoct the script as he went along. It would revolve around a news cameraman, to be played by Robert Forster, who was filming the violence on the streets but who also found himself involved with a young schoolteacher whose little boy had become lost in the maelstrom.

Wexler vowed that he would come up with "combat" footage of the convention that had never been seen in an American film. "No one in your corporation will ever be able to claim you said yes to this project," Wexler reiterated. "All you did was hang up on me."

I was grateful for Wexler's protectiveness (though dubious about its effectiveness), and I also felt deep satisfaction that we were making his movie. This was the mirror opposite of *Darling Lili*. This was real. Wexler even wired me a suggested title for his guerrilla film: *Medium Cool*.

I did not inform my colleagues at the studio about the details of my Wexler arrangement. I told Evans that Wexler had decided to shoot a different story which I had approved; it would be set against the backdrop of the Democratic convention. He responded with a conspiratorial nod and said no more.

Wexler started shooting, his production shrouded in secrecy. Now and then, dailies would arrive at the studio. I saw them alone. It was war footage—the nightmare of the convention protesters being gassed and beaten. The snatches of dialogue were almost incidental to the overall devastation.

"It's great material but don't lose the personal story," I urged Wexler on the phone.

"It'll work. I promise," he replied.

When *Medium Cool* was shown to the studio, the shock waves could be felt across the company. The movie carried a ferocious emotional impact. No American movie had ever depicted the nation's incipient political anarchy. One or two of my colleagues pointed out that the central story was thin. A love scene between the two lovers crossed the censorship bounds with full frontal nudity on display.

But protests soon started emerging from New York. A key member of Gulf & Western's board of directors was also a top leader of the Democratic Party and he demanded that Paramount ignore its distribution commitment and suppress the movie. Picking up on this, a couple of the more senior marketing executives dispatched memoranda predicting that *Medium Cool* would never find an audience.

Wexler and I had been conspiratorial in fostering *Medium Cool*, but I watched in anger as yet another conspiracy formed within the company. I hammered away at the marketing and distribution executives, but could elicit only vague promises. Yes, the movie would open, but nominally. Yes, there would be advertising support, but marginal.

The critics by now had discovered the movie—I had seen to that much—and their response was exuberant. Screenings in Los Angeles and New York brought rave reviews. Wexler was winning praise for his bravery as well as his talent.

But his movie was disappearing into studio quicksand. It was as if the old Paramount had decided to swallow up the initial product of the new Paramount.

When I confronted Bluhdorn and his ever-hovering sidekick, Martin Davis, their response seemed synchronized. "Movies and politics don't mix, kid," they said together. They were right of course—at Paramount, that is.

Since Paramount essentially pulled the rug out from

under *Medium Cool*, the studio perhaps deserved the nightmare of yet another failed political film several months later. While *Medium Cool* had effectively come in through the transom, a project with the unfortunate title of *WUSA* arrived proudly through the front door. Its advocate was none other than Paul Newman, a superstar with strong liberal ties.

The plot was set at a radio station in New Orleans—WUSA—that espoused ultra-right-wing propaganda. Newman played an announcer on the station who nonetheless hated its bias. His wife, Joanne Woodward, was cast as a prostitute who'd been arrested during a political protest. Directed by Stuart Rosenberg, who had guided Newman through *Cool Hand Luke*, the movie had an illustrious supporting cast that included Laurence Harvey as a bogus evangelist, Pat Hingle as a demagogue, and Anthony Perkins as a deranged welfare worker.

When agents for Newman and Woodward marched into the studio to submit their star-laden project, the studio stood up and saluted. Having read the script, I promptly told Bluhdorn and Evans that the material was shrill and depressing. Evans was quick to align himself with me; he hated political movies and reminded everyone that the studio had subverted *Medium Cool*.

Bluhdorn predictably liked the idea of a Newman-Woodward movie. He pointed out that the script was based on a well-reviewed novel by Robert Stone, titled *Hall of Mirrors*. How bad could it be?

The inevitable face-to-face confrontation took place. I told Newman I respected his commitment, but I was candid about my opinions. The movie was shrill. It simply didn't work.

The star did not disguise his disdain for my position, reminding me of my origins with the *New York Times*. "I'd expected a more intelligent response to a gutsy project," he said.

My colloquy with Newman was mild compared with the

one to follow. When Frank Yablans saw *WUSA* at a test screening in Boston, he became livid. Yablans bluntly declared that he hated the movie and wished he could flush it down the hotel toilet. Incensed, Newman rose from his seat and started toward Yablans. His producer, a former agent named John Forman, restrained him, but started shouting insults at Yablans, which were returned at a higher decibel.

As with *Medium Cool*, *WUSA* did not find support at Paramount. The studio's era of political cinema had now stalled out.

LESSON: Satire doesn't work on the screen either.

When I read the first draft of *The President's Analyst*, I found myself laughing out loud. Concocted by a TV comedy writer named Theodore Flicker, *TPA*, as it came to be known, revolved around a psychiatrist who was conscripted to treat the president of the United States. The shrink, played by James Coburn, was besieged by spies of various nations who hounded him for political secrets. Ultimately he, like the president, became convinced that he was surrounded by conspiracies, with the bad guys including the FBI and even the telephone company. As in most sixties movies, the shrink takes refuge in a hippie commune where even further insanity unfolds.

Evans shared my enthusiasm for the movie and felt that the heavy dose of slapstick made the satire palatable. Initial results from test screenings were encouraging.

Immediately after the movie opened, however, Evans's fondness for the movie darkened. Two men in dark blue suits pulled up to his house. "They say Mr. Hoover sent them," the housekeeper announced. Since Evans had hired an agency to find a new butler, he assumed they were candidates for the job and had been sent by the Hoover Agency. He sent for them and started to question them on their experience. The men quickly clarified their mission. The "Mr. Hoover" was J. Edgar Hoover and they were FBI agents who had been dispatched to question Evans about Paramount's motivations in frivolously depicting the agency's work.

Evans was bewildered. He explained that *The President's Analyst* was a comedy, that the agency's name had been changed to FBE. The two visitors did not seem to buy this explanation, but left after a half-hour conversation.

In the coming weeks, Evans came to understand the impact of their visit. His phones were now being tapped. His home was watched. The Hoover Agency, he learned, did not have a sense of humor.

TPA ultimately opened to favorable reviews, but to many filmgoers the movie seemed more disturbing than entertaining. As for Bob Evans, he wished we hadn't made the film at all. He didn't like the idea that someone out there was peering at him.

LESSON: Directing represents a complex skill set, and it's dangerous to entrust neophytes to the process.

My enthusiasm about opening the doors to new talent would turn out to be riskier than I presumed. It was one thing to bring a Francis Coppola to the studio—he had made student films, had studied filmmaking and had honed his craft—but it was a far different proposition with an individual who was not only unprepared but indifferent to mastering the intricacies of filmmaking.

When I first learned that Elaine May had written a romantic thriller called *A New Leaf*, I hurried to get my hands on her script. May was not only an accomplished writer but also, together with Mike Nichols, was a brilliant practitioner of an idiosyncratic brand of stand-up comedy.

While *A New Leaf* was not officially available, a friend at the William Morris Agency sneaked me a copy of the screenplay. I promptly read it and communicated to colleagues that

May's work was witty and bizarre—she had even tossed in a couple of murders to seduce her audience. When I phoned my friend at the agency, however, I learned that May and her producer, Hillard Elkins, were doing some furtive packaging. They had approached Walter Matthau to costar, and he had expressed interest. The reason they had gone star hunting was that May had made an unexpected decision. She wanted to try her hand at directing, and she knew that the "muscle" of a star was necessary to find financial backing.

To my surprise, all my colleagues—Bluhdorn, Evans, Yablans—were willing to go with Elaine May as a director without even testing her or, for that matter, restricting her creative control over the material she would shoot. Indeed May demanded, and won, a wide degree of autonomy. Once a shooting script had been accepted, the studio was barred from demanding changes. It was unclear whether these constraints would also affect the final cut—an issue that would later come to haunt us.

I had a short meeting with May before the movie started shooting, and, as with Silvio Narizzano on *Blue*, was surprised by her shoddy preparation. Furthermore, she was not interested in taking meetings to discuss her script or shooting schedule. This was going to be her show and comments or ideas from the studio would not be welcomed.

I told Evans and Yablans that I didn't like or trust Elaine May and suspected that she didn't know which end of the camera to look through. They dismissed my fears as alarmist. Like a ship headed for an iceberg, *A New Leaf* drifted toward production.

After the first week of principal photography, Howard W. Koch, the executive producer, called me to confide that Elaine May had not composed a shot list nor had she ever inspected key locations. "We're headed down the road to disaster," he

said. "Who do I have to fuck to get off this picture?" It was a
twist on an old joke, but I could tell he was not joking.

I heard Koch's words loud and clear; what was not clear
was what I should do about them. It would be difficult to re-
move her—Matthau might quit and there would be long delays. And it seemed all but impossible to reason with her.

Two or three weeks into the schedule, Bluhdorn and
Evans advanced their solution: Since Howard Koch wanted
out, they would put Stanley Jaffe on the movie as executive
producer. He'd be the man in charge. Jaffe would not be intimidated by May. Indeed, he had just brought in his first production, *Goodbye, Columbus*, on budget and on schedule and
his team had been impressed.

Was the twenty-nine-year-old neophyte producer the
right man for the job? Alarm bells went off when Jaffe reported
the results of his first foray on the film. "She has finished the
first thirty of her thirty-four-day schedule," he said. "But she
is incredibly thirty days behind schedule. She's managed to get
nothing done."

I wondered whether Jaffe, in advancing this report, really
wanted the movie to be summarily canceled. That way he
could escape the blame.

But Bluhdorn was adamant that Jaffe and May were to
work as a team, however unlikely a team that would be. The
movie would go forward and his orders were to be obeyed.

Each day on the set, however, new combat erupted: Jaffe
resolutely pushed for a quicker pace as May constantly changed
her mind about the actors' lines and the camera angle.

"This movie is never going to end," Jaffe moaned to me
one day. Remarkably, it finally did. While Elaine May went off
to edit her picture, Stanley Jaffe went on vacation, and the entire studio breathed a sigh of relief.

It was short-lived. If May's behavior on the set seemed in-

Paramount Pictures
1938

OPPOSITE PAGE: A hopeful star-in-the-making, Robert Evans wields his cape for *The Sun Also Rises*, 1957.

LEFT: Evans and Peter Bart confer prior to a 1968 press conference to announce their new slate.

BELOW: Evans and Bart, 2010, at an industry event.

PHOTO COURTESY OF THE AUTHOR

ABOVE: Mario Puzo, author of the world-wide bestseller *The Godfather*, with director Francis Ford Coppola, Robert Evans, and producer Al Ruddy as they officially sign on to start their movie.

LEFT: Evans and Coppola on the set of *The Godfather* debate a story point.

Adolph Zukor (seated),
at his 100th birthday
party with (from left
to right) Frank Yablans,
Charles Bluhdorn, and
Robert Evans, 1973.

LEFT: William Friedkin on the set of *The Exorcist*, 1973.

BELOW: Robert Redford and Gene Hackman, *Downhill Racer*, 1969.

OPPOSITE PAGE: Clint Eastwood and Ingrid Pitt, *Where Eagles Dare*, 1968.

ST. ANTON A.A.

OPPOSITE PAGE: Evans and Ali MacGraw reflect on their upcoming marriage, 1969.

RIGHT: Warren Beatty and Paula Prentiss, co-stars of *The Parallax View*, 1974.

BELOW: MacGraw and Ryan O'Neal during rehearsals of *Love Story* in Boston, 1970.

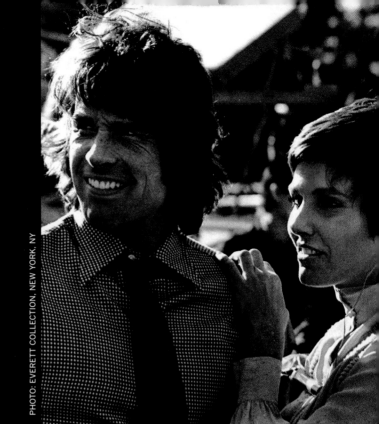

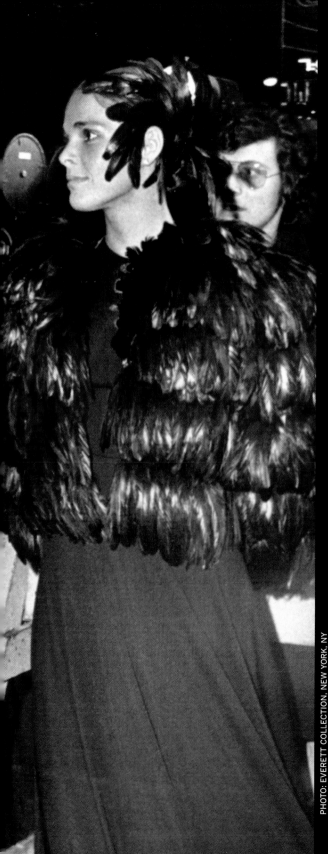

Henry Kissinger lends his gravitas to the premiere party of *The Godfather*, 1972.

OPPOSITE PAGE:
Evans tries to buoy
Mia Farrow's morale
during production
of *Rosemary's Baby*,
1968.

ABOVE: Polanski and
Jack Nicholson
ponder a key scene
in *Chinatown*, 1974.

RIGHT: Newlyweds
Polanski and
Sharon Tate on
the Hollywood
party circuit, 1968.

ABOVE: Bud Cort and Ruth Gordon developed a bond during *Harold and Maude*, 1971.

LEFT: Bart (center) and director Franklin Schaffner (right) in Kauai in midproduction on *Islands in the Stream*, 1976.

OPPOSITE PAGE: Director Hal Ashby and Jack Nicholson share a laugh during filming of *The Last Detail*, 1973.

DAILY VARIETY DAILY

VOL. 155 No. 54   Hollywood, California-90028, Thursday, May 18, 1972   12 Pages   15 Cents

PAR DISPLACES 20TH AS NO. 1

Tv Academy Awards Revamp; 2 More Added

By DAVE KAUFMAN

National Academy of TV Arts & Sciences has revamped its awards structure, with the net result being addition of two new categories.

Lee Schulman, awards committee chairman, disclosed plans at an Academy press conference, following approval of the restructured awards setup at a meeting of the national trustees.

For the first time, the Academy has established a category for the so-called "limited" series, those with a few segments, and they will no longer be in competition with regular series.

Academy has also eliminated situation where a single seg of a series is in competition with spex or a one-shot dramatic show. Henceforth series will compete only with series.

AM Separation

Awards structure in daytime tv also has been revised. Under the old setup daytime had two areas, one for dramatic, the other non-dramatic, and in these areas they lumped them together so that a program and people associated with it could win—any number could come out winners.

Now, however, Academy has taken both dramatic and non-

(Continued on Page 11, Column 2)

Cavett's Fate Should Be Public Issue, Nader Says

Chicago, May 17—Ralph Nader proposed before the National Cable Television Assn. convention today that the potential demise of the Dick Cavett Show should be made a public consumer issue. He held that the ABC latenite talkshow was a consumer commodity no less important than, say, auto safety, and that it was irresponsible to leave such a social issue up to the Nielsen ratings. He suggested that the network hold public hearings before making a decision as to whether to cancel or continue the show.

In his wide ranging speech, Nader urged the cablers not to repeat the mistakes of the "older communications technologies" which he expects cable to displace.

(Continued on Page 11, Column 2)

'CLOWNAROUND' NO MORE; ENDS AS 750G LOSS HINTED

"ClownAround," the arena show put together by William Cohen of Theatre Now and set for numerous bookings this summer throughout the country before opening Madison Square Garden in the fall, has closed down, reportedly losing all of the $750,000 investment.

Show shuttered May 7 after San Francisco opening engagement. It is said to have suffered a $50,000 loss in the 10-day stand.

Directed by Gene Kelly and starring Ruth Buzzi, show featured huge set that required 24 hours to assemble and 12 hours to dismantle. It was to have played convention centers such as the Inglewood Forum here and others in San Diego, Houston, Dallas, Pittsburgh and Cincinnati.

The Forum performance was postponed while show was still in Frisco because of the basketball tourney playoffs, but was not rescheduled before closing notice was posted.

Kelly said that with cancellation

of the Forum date, show also had to cancel the Dallas booking which was sold out. "We couldn't just sit around for two weeks," he added.

Promotion for "ClownAround" as a "new" show was thought not to be enough and the response in Frisco didn't bring the word-of-mouth reaction needed. Likened to "Disneyland on Parade," which lost money in the first several months of its run, "ClownAround" apparently didn't have the reserve funds to keep the production going. "Disneyland" had a hard time catching on, but its backstop was NBC.

Cohen made the decision to shut down, but Kelly is confident show will go back into production at some future date. "As director (he worked on a salary plus percentage), I was very pleased with the show. I'm disappointed it didn't play L.A., but I'm confident we'll come back. We're reorganizing now to get bookings for the fall. Just call this a 'hiatus'."

L.A. FILM OFFICE REPORT WILL RECOMMEND STANDARD FEES, COSTS

Standardization of city fees and costs to the film industry—which would mean lower costs in the long run—will be recommended to the City Council shortly in the first comprehensive report it has received on how the city can aid the industry.

Report is being prepared by city's new Office of Film Coordination under the Board of Public Works and economic development coordinator Milt Renzler following

Dortort Plans 'Road' As Feature Film

Producer David Dortort has acquired motion picture rights to "The White Man's Road," by Benjamin Capps and added it to his slate along with previously acquired "A Beggar In Jerusalem," by Elie Wiesel.

"Road," tagged by National Heritage as best historical tome of 1971, is based in Oklahoma at the turn of the century, and relates the Indian point of view.

Dortort has just returned from a trek to Israel where he was scouting locations for the Wiesel tome. Screenplay is being written by his son, Fred.

several meetings with industry reps.

According to Renzler, some city departments charge as much as $250 a day for use of their facilities for shooting. The report will recommend the city establish a set $100 for exterior locations and $125 for interior locations for shooting anywhere on city property.

In addition to permit fees, producers are required to pay for any costs incurred by filming. The report will recommend the council require departments to cut costs wherever possible.

Location Book

It will also recommend establishment of a city location book and ask that the one-step permit center, which has been in operation for several months, be made permanent and official.

"Both the council and the mayor have been very, very concerned about the exodus of the film industry from Los Angeles," Renzler said. "We're trying to come up with some sort of program that would assist the industry, not subsidize it. One of the biggest complaints the industry has had is the myriad of offices they have to go to

(Continued on Page 8, Column 5)

Leads Majors In Survey Of '71 Domestic Market Share; WB, MGM Gain

By A.D. MURPHY

A survey of the 1971 domestic film market reveals major shifts over 1970 in the share obtained by the most prominent production and distribution companies. Leading the pack in 1971 was Paramount, with an estimated 17 percent of the U.S.-Canadian film rental pie. In 1970, 20th-Fox was in top position with an estimated 19.4 percent of this market, but in 1971 that company dropped to second place, with an estimated 11.5 percent share.

These corporate rankings, inaugurated by *Daily Variety* last year, derive from an analysis of several sets of figures.

First, the annual list of top-rental films, published annually by *weekly Variety*, serve as a major point of departure. Historically, the smash hits in a given year not only have a tendency to scoop up a large share of the b.o., and hence related film rentals, but also provide the company releasing those hits with enough clout to move less spectacular merchandise and to

(Continued on Page 8, Column 3)

Tv 'Staged News' Probe Opens; No Fireworks So Far

By LARRY MICHIE

Washington, May 17—"Staged news" was the subject of a House investigations subcommittee hearing today, but no spectacular charges surfaced and even subcommittee chairman Harley O. Staggers (D-W.VA.) admitted that though "there has been staging" at times, "I believe now it is being stopped."

Several staging charges were leveled by Robert Jennings, ABC news staff cameraman in Los Angeles, involving filming done under the auspices of Bruce Cohn, now executive producer of National Public Affairs Center for Television in Washington. In a telephone interview this afternoon, Cohn said that he was never interviewed by subcommittee investigators, much less asked to testify,

(Continued on Page 8, Column 1)

CINEFX

decisive, her work in the editing room carried those traits to another level. Her cut turned out to be almost three hours long.

The moment the lights went on after the first screening, the argument started. "It's too long," Evans admonished. "The comedy has been lost. It's not funny."

"It's not supposed to be a comedy," May shot back, and the conversation went downhill from there. This was her cut and she didn't intend to change it. She apparently truly wanted a three-hour movie.

Evans, Jaffe, and I met the following morning and decided on a new course. We would hire a new editor and make our own cut. This was not a course of action we would follow with a respected filmmaker, but none of us respected Elaine May. She had worn out every shred of goodwill.

In hiring a new editor, my edict was to be respectful to her original script. In accordance with her first draft, the pacing should be brisk, and any opportunity for comedy should be exploited.

After the new cut was shown to May, we did not hear from her, but rather from her attorney who let it be known she was suing not only the studio but also Stanley Jaffe personally. The legal argument was opaque: May's contract provided that the studio could not alter her shooting script without her permission and by altering her cut, the lawyer argued, Paramount was effectively altering her script.

Since a release date was looming (the film was scheduled to open at the prestigious Radio City Music Hall), a judge decided to cut through the conflicting arguments and watch both versions. The result: he liked the studio cut and found hers tedious. May lost her case before a judicial film critic.

A New Leaf opened to solid business and generally favorable reviews. Critics decreed that she had delivered a clever, if mordant, comedy.

My own critique of the experience was somewhat harsher. I made a vow never again to advocate a project with a first-time director, no matter how prestigious, unless I had personally spent time with that wannabe filmmaker and was persuaded that he or she would do their homework and entertain outside opinion. Indeed, if another Elaine May type came along I would be dogged in derailing that movie, as I should have done with *A New Leaf*.

Lesson: Literary inspiration does not necessarily translate into cinematic inspiration.

In the early seventies, John Schlesinger seemed to dwell in an orbit aglitter with talent and celebrity. Wherever he'd appear, the likes of Julie Christie, Alan Bates, Tom Courtenay, and Maggie Smith seemed to swirl around him. Other English directors had achieved success (witness Tony Richardson's *Tom Jones* or Lindsay Anderson's *If*) but Schlesinger's hits, like *Midnight Cowboy* and *Darling*, were defiantly provocative. They simply dominated the cinematic conversation of the moment.

I had encountered Schlesinger several times in London and Los Angeles and found him to be a brilliant, self-effacing man who was bemused by his own fame. Portly and balding, Schlesinger was openly gay—indeed, among the first of his generation of filmmakers to acknowledge that fact, which, in turn became part of his celebrity.

In my mind, Schlesinger was linked to the glitz and panache of the London film scene, its hot clubs and parties. I was therefore surprised one day when he told me of his ambition to shoot a film in Hollywood, indeed to shoot the ultimate Hollywood film. We had been trading stories about our favorite books of the moment when he said that he was obsessed by the Nathanael West novel *Day of the Locust*. The book was dark, the story disjointed and the ending apocalyptic, but he was convinced it could be the basis for a powerful movie. And he would readily shoot it exactly where it was set—in Hollywood.

It took me a while to assimilate Schlesinger's words. *Locust* seemed antithetical to everything Schlesinger embodied: Set amid the shacks and bungalows that were the true underbelly of Hollywood, *Locust* told the story of the industry's struggling wannabe artists and artisans. Schlesinger explained that *Locust* evoked the Hollywood of the thirties just as *Darling* had reflected London in the sixties. Its allegories also fascinated him; the portents of the novel all pointed to war and economic collapse. The novel was about Hollywood, but it was also about a society that was coming unhinged.

Over the next few weeks I did some research on *Locust*. Schlesinger had earlier tried to develop it at Warner Bros., but the talks had gone nowhere. Hence his was not a casual interest but rather a serious commitment to the material.

When I learned Schlesinger was shortly returning to Hollywood, I pursued our discussion. Over drinks one afternoon, I asked him whether an audience would empathize with these pathetic characters who, mothlike, were drawn to the luminous glow of Tinseltown?

The filmmaker did not waver. The movie industry was entering an entirely new phase, he insisted. Audiences yearned for films that challenged existing value systems and that cleaved away from the traditional formulas.

I was uneasy, but I was also thrilled at the prospect of working with this vibrant and robustly optimistic man, albeit on a downbeat movie. Paramount would develop *Locust*, I told him, and we would all see where it would take us.

To craft the script, Schlesinger brought in Waldo Salt, who had written *Midnight Cowboy*. He also wanted Jerome Hellman, his producer on that film, to supervise *Locust*. Before long a $7 million budget was presented to the studio with Paramount putting up half the production budget, the rest coming from a tax shelter group.

Bluhdorn, Yablans, and Evans all quickly signed on—this would be a go project. Even as the casting was being lined up, however, the cofinancing group suddenly changed its mind. I called Yablans and told him Paramount would be on the hook for the entire budget. Courageously, Yablans said, "Let's make it anyway." Schlesinger and Hellman agreed to defer most of their salaries. The production would be kept lean.

While I was proud of my studio for backing *Locust*, decisions about casting began to worry me. The central character, Tod, was an individual who, like Fitzgerald's Gatsby, did not motivate the action. He was a literary device—more poetic vision than character. Jon Voight was nonetheless eager for the part. Alan Bates and Tom Courtenay were also possibilities. Schlesinger, however, was persuaded that the role should belong to a newcomer—a young actor named William Atherton was his choice. I saw his test and felt he lacked the charisma of a potential leading man. Schlesinger assured me that he wasn't looking for charisma.

Sally Struthers, from *All in the Family*, wanted to play opposite Atherton, but Schlesinger preferred Karen Black, who had appeared in a cult film called *The Pyx*. Supporting roles went to Donald Sutherland, Geraldine Page, and the great character actor Burgess Meredith. Schlesinger was confident that his cast would deliver.

From the outset Schlesinger was troubled by the technical challenges of his climactic scene—an opulent movie premiere which would end in an apocalyptic riot. The scene would be both real and surreal. Three soundstages on the Paramount lot were linked together in a maze of black plastic, the facades of Hollywood Boulevard re-created with stunning vividness. Nine hundred extras all but choked the space. Some were found who resembled thirties stars like Ginger Rogers and Dick Powell.

According to the script, the character played by Donald Sutherland would be lynched by the mob, and Sutherland volunteered to do the stunt himself. With the crowd raging, the destruction of Los Angeles was completed in ten days of shooting, with a hint that some would survive the nightmare.

Even as an exhausted Schlesinger went home to England, he exhibited signs that he, too, was now uneasy about how his film would be received. Upon seeing a rough cut, Schlesinger wrote to his assistant director, "I know the film cannot by its nature please everyone. I simply hope it pleases enough."

Alas, it failed to please anyone. The premiere in Westwood ended with the audience filing out in stony silence. Schlesinger and his companion, Michael Childers, took refuge at La Scala, a favored restaurant in Beverly Hills, only to find Warren Beatty and Julie Christie dining across the room, having just come from the screening. There was no interaction until the end of the meal, when Beatty stopped by and mumbled some embarrassed vagaries of encouragement. Schlesinger understood the subtext.

The critics were not kinder. Pauline Kael commented that "Schlesinger's direction seems to grow worse in direct relation to the number of people on the screen." The box office results were no more encouraging. The film ended up grossing a paltry $2.3 million, failing to cover its advertising costs.

Paradoxically, the failure of *Locust* was interpreted by many as a reflection of John Schlesinger's hatred for Hollywood. I knew this to be a misconception; his fascination with the subject matter mirrored his fascination with Hollywood as a dream factory. By the end of the movie, Schlesinger was considering the purchase of a house in town; he ultimately bought one in Palm Springs, where he spent his final days with Michael Childers following a stroke.

In his thoughtful biography of Schlesinger, William J. Mann argued that *Locust* took the heart out of its auteur. "Never again would John Schlesinger attempt so lofty, so sweeping an observation," Mann wrote. "*The Day of the Locust* would remain his grandest, most ambitious expression as an artist."

By the time *Locust* came out, Bob Evans was caught up in *Chinatown*.

Yablans was engaged in bitter corporate battles both with Evans and Charlie Bluhdorn. Everyone was too distracted for recrimination. No one said to me, "How could you have fostered such a uniquely uncommercial venture?"

The admonitions were unnecessary anyway; I was already keenly aware that Nathanael West's novel should have been left as a literary phenomenon. It was not the grist of cinema.

CHAPTER 10

Rising Stars

With Hollywood's studio system crumbling in the 1950s and 1960s, movie stars were among the most visible casualties. Ironically, the top stars had always complained about the studio mandarins who'd dictated their roles, their salaries, and even, on occasion, their wives (or husbands). The Jack Warners and Louis B. Mayers had final say on whether an actor would become a lover or a gangster and whether their renown would be that of bravery or buffoonery. Stars were often suspended by studio bosses for turning down roles or otherwise defying decrees. The gossip columns of that era were steeped in angry rhetoric from actors directed against their career tsars.

But when the studios fell apart, these same irate actors suddenly realized that their dreaded employers had served as protectors as well as exploiters. Suddenly no one was around to develop projects or otherwise provide a protective cocoon within which an actor could build a career. Hence, just as the dream factories were falling apart, so were the careers of the pampered stars.

By the time I arrived at Paramount, in 1967, some stars were behaving like frightened creatures that had been unexpectedly removed from their native habitat. I was stunned at the absolutely terrible career choices being made by panicked performers when faced with the specter of unemployment. Paramount's release schedule bulged with vivid examples: Lee Marvin singing in *Paint Your Wagon*, Rod Steiger blustering as Napoléon in *Waterloo*, Rock Hudson being seduced by Julie Andrews in *Darling Lili*.

Other career casualties littered the landscape: Peter Finch in *The Red Tent*, Tommy Steele in *Where's Jack?*, Sean Connery in the *The Molly Maguires*, Liza Minnelli in *Junie Moon*, Elizabeth Taylor in *Ash Wednesday*, Kirk Douglas in *Once Is Not Enough*, Richard Burton in *The Klansman*, and Peter O'Toole in *Murphy's War*. These were not so much roles as career enders.

Stars were accepting any role offered them because they realized that a new era had arrived in Hollywood. Studios were looking primarily to directors, not to stars, in assembling their pictures. Equally alarming: the hot young filmmakers didn't want to work with established actors, preferring to create their own stars rather than cope with the huge egos (and salaries) of the old guard.

There was also another factor in play, as I soon discovered. Left to their own devices, many, if not most, stars simply didn't know how to read scripts. They would study their own lines, obsess over a specific scene, but systematically ignore the overarching quality of the material.

Sometimes they turned out to be either smart or lucky. Mia Farrow was so captured by the lead role in *Rosemary's Baby* that she put up with the taunting of her director, Roman Polanski, and the threats of her husband, Frank Sinatra. Sinatra felt that Polanski was brutalizing his wife; more importantly, he wanted her to finish on schedule so that she could next costar in his own movie, which was supposed to start right after *Rosemary's Baby.*

Early on I realized that the most interesting projects tended to involve not the hottest actors, but those who had not as yet reached their zenith. Such was the case with Woody Allen, who had written a play titled *Play It Again, Sam* that Twentieth Century-Fox was interested in filming. Allen's ambitions were not only to star in the adaptation but also to direct it. The studio, however, wasn't interested in either option; they just wanted the property.

Given the impasse, I approached Fox about selling the project. They rejected my entreaties—studios have always been notoriously paranoid about putting a project into turnaround for fear a rival will turn it into a hit. My sources at Fox, however, disclosed that Fox was keenly interested in an action film I had developed titled *Emperor of the North Pole.*

I decided to approach Richard Zanuck, the boss of Fox, about an unorthodox trade: I would give him *Emperor* in return for *Sam*, with no money changing hands. To my surprise, he agreed. He really wanted to make *Emperor* but felt Woody was a lost cause.

My last challenge was to inform Woody's very protective handlers that Paramount would now be making *Sam* with Woody starring, but not directing. The director would be Herb Ross, the esteemed director of *Funny Girl.* My hunch (and Bob concurred) was that Ross's work was more accessible and that he would bring a wider audience to Woody's film.

Woody reluctantly agreed. *Sam* turned out to be a major hit and would be the last successful movie in which Woody appeared as an actor but did not direct.

While Evans and I were trying to identify new stars, Charlie Bluhdorn decided that he, too, could be a star maker. His entry was a fierce-looking Yugoslavian named Bekim Fehmiu—an actor with a thick accent and a complicated name (which he didn't want to change). To the chairman, he had star quality written all over him.

Fehmiu was to star in several high-profile Paramount films—the melodrama called *The Adventurers*, based on the Harold Robbins bestseller, and an action film titled *The Deserter*. Both bombed. Few filmgoers could understand his dialogue.

When it came to rancorous quarrels over casting, it was usually Evans who bore the brunt. As an ex-actor, Evans had passionate, and usually accurate, instincts on casting, but I found the process to be utterly exasperating.

The mechanism of the screen test itself struck me as desperately inadequate. An actor would sit in a cold room, looking utterly terrified, and be fed lines by a casting director. The tests revealed little to me beyond surface attractiveness or nervous tics. But sitting in a screening room, my studio colleagues would become passionate advocates or critics.

After enduring several such sessions, I asked the studio casting director to do some research for me. I wanted to see great screen tests from the past; what did Brando or Newman look like when they were starting out? Would even I—an admitted newcomer to this business—be able to discern their genius?

The studio casting guru, a bulky and forceful woman named Joyce Selznick, was delighted to take me up on my challenge, marshaling footage of old auditions. For two hours the two of us stared in awe as Brando and Newman, both raw and obviously intimidated, read their lines and tried to impress their peers. When the lights came on again, Selznick turned to me with a grin.

"So?"

"What cliché should I use?" I stammered. "They blew me away. They tore up the scenery . . ."

"You're damned right." She smiled.

"Where can we find actors like that?" I asked dumbly.

"Beats me," she replied with a shrug. "I'm trying. That was a different era. Actors in those days had done Broadway, studied at the Actors Studio. But today we're looking at mannequins."

The next morning I advised Evans that I was officially removing myself from casting sessions. Unless, that is, he had found the next Brando or Newman.

I soon discovered that I was not alone in my impatience with the conventions of casting. Given the collapse of the studio system, more and more young actors saw that their career aims would not be served by making the rounds of casting directors. The process of "discovery" was too happenstance. They'd do better buying a lottery ticket.

In my initial months at Paramount, I came into contact with three young actors who, despite their obvious differences in background and appearance, struck me as especially aggressive in this pursuit. All three had had promising breaks at the beginning of their careers. Their surface talent and their unique look had gotten them that far. But all realized how tough it was to take that next step. So many in their age group had stalled. They were determined to take that leap, even if it meant developing their own material and packaging their own projects.

The three in question were Warren Beatty, Clint Eastwood, and Robert Redford. At that moment in time, all were exhibiting both big talents and big appetites. And as budding students of the system, they knew that Paramount offered opportunity amid the chaos and that we would take chances that other studios were unwilling to take.

Of the three (all then entering their thirties) Beatty was the most astute, Redford the most cunning, and Eastwood the hardest to read. Beatty wanted to register the fact that, despite his mythic social life, he was also the smartest kid in town. He played the girls, but he also did his homework. Redford, by contrast, was a serious, very guarded young man who was almost pathologically suspicious of the studios—even in their present disarray. He had a vision of Redford, the Star, but it was still an unformed vision. He knew who he didn't want to become but wasn't sure what he was chasing.

Eastwood, oddly, was the most accessible, though inscrutable. Always attired in jeans and a T-shirt, he seemed comfortable as the handsome, but dim kid who'd made a name for himself in *Rawhide*. He enjoyed having a beer and talking about girls, but occasionally he would drop his guard: Beneath the pose was an intensely intelligent young man who had no intention of going through life as the hick who played in westerns. When Eastwood decided to "get serious," his well-concealed intellect was easily as sharp as those of Redford or Beatty.

The three actors also had this in common: intuitively they knew that they had come along at the right time. The few remaining studio stars, like Kirk Douglas, Burt Lancaster, and Spencer Tracy, were too old to compete for the leading-man roles. Montgomery Clift and James Dean had already self-destructed. Young filmmakers didn't want to be stymied with studio-bred leading men like Troy Donahue, Rock Hudson, or Tab Hunter. And Brando was being Brando—turning up in disasters like *Burn* amid reports of bad behavior. No one could compete with Paul Newman or Steve McQueen, but they were older and more expensive. There was definitely room within the ranks of the leading men for the likes of Beatty, Redford, and Eastwood.

Despite their surface macho and self-confidence, however, the three young actors were finding the road to stardom to be a bumpy ride, with abundant traps and dead ends along the way. Beatty had managed to shed his TV stigma (he had a recurring role on *The Many Loves of Dobie Gillis*) and achieve a brief glimpse of potential stardom opposite Natalie Wood in *Splendor in the Grass*. He'd become an instant fixture in the gossip columns, and producers were showering him with scripts. Still the seemingly shrewd young actor had proceeded to involve himself in a succession of box-office flops, which cumulatively labeled him both "difficult" and "noncommercial." By 1967, when I arrived at Paramount, the word among studio executives was that Warren Beatty was more trouble than he was worth.

Clint Eastwood, too, had fled his TV career after some angry salary battles on *Rawhide*, but his initial forays in film had left him unsatisfied. The Italian director, Sergio Leone, had made him a semi-star in Europe as the silent, steely-eyed hero in *A Fistful of Dollars*, but Clint knew a career could not be built around spaghetti westerns. By the late sixties, Clint Eastwood was regarded as an aging TV star whose ambitions were getting in his own way.

Like Beatty and Eastwood, Robert Redford, too, was having trouble making his way as a young actor. His native talent and Middle America good looks were landing him interesting roles, but his movies, *The Chase* and *This Property Is Condemned*, were tanking. He was the third or fourth choice for the lead in *Barefoot in the Park*, in '66, but won the role, and the movie gave the young actor positive buzz. Redford was now getting offers to do light comedy, but those were not the roles that interested him. He wanted to be accepted as a serious actor and as a serious person, but that was not the way Hollywood saw him.

By the end of the sixties, an abundance of actors in Hollywood found themselves frustrated by the chaos of the system, but what set Beatty, Eastwood, and Redford apart was that each was about to seize their moment.

* * *

Even as a raw young actor, Warren Beatty seemed determined to be active in his own rescue. He understood that he was initially dismissed by some directors as yet another pretty boy. If he got lucky, he'd become another Troy Donahue, a career that had no interest for him.

Beatty observed that, both in Hollywood and on Broadway, there existed small enclaves of talent who fed off one another. It was as though the shrewd, truly gifted individuals in the creative community built walls to fend off the losers and the talentless. In his head, Beatty began to formulate his own list of the elite and to figure out scenarios on how he could join them.

On Broadway, he laid siege to the two hot playwrights of the moment, Tennessee Williams and William Inge. A gay Midwesterner, Inge had become an instant icon with hits like *Come Back, Little Sheba* and *Picnic*. And though Beatty was aggressively straight, he was also downright attractive to Inge. Indeed, the playwright saw to it that his young protégé played a lead role in his new play, *A Loss of Roses*. It flopped, but Inge's theater friends labeled him Beatty's "fairy godfather."

Beatty's quest continued in Hollywood, where he courted publicity as aggressively as he courted roles. Beatty's ongoing affair with Joan Collins and his kinship with R. J. Wagner and Natalie Wood ensured his continued appeal to the gossip columnists. The agent turned producer Charlie Feldman decided Beatty would be a desirable addition to his salon, which meant introductions to filmmakers like Billy Wilder as well as stars like Cary Grant and Rita Hayworth.

Beatty had campaigned zealously for the lead opposite Natalie Wood in *Splendor in the Grass*, directed by Elia Kazan. At age twenty-three, Beatty was thrilled about working with Kazan, yet insecure about his acting talent. In an interview in the *New York Times*, he admitted, "I suppose I have a method—sloppy method."

Yet the film earned some positive reviews for Beatty, with *Time* magazine pointing out his "startling resemblance to the late James Dean," and the *New York Times* describing him as "a surprising newcomer."

Most important to the young actor, however, was that the movie presented him as a symbol of male sexuality. It was Beatty's fantasy: his career had been eroticized. The gossip columnists helped by pointing up his affair with his costar, Wood.

Beatty had by now launched himself into two other projects—a drama titled *All Fall Down*, also written by Inge, and a turgid piece titled *The Roman Spring of Mr. Stone*, in which Beatty was cast as an Italian lover. According to Bosley Crowther, the *New York Times'* esteemed critic, Beatty was "hopelessly out of his element playing a patent-leather ladies' man in Rome." Crowther was even tougher on *All Fall Down*, in April 1962, writing that Beatty's character emerged as "sloppy, slow-witted and rude."

To the celebrity press, Beatty was brimming with superstar self-confidence. After the opening of *All Fall Down*, he left for a two-month vacation with the newly divorced Natalie Wood, who adorned the cover of *Life* magazine. Yet Beatty's interactions with studio executives were earning him a reputation for indecisiveness. He committed to *Youngblood Hawke*, then changed his mind. He turned down commercially promising projects like the film adaptation of *Barefoot in the Park* (which Robert Redford eagerly accepted) as well as Visconti's *The Leopard*. Studio chiefs like Jack Warner openly expressed their dismay with Beatty's behavior. Hollywood's working filmmakers felt he was a *poseur* who would court an Inge, but turn up his nose at studio projects.

Beatty compounded his problems by committing to yet another film that had snob value but little else. Robert Rossen, who had won awards for *All the King's Men* and *The Hustler*, asked Beatty to play the lead in a downbeat drama called *Lilith*, which was set in a mental hospital. Beatty admired Rossen and the script reminded him of *The Snake Pit*. The character of Lilith, a nymphomaniac, also appealed to him. Rossen invited Beatty to join him in working on the screenplay and choosing his costar. She turned out to be Jean Seberg, an actress who had made an impact in *Saint Joan*.

Throughout principal photography, dire rumors spilled from the set of *Lilith*. Beatty was quarreling with his costar, Peter Fonda, and with his director. Rossen was quoted as saying, "If I die, it'll be Warren Beatty who killed me." In September 1964, *Lilith* was greeted with negative reviews and skimpy box office results.

A worried Beatty now did not want to let any time elapse between jobs. He quickly agreed to shoot an existential New Wave crime drama directed by Arthur Penn titled *Mickey One*. Penn called the plot a metaphor for McCarthyism. Most studio executives who read it couldn't figure out what it was about.

Beatty's troubles were mounting. *Mickey One* was destined to be yet another pretentious disaster. Meanwhile, Beatty was battling his friend Charlie Feldman, who was trying to develop a comedy with Woody Allen titled *What's New Pussycat?* The producer let it be known around Hollywood that Beatty had accepted a rich deal to star in *Pussycat*, but had reneged. At the same time, the ubiquitous gossip columnists were reporting that the actor was having a secret love affair with Leslie Caron, breaking up her marriage to Peter Hall, director of the Royal Shakespeare Company (they'd had two children).

What's New Pussycat? turned out to be a hit, with Beatty's role assumed by Peter O'Toole, who had just finished *Lawrence of Arabia.* Peter Sellers came aboard as his costar. Once again, Beatty had misjudged an important property.

I would run into Beatty now and then during this period and was always confounded by him. When he walked into a party it seemed as though a neon banner proclaiming "super-star" lit up over his head. He always knew how to work the room, flirting with the women, paying homage to the heavy-weights. The fact that I'd worked for the *New York Times* had been implanted in his memory bank, and when he saw me, he was uniformly polite and attentive. Within minutes, it was clear that he had read everything and was up on every rumor and intrigue both in Hollywood and in Washington. Beatty was smart and intended that I know it. There was no personal subtext to all this, but once, early on, he gave me a quick once-over and said, "You're a married guy, right?" When I nodded my affirmation, I felt that I had shifted from one category to another in his mind. I would not have access to Beatty's for-midable inventory of spare girlfriends.

By 1965 Beatty had decided to recast himself as a cultural rebel. Though a product of middle-class mainstream America, he felt an urgent need to break out of that mold. The pressure was now on to find a project that would express sixties rebel-lion and present him in a new aura.

Beatty had negotiated a meeting in London with Francois Truffaut to determine whether the French director might cast him in *Fahrenheit 451*, a project Beatty admired. To the young American, Truffaut was the personification of the New Wave auteur who was rewriting the lexicon of cinema. To the Frenchman, however, Beatty seemed at once egotistical and unsophisticated; indeed, he had no interest whatsoever in casting him in his picture. During their conversation, how-ever, Truffaut explained that he had been flirting with a screenplay titled *Bonnie and Clyde.* He related the story line, and then explained why he had decided that the movie was not right for him as a director.

Beatty was intrigued. If Truffaut liked the story, it had to have something going for it. Upon returning to New York, he learned that yet another French auteur, Jean-Luc Godard, also had read *Bonnie and Clyde* and found it compelling.

In New York, Beatty obtained the phone number of Robert Benton, the cowriter of *Bonnie and Clyde*, and made an impromptu phone call. Benton, who worked for *Esquire* magazine at the time, had never met Beatty. He was convinced the call was a practical joke on the part of his cowriter, David Newman. Hearing the skepticism, Beatty explained with his customary low-key nonchalance that he wanted to read the script—indeed, that he would personally drop over to Benton's apartment to pick it up.

Now Benton was certain this was a joke, and he was glad he had not mentioned the call to his wife. When the doorbell rang, however, she answered it wearing her hair in rollers, no makeup on, and her usual hang-about-the-house clothing. When she recognized her visitor, she almost fainted, but Beatty got his script.

Shortly thereafter came another Beatty bulletin. He liked the script and wanted to produce it.

Benton and Newman were delighted but also dubious. They knew Beatty's reputation for procrastination. They also knew that all the studios had already read *Bonnie and Clyde* and turned it down. To Hollywood executives, it was a downbeat period piece. Its sexual subtext was a turnoff, and the ménage à trois scene rang the alarm bell.

Soon Beatty began second-guessing himself. *Mickey One* had opened to damning reviews and dismal box office results. *Variety*'s review called it "strange and confused." Columbia Pictures was not promoting the film, merely booking it into a few theaters as though embarrassed by the project. Beatty was a few months short of thirty years old, worried now that stardom seemed to be escaping his grasp.

In November 1965, Beatty made two moves on his project of the moment that displayed both decision and indecision. He wrote a check for $10,000 to option the screenplay of *Bonnie and Clyde*, telling friends that he intended to create an American New Wave film. At the same time, he started submitting the script to exactly the sort of Hollywood directors who had no desire to make that sort of movie—establishment filmmakers like George Stevens and William Wyler. Neither "got" the material, nor did they understand why Beatty had decided he was qualified to be a producer.

Shaken, Beatty decided to return to the one filmmaker he knew sympathized with his take on the material. Like Beatty, Arthur Penn had felt whiplashed by the failure of *Mickey One*. He had already read *Bonnie and Clyde* and hadn't responded favorably. Stirred by Beatty's conviction, however, he now reversed course and decided to take a shot with his charming and determined young star.

Funding was now the key issue. David Picker, a young executive at United Artists, liked the script, but his zeal faded when Beatty submitted a $1.8 million budget. Beatty knew his likeliest target was Jack Warner, the seventy-five-year-old patriarch of Warner Bros. Warner was displaying occasional moments of senility, but still held tenuous control over the studio. His attitude toward Beatty had shifted as quickly as his moods: He had seemed satisfied with *Kaleidoscope*, a modest thriller Beatty had starred in for the studio. However, he'd also been irritated by Beatty's refusal to say yes to studio projects like *Youngblood Hawke* or *PT 109*, which had been offered him.

Warner Bros. needed product, however, and Walter McEwen, a longtime Warner aide, felt he could engineer a green light at the studio provided Beatty handled the boss shrewdly. A meeting was set up and Beatty was suitably obsequious. Indeed, he even got on his knees and offered to lick Warner's boots if he was awarded a deal. The young producer made his score.

When Beatty finally delivered his film, however, Warner made no effort to disguise his distaste for the movie. Beatty told the old studio chief that he should think of *Bonnie and Clyde* as an homage to the studio's classic gangster pictures. Warner replied, "What the fuck's an 'homage'?" The film's only internal supporter was a young marketing executive named Richard Lederer, but he clearly was a voice in the wilderness.

Beatty knew his movie would be dumped and he was right. The critics weren't offering encouragement. Bosley Crowther, never a Beatty fan, termed the movie "a cheap piece of bald-faced slapstick." The only affirmative voice was that of Pauline Kael, then a reviewer who was auditioning for a job at the *New Yorker* and hence eager to cause a stir by taking on the *New York Times*. Her review started with the rhetorical question, "How do you make a good movie in this country without being jumped on?" She then launched a stalwart defense, arguing that *Bonnie and Clyde* needs its violence; "violence is its meaning."

Kael's ringing endorsement got *Bonnie and Clyde* a few release dates. It even earned it an opening in Paris, but the movie still was not performing well at the U.S. box office in its limited releases. To Warner Bros., it was still a "critics' picture." Not until the movie gleaned ten Oscar nominations did Warner Bros. finally give the film a wide opening—which yielded banner box office results. *Bonnie and Clyde*, together with *The Graduate*, suddenly were heralded as precursors of a new movement in American cinema—the long-awaited Hollywood New Wave.

By the time I met Beatty, in 1967, he was not only a reborn

movie star but also something of a folk hero. He had taken on the Hollywood establishment and won. The bad calls of his earlier career were now forgotten. He was being flooded with offers as both actor and producer and, true to form, was turning them all down—even *Butch Cassidy and the Sundance Kid*. He was now above the Hollywood fray and let it be known that his primary concern was Robert Kennedy's presidential campaign. He was also immersing himself in books about John Reed and the Russian Revolution—tracts that would, some years later, lead to his involvement in his grandiose movie *Reds*.

Warren Beatty was no longer an actor for hire. Beatty was starring in a grander scheme—the Beatty Legend.

Life as a legend provided a delicious complement to political celebrity. George McGovern and his campaign chief, Gary Hart, devoured Beatty's endorsement and support. Beatty cajoled Carole King, James Taylor, and even Streisand to bring glitter to fund-raisers and rock concerts. Beatty and his then companion, Julie Christie, were stars at the '72 Democratic convention in Miami Beach. The Democratic cause was clearly headed for defeat at the hands of Richard Nixon, but the McGovern primary campaign was an exciting distraction for the star. Despite Beatty's entreaties, Christie had flown off to Venice to star in *Don't Look Now*, opposite Donald Sutherland. *Dollars*, Beatty's third follow-up to *Bonnie and Clyde*, had opened to patchy reviews and mediocre business. Previous films, *The Only Game in Town* and *McCabe & Mrs. Miller* had failed to generate the sort of box office heat Beatty had hoped for.

Beatty again yearned for a hit, but found it impossible to leave politics behind him. "I understand politics and I'm damned good at it," he told me earnestly. At the same time, the thought of running for office was anathema to him, defying all his self-protective instincts.

Given Beatty's mood, a screenplay titled *The Parallax View* provided the ideal lure. The property, based on a novel by Loren Singer, was a deftly dramatized study in political paranoia. A presidential candidate is mysteriously murdered. Several witnesses meet suspicious deaths. A conspiracy looms.

The script had been brought to my attention by Alan J. Pakula, a smart filmmaker whose first directing effort, *The Sterile Cuckoo*, had been distributed by Paramount in '69. Pakula had followed up with a vastly more commercial film, *Klute*, in '71, and he had been looking for a thriller that had social relevance. A thoughtful but fastidious man, Pakula knew of Beatty's interest but was worried about getting into business with him. Was Beatty serious about *Parallax*, or would this become another notch on his development list?

Bob Evans, too, was wary of Beatty. There was always a tacit competitiveness between them—one that involved business, women, and matters of style. "In Warren's mind, he's the biggest star in the world," Evans told me. "But look at the numbers; his movies don't make any money."

Personally, I was eager to get *Parallax* moving. A Beatty-Pakula thriller was a solid commercial bet, but also one that could capture the attention of smart young filmgoers. The Nixon landslide had stirred a paranoia that Washington was out of control, and Vietnam seemed like a struggle without end. Further, the Watergate hearings were coming to a boil, with charges of conspiracy and cover-up. This could be a perfect moment for *Parallax*, provided I could move it forward quickly.

But that in itself posed problems. The original screenplay by Lorenzo Semple Jr. needed work, and David Giler, a solid rewrite practitioner—"body and fender" man was his informal job description—had been hired to sharpen it. In script meetings, Beatty's mind tended to wander. He would come up with an idea, then back away from it. Pakula, by contrast, was precise, but pedantic in his presentation.

I had long since learned that every star had a favored writer and that the only way to pacify their story concerns, real or imagined, was to hire that writer at the eleventh hour. For Beatty, that writer was Bob Towne, with whom he had worked on *Bonnie and Clyde*. The problem was that Towne, too, was famously slow in delivering script changes.

I knew I had one card to play and I decided to play it. The Writers Guild was threatening an imminent walkout. Unless we jammed on the script, I pointed out, no writer—even Towne—could do a rewrite without facing banishment from the guild. The time had come to push forward.

Over dinner with Pakula, the director endorsed this strategy. "We know the direction of the narrative," he reasoned. "Warren and Bob Towne need to stare at a deadline."

Beatty himself turned up at my office one afternoon, looking troubled. "Alan has told me of your conversation," he said. "I just want you to know that I'm ready to start the picture. If there's a strike and changes need to be made in the script, I'll make them myself."

His comment surprised me and also left me stymied. "I appreciate your attitude," I responded. "But the writing . . ."

"I know how to write," he reassured me. "I'm a good writer."

I didn't think it prudent to argue with him about his literary talents. Knowing the cadence of his speech, meandering and absent of structure, my every instinct was that Beatty's talents did not lie in writing.

Alan Pakula agreed. "We'll figure a way through it," he said. "Besides, the writers may very well call off the strike at the last moment. Writers don't strike. They're not Teamsters."

Even as the movie started, however, the writers' strike

commenced. By the end of the first week, the pace of shooting had already slowed. The company would arrive on set ready to start, and Pakula and Beatty would retire to discuss script changes. By midday, the cameras would start to roll.

But pages of the rewritten script would then start arriving. The official word was that no one knew where they came from. The young assistant director, Howard Koch Jr., son of the former studio chief, would distribute the mystery pages with a genial wink. I would read them, along with Pakula and Beatty. And none of us would discuss their source.

"Where the fuck are the pages coming from?" Frank Yablans asked one day.

"I don't know and I don't want to know," I replied.

"Beatty's pal Towne is writing," Yablans said. "Towne's the only guy in the business who's as big a mind-fucker as Beatty."

If last-minute rewrites were slowing the shoot, so was Beatty's desire for multiple takes. In one scene, Beatty demanded repeated shots of him sitting at a table, stirring soup. I happened to be on the stage that day and, despite my impatience, had to admire the way Pakula indulged him. If his star was worried about the lack of steam rising from the cup, Pakula would let him play.

When I visited Beatty in his dressing room, however, he seemed unconcerned about the sluggish pace. Thumbing through newly arrived pages, Beatty was wearing nothing but red-and-white-striped underpants, which struck me as oddly patriotic. "I think the story is unfolding well," he said, "but Gordie Willis is costing us time. There was one scene yesterday—Alan said it was so dark it was unusable."

The man he referred to, Gordon Willis, the gifted cinematographer, previously had worked on *The Godfather* where, again, his tendency to underlight scenes had caused some reshooting, but the finished film was superb. On *Parallax*, Willis was seeking a darkly moody atmosphere to reinforce the sense of paranoia.

Ultimately, *Parallax* wrapped with no writer admitting authorship, but when Evans and I viewed the first cut, we were both disappointed. The movie was intelligent and well acted but oddly unsatisfying. Beatty's character had pinpointed the dreaded Parallax Corporation as being responsible for the murders, but the point of the exercise still seemed unclear.

"As I said at the start, Beatty's movies never make money," Evans grunted.

The *Parallax View* was released on June 14, 1974, but instead of causing a stir, it seemed to stir disappointment. "You're likely to feel cheated, as I did," wrote Vincent Canby in his review in the *New York Times*.

Beatty and Pakula, too, felt cheated, but for a different reason. In their view, the campaign for their film had been vastly overshadowed by the publicity blast greeting *Chinatown*, which opened only a few days later. *Chinatown*, of course, was the first production from Bob Evans's new production label at Paramount, and, as such, commanded the major share of attention from the marketing teams at the studio—at least to the mind of Beatty and Pakula.

Release of the two films side by side should have resonated as a triumph for Paramount. Here were two ambitious films announcing a reenergized studio.

Instead, the openings marked the beginning of a new frenzy of anger and bitterness. To Pakula, the release of *Chinatown* had "doomed" his movie—a view he expressed to Bluhdorn with great passion. Beatty, too, felt that his longtime friend, Evans, had betrayed him. Evans, he knew, had a percentage of the profits in *Chinatown*. He thus had every incentive to make that film the winner, not *Parallax*.

When I first learned of the release dates of the two films— they were set very late in the game—I warned Yablans of my apprehensions, but he was sternly dismissive. "They both have great dates," he countered. "They are our summer pictures. Anyone who complains about it can go fuck themselves. That goes for Evans, too."

What I did not realize was that Yablans and Evans were themselves battling at that moment over shares of *Chinatown* profits. If Pakula and Beatty were alarmed about conflicts of interest on Evans's part, they should have been even angrier about Yablans's cut.

Their movie about paranoia, it turned out, was even more relevant than they had imagined.

From the outset, Clint Eastwood didn't seem comfortable on a movie set and certainly didn't display the natural gifts of an actor. Tall and chiseled, his gaze nonetheless seemed distanced and disinterested. His teeth were yellow and he moved awkwardly. He looked like what he was—an awkward kid who pumped gas during the day and took acting classes at night. In 1953, shortly after getting married, he lucked into a modest contract at Universal where he started earning bit parts in movies. Always the realist, however, Eastwood sensed that his career as a film star wasn't going to happen. He considered going to college and looked for other jobs.

But then he got lucky again. TV westerns like *Gunsmoke* and *Wagon Train* were registering solid ratings, and he caught the eye of CBS executives who were casting a rip-off titled *The Outrider*, later retitled *Rawhide*. To his surprise, Eastwood got the nod for the young lead, Rowdy Yates. The show was a hit from the start and rolled on to seven seasons, with Eastwood playing the fast-drawing young stud opposite Eric Fleming.

One unexpected fan of the show was the Italian film director Sergio Leone, who yearned to make a western. Leone needed a believable young American cowboy and was keenly aware that the top Hollywood actors weren't interested; even Eric Fleming had turned him down.

Eastwood was wary when he got the offer. For one thing, he didn't think of himself as a cowboy, yet feared being typecast as one. On the other hand, he had never been to Italy, and the $15,000 offer, with *Rawhide* on hiatus, was tempting.

It was not long into the shoot of *A Fistful of Dollars* that Eastwood realized that while Leone was shooting a traditional revenge movie—the stranger who helps folks, is left for dead, then comes back against the odds—his rhythms and stylized camera angles were vastly different from those of TV directors. The Man with No Name, in sheepskins and poncho, was a mythic figure in the making. And since the character had little dialogue—Leone was shooting in three languages simultaneously—Eastwood began to come to terms with the power of his physical presence, his eyes and his gestures.

Eastwood went into his Leone experience as a television actor but emerged from it as a director-in-the-making, with a heightened sensibility about the possibilities of cinema.

Meanwhile, the young actor was also aware of the fact that he was beginning to occupy a precarious never-never land in the pop culture. Serious critics were fascinated by his Leone films. Andrew Sarris wrote, "What Kurosawa and Leone share is a sentimental nihilism that ranks survival above honor and revenge above morality." Sarris concluded, "The spaghetti western is ultimately a lower class entertainment."

Eastwood noticed that while his Leone sequel, *The Good, the Bad and the Ugly* was outgrossing most Hollywood movies, its reviews were still dismissive. Charles Champlin, the critic of the *Los Angeles Times*, dubbed the movie *The Bad, the Dull and the Interminable* and Pauline Kael, writing in the *New Yorker,* called the film both "stupid" and "gruesome."

In a 1974 interview in *Playboy* magazine, Eastwood observed petulantly that while his spaghetti westerns were increasingly popular in the U.S. and overseas, "I'm having a rough time cracking the Hollywood scene." He added, "Not only is there a movie prejudice against television actors but there is a feeling that an American actor making an Italian movie is taking a step backward."

I occasionally ran into Eastwood in and around the Paramount lot during this time, and he was candid about his frustration. Though reserved and spare in his conversation, Eastwood was always good company. He liked drinking beer and his gaze would dwell on any attractive woman who happened by.

Though a married man, his reputation as a player was well known and well deserved. Yet he also saw lots of movies and studied scripts and, if pressed, commented on them concisely and lucidly. His tastes were populist, but he particularly admired filmmakers whose work was lean and disciplined. While Warren Beatty sought out the top playwrights and auteurs, Eastwood was drawn to the working artisans of the business. His friend and mentor was Don Siegel, a Hollywood veteran of B-pictures. "He shoots lean and he shoots what he wants," Eastwood observed. "He knows when he has it and he doesn't need to cover his ass with a dozen different angles." Siegel's films ranged from *Baby Face Nelson* to *Hell Is for Heroes* and the studios considered him dependable but pedestrian.

To Eastwood, the time had now come to mobilize his own company and turn out films to his liking. Since he owned land in Big Sur that encompassed the Malpasso Creek, he named his company Malpasso and decreed that its initial production would be a contained little western titled *Hang 'Em High.*

The project was classic Eastwood: it represented a step forward, yet a very guarded one. The $1.5 million movie followed a Sergio Leone–type plot—Clint pursuing the men who tried to kill him, all of it ending in a shootout. He selected as its director a veteran from TV, Ted Post, a safe choice, who had shot several *Rawhide* segments.

Funded by United Artists, which had distributed the spaghetti westerns, *Hang 'Em High* turned out to be a solid business venture and a help to Eastwood as a filmmaker. Upon seeing it, Universal offered him $1 million to star in *Coogan's Bluff*, in which he would play a deputy from Arizona assigned to bring back a murderer hiding out in New York. In his new venture, Eastwood was invited to function as a producer, working with the writers and appointing his friend, Don Siegel, to direct.

While his first Hollywood films gave him credibility as a producer, they also raised his price as a movie star, and Eastwood was eager to exploit that franchise as well. He accepted the lead in an action film titled *Where Eagles Dare*, opposite Richard Burton. Clearly the notion of hanging out with the brilliant, hard-drinking Welshman and his wife, Elizabeth Taylor, in Salzburg, Austria, was appealing to an actor who had been locked into low budget westerns. The film was a potboiler but represented a good payday.

Upon its completion offers were streaming in for other action films and westerns, but Paramount put another scheme before him—one that would provide a bizarre diversion in his career path.

When Bob Evans first informed me that Alan Jay Lerner had offered Eastwood a role in *Paint Your Wagon*, I laughed it off. "I know Clint a little bit," I responded. "His mind is set on becoming a filmmaker. There's no way he's going to do a singing western."

I was dead wrong. Having made his "secret" album of western songs, Eastwood was, in fact, thrilled that the Broadway legends Lerner and Loewe were now pursuing him. Years later, when I discussed the film with him, he seemed embarrassed by the entire episode. "These great men of the theater . . . they actually were courting me. And they wanted me to sing!" he said.

In the end, of course, *Paint Your Wagon* proved to be a career embarrassment. Eastwood now found himself caught up in a series of almosts: He was almost a TV star, almost a movie star, almost a producer. His frustration was exacerbated by bad luck in the release schedules. Three Eastwood movies, *Paint Your Wagon*, *Kelly's Heroes*, and *Two Mules for Sister Sara*, were all opening in close proximity—a daunting triple-header that dramatized the lack of direction in his career.

In an unusually candid interview with a *Los Angeles Times* reporter at the time, Eastwood declared, "After seventeen years of bouncing my head against the wall and watching actors go through all kinds of hell without any help, I'm at the point where I'm ready to make my own pictures. I stored away all the mistakes I made and saved up the good things I learned and now I know enough to control my own projects and get what I want out of other actors."

Clint Eastwood was determined now to transform himself into a director, but typically, he would do so on his own terms. *Play Misty for Me*, his first turn as a director, would be modest in design and conventional in plot, as *Hang 'Em High* had been. *Misty* was a thriller about a disc jockey who had a one-night stand with a caller, but then turned violent when she subsequently refused his advances. The plot seemed somewhat dated, but the performances were solid.

Eastwood completed his film in under five weeks in the fall of 1970. It received respectful notices. Studio reps who saw it complimented him. They treated him as though he were a diligent student who had now received his diploma.

But *Misty* was to be overwhelmed in the marketplace. The screens seemed ablaze with films that were redefining the lexicon of cinema—*A Clockwork Orange, The French Connection, The Last Picture Show.* In comparison, Eastwood's foray seemed bland and dated. It was a start—but Clint Eastwood knew he had to do better.

The inability of *Misty* to attract the attention it deserved played a part in Eastwood's decision to take on the role of Dirty Harry Callahan. Here was a character who demanded attention. Frank Sinatra and Paul Newman had both turned down the movie, fearing that the public would reject the movie's violence and its lowlife protagonist. Callahan had set himself up as both judge and jury, tracking down a bad guy named Scorpio who had earlier been set free because his rights allegedly had been violated by other cops. Eastwood felt he could capture Callahan's antiauthority rage. But, following the disappointment of *Misty*, he wanted the assurance of having his alter ego, Don Siegel, serve as director.

Dirty Harry was released in December 1971, two months after *Misty*. The audiences loved it and the critics were appalled. Writing in the *New Yorker*, Pauline Kael described it as an exercise in "Fascist medievalism." The *New York Times* critic Roger Greenspun said Eastwood's performance amounted to "iron-jawed self-parody."

To Eastwood himself, the chorus of criticism reflected the ideology of what he liked to call "the pussy generation." He felt great about the movie. Perversely, the intensity of the response to *Dirty Harry* guaranteed Eastwood's ascent to stardom.

Among the young actors coming into their own in the late sixties, Robert Redford seemed the best bet for conquering the studios. Born in Santa Monica, he instinctively understood Hollywood's schemes and idiosyncrasies. He was intelligent and handsome in a stolidly conventional way. Hollywood always needed a young star with an all-American look, and Redford not only had the look but also knew how to market it.

But he wasn't who he seemed to be. Though an LA brat, he was reserved and rather conservative in his personal habits and liberal in his political beliefs. Seemingly open in discussions, he would walk away from confrontation. If a negotiation became an argument, Redford would simply disappear. "Redford is someone you can easily get to know, but you never really know him," Judd Bernard, the producer, warned me early on.

One clue to his behavior was that Redford distrusted the studios and their executives perhaps more than any other actor. His dream was to construct an institution that embodied the mirror opposite of Hollywood processes and values—a vision that ultimately came to life as the Sundance Festival. But to achieve his aims, Redford understood he would first have to exploit the resources of mainstream Hollywood without becoming a servant of the system.

Inevitably, Redford would turn out to be the most difficult to deal with of his generation. With Redford, all commitments were tentative, all relationships arm's-length. In my dealings with him, I sensed his distrust, but felt it was an institutional antipathy, not a personal one. I represented studio power and Redford hated studio power in all its iterations.

Since he generated so many mixed signals, Redford's ride to stardom was a bumpy one. He was the clean-cut young leading man in *Barefoot in the Park*, displaying solid instincts for comic understatement. Cast in somber melodramas like *The Chase* and *This Property Is Condemned*, Redford received tepid reviews and his films generated meager box office results. *Inside*

Daisy Clover, too, demonstrated his competence as an actor, but the movie simply didn't work.

Keenly self-aware, Redford realized that his Waspy appearance often worked against him. Mike Nichols auditioned him for the lead in *The Graduate*, but opted instead for the more ethnic and idiosyncratic Dustin Hoffman. The movies that were stirring excitement were not about blond, blue-eyed Protestants but rather about freaks.

Mindful of Redford's shifting moods, producers began to approach him with more complex roles, and *Blue* was such a project.

Redford liked his character—a tough cowboy raised by Mexican bandits—and also related to the milieu (the Mexican border), but had reservations about both the script and the director, Silvio Narizzano. Fearful of potential failure, he simply walked away. Lawsuits were threatened but Redford would not reconsider.

When *Blue* imploded, several issues became clear to me. There was no sense developing a script with Redford, because he was simply too difficult to communicate with. He would show up an hour or two late for a meeting, never offering an explanation or apology. His comments on material were opaque and he didn't show much interest in the points of view of others.

Though Redford's sudden exit from *Blue* had caused a chill in his relations with the studio, I still felt that the right Redford project at the right time would be a win. With this in mind, I kept in touch with a shrewd young British agent named Richard Gregson, who I knew had a solid relationship with the actor and who also yearned to become a producer. One day I told Gregson that I'd read a gripping screenplay titled *Downhill Racer*, which dealt with Olympic skiers. Given

Redford's passion for skiing, I said, this was a subject that might stir some interest.

A week or so later Gregson phoned to say that we'd hit pay dirt. Redford was not only a passionate skier but had also wanted to buy property in the Wasatch Mountains of Utah—an undeveloped area some 6,000 feet up. Within a decade, not only would the actor purchase thousands of acres in that area, but they would become home to his Sundance Institute and to its resident festival—the mecca of independent film.

Richard Gregson was witty and worldly and I felt I could be candid with him. If *Downhill Racer* became reality, I would help him through the Paramount intricacies if he would deal with Redford. I was intent on keeping my distance from his star and from his resentments. The project, I warned them, already had become politically complicated because it had been dangled before Roman Polanski as part of a possible two-picture deal involving *Rosemary's Baby*. The Polish filmmaker, too, was a devoted skier. On top of that, Polanski was at that point considering Redford as the possible lead in *Rosemary's Baby* (a role which ultimately went to John Cassavetes).

In the end, Redford decided to focus on *Downhill Racer* and Polanski on his demonic thriller.

Gregson and Redford decided to hire a novelist named James Salter to rewrite their skiing script, which was based on a 1965 novel written by Oakley Hall. They went to Grenoble, to hang out with the U.S. ski team, traveling with them on buses and taking notes. When they returned, Gregson and Salter filled me in on the specifics of their central character, to be named David Chappelet. He would be something of a golden boy, remote and self-centered, a humorless young athlete who, while a member of the Olympic team, was never a team player. As they described Chappelet, I realized that, consciously or not, they were also describing Redford. The central character of this movie would be as emotionally inaccessible and fiercely focused as the movie star who would play him.

With the new script in development, the search for a director became crucial. I had become friendly with a bright young filmmaker named Michael Ritchie, who'd been working mainly in long-form television. Ritchie was an articulate Harvard graduate and an avid skier. I felt Ritchie would be an interesting match for *Downhill Racer*, but, as I'd learned on *Blue*, Redford would never be comfortable if he felt he'd been assigned a director. It would have to be Redford's idea.

That would become Gregson's problem, and he negotiated it well. He showed some of Ritchie's work to his star before setting up a meeting. Ritchie's intellect impressed Redford. Since Ritchie was six feet eight inches tall and Redford, like many stars, was somewhat undersized, the height differential also made the director's arguments more persuasive. Ritchie was signed to direct the film.

Even as *Downhill Racer* was being prepped, yet another important screenplay possibly involving Redford was stirring interest at Paramount. Titled *Butch Cassidy and the Sundance Kid* (and written by William Goldman), the script was put up for auction by the writer's agent and the bidding quickly passed $300,000—a formidable figure at that time for an original screenplay with no "elements" attached. I offered a bid for Paramount, telling my colleagues that the two leading roles would surely attract top stars and that our studio could benefit from another star vehicle. Redford was clearly a possibility, but he had not as yet read the script, nor had Paul Newman, who would finally get the other lead role.

Ultimately, my bid was topped by Twentieth Century-Fox. Within a couple of weeks, firm offers went out to Newman and Redford and Fox had itself a superb package.

Meanwhile, *Downhill Racer* rolled into production on

colorful Alpine locations in Wengen, Switzerland, and Kitz-
bühel, Austria. The racing scenes were made vividly realistic
through the use of handheld cameras. Redford's skiing double
managed to ski downhill at upwards of fifty miles per hour tot-
ing a 35 mm Arriflex camera weighing forty pounds. The audience would feel the swerves and bounces, all the while hearing
the crunch of snow and sensing the bone-chilling blast of air.

The finished film was superbly spare and understated.
Chappelet remained a man of few words; though he didn't
get the girl, he won his Olympic medal and emerged a classic antihero.

In test screenings, filmgoers reacted with admiration to
Downhill Racer, but their praise seemed tentative. Some commented that the characters seemed as chilly as the setting. They
wanted a story that was both warmer and more entertaining.

They got it in *Butch Cassidy and the Sundance Kid*, which
opened on September 25, 1969, six weeks ahead of *Downhill
Racer* to ecstatic reviews and audience reaction. Indeed, *Downhill Racer* seemed to be pale and spartan compared with *Butch
Cassidy*. It was a well-crafted art picture, and *Butch Cassidy* was
a classic Hollywood blockbuster.

Evans and I were both disappointed in *Downhill Racer*, but
we were already developing yet another Redford picture—one
that was also a racing story. In *Little Fauss and Big Halsy*, however, the setting was far from the clean white slopes of Olympic
skiing. This was a down-and-dirty script by Charles Eastman,
a cult favorite among writers and young directors, and it was
set in the dusty Southwest biking circuit. It was a buddy picture that focused on a homely but earnest loser and his wom-
anizing, thieving partner on the circuit. The project was
brought to me by Albert S. Ruddy, a tall, fast-talking young producer with a gravelly voice and an off-center sense of humor.

Ruddy's notion was to match Redford with a hilariously

eccentric young actor named Michael J. Pollard. And the director would be Sidney J. Furie, a young Canadian, who had made an impact with his thriller *The Ipcress File.*

To my surprise, Redford liked the lowlife role and the colorful setting, and felt Furie had an original take on the material. He also was intrigued by the sexual tension generated by a sex object named Rita Nebraska, who was to be played by Lauren Hutton. The bike racing, too, interested him, even though Big Halsy was anything but a champion.

Redford's behavior on the movie was typically cool and professional. Consistent with the subject matter, Ruddy put together a boozing and hard-living cast and crew. Redford showed up every day on the Arizona location looking like the down-and-dirty Halsy, but he and his wife opted to live at an upscale resort far from the gritty location. He did not "hang" with the cast, and while other actors tended to ham it up during the shoot, Redford's performance was carefully understated. It was as though he was buying into the funky setting but also Redfordizing it.

Little Fauss did not especially embellish Redford's career. If anything, it was irrelevant to it. By the time of its release, a different destiny in the film world had taken shape in Redford's mind. He had yearned to be a movie star, but that was now a means to an end. The vision of Sundance had captured his imagination, the notion of establishing an environment for independent filmmakers that would become at once an alternative to Hollywood, and also a preparation for it. Redford would himself mature as a skilled director of films that occupied a shadow world between the two domains. *Ordinary People* reflected the sensibility of independent filmmaking but achieved widespread mainstream recognition. *Lions for Lambs*, by contrast, aspired to challenge mainstream sensibilities, but turned out instead to be a failed polemic.

* * *

Redford's contemporaries Beatty and Eastwood each went on to momentous achievements as filmmakers. Beatty's supreme moment, *Reds*, surpassed expectations in every way. It was challenging as a work of pop culture; it was wildly excessive in terms of cost, and, finally, it achieved recognition on a scale that exceeded even Beatty's formidable ego. The depth of Clint Eastwood's work similarly mirrored the star's own personal growth. In a sense, *Gran Torino* was a response to *Dirty Harry*; *Letters from Iwo Jima* was a counterpoint to *Kelly's Heroes*. The Man with No Name had molted into a sort of Everyman, who was determined to teach as he was himself learning.

When I first encountered them, Redford, Beatty, and Eastwood, each was desperate to find a good role in movies and in life. Surely none would have imagined the mythic roles they were destined to play out.

CHAPTER 11

Unholy Alliances

During my years at Paramount, I grew to admire the company's ability to cope with failure. The failure of many of our films fostered a certain fatalistic civility among the principal executives; since no one seemed to expect the best, it was easier to accommodate the worst. Besides, the blame-it-on-Bluhdorn syndrome provided a convenient channel for explaining away mediocrity.

By mid-1971, however, I sensed a dramatic shift in the metabolism of the company. As *The Godfather* worked its way through production and postproduction, with all its intrigues and controversies, the change in mood was discernible. Failure was no longer considered an inevitability: a more ominous phenomenon was now looming—the anticipation of success. And, judging from the neuroses that were beginning to emerge, I was dubious whether the cast of characters running Paramount would be able to cope with success as deftly as they had coped with failure.

Certainly, there had earlier been some bright patches amid

the aura of gloom. Hits like *Rosemary's Baby* in '68 and *True Grit* in '69 and, of course, *Love Story* in '70 had provided glimmers that a new sensibility was working its way into the studio's mind-set. Still, the abject disasters not only of the big musicals but also of *Catch-22* and *The Molly Maguires* continued to cast a pall over the Paramount landscape, reinforcing the notion that this was a creaky company that could not escape its past.

The community sensed there were new forces at work. The roster of filmmakers now included Hal Ashby, Francis Coppola, Peter Bogdanovich, Peter Yates, Karel Reisz, Nicolas Roeg, and Roman Polanski. And it was no longer Charlie Bluhdorn who dominated the news about Paramount. Robert Evans, fortified by the success of *Love Story*, and by his megapublicized marriage to Ali MacGraw, was now gaining acceptance as a savvy player in Hollywood's power pyramid, as was Frank Yablans, the forceful and outspoken new president. Both reflected a new confidence and brashness, yet shared a self-image as outlaws.

The media suddenly was touting Paramount's new power team even as I was observing the seeds of its self-destruction. Indeed, as *The Godfather* was nearing its release, I became convinced that there was no way Evans and Yablans could survive their own success.

Evans had been apprehensive about Yablans from the moment of his ascension to the Paramount presidency in February 1971. He was baffled that Stanley Jaffe, only thirty years old, could have blown his relationship to Bluhdorn so quickly. "Stick your opinions up your ass," Jaffe had shouted at Bluhdorn and had refused to apologize for his outburst. Bluhdorn had been more shocked than offended, but he'd also come to realize something more important: that his "boy wonder" (Jaffe) was not temperamentally mature enough to fulfill his responsibilities.

But would Jaffe's successor, the bantam-size Yablans, prove

any more stable? Jaffe had warned Evans that Yablans had been aggressively taking credit for Paramount's creative decisions. Even as a humble assistant sales manager, Yablans had boasted that he'd "saved Bluhdorn's ass."

Among all Paramount executives, the individual who was most shaken by Yablans's appointment was his brother, Irwin Yablans, who had worked for several years as West Coast sales manager for the studio and was well liked within the company. Upon learning the news, Irwin Yablans took Evans aside and confided: "This is never going to work. Trust me—Frank Yablans is crazy. I should know—I'm his brother. He's doing well where he is, but he'll never be able to handle this much power."

Evans was shaken by Irwin's warnings—even more so a day later when Irwin Yablans was summarily fired by his newly appointed brother. "I think we've ended up with the wrong Yablans," Evans told me during our drive home that evening.

Early into his presidency Yablans had begun to show signs of incipient megalomania. Visitors to his office in New York noticed that his desk was now positioned on a platform so that Yablans, self-conscious about his diminutive stature, would now look down on his guests.

Amid all this, Yablans could mobilize great charm and display extraordinary intelligence in tackling company problems. He instinctively understood the complex superstructure of the distribution and exhibition business, knowing what buttons to press to trigger action—or panic. "I respect Frank Yablans—I even like him," one crusty exhibitor, Sumner Redstone, told me at the time. "That doesn't mean I trust him."

One key source of Yablans's insecurity was the decision to move Paramount's creative team to new offices on Canon Drive in Beverly Hills. Though Yablans had participated in the decision, it was a precedent-setting move. Before this, no studio had severed its umbilical cord to its back lot.

The abrupt move away from the studio had been prompted by the sale of the acreage and the soundstages to the Italian company Immobilière, but it also provided an extraordinary opportunity to cut costs. Fully 75 percent of the staff had been let go, leaving a skeletal production team consisting of Evans, myself, and three creative aides. And instead of a commissary and several screening and conference rooms, the Canon Drive facility offered one small conference room and a screening room seating twelve. Instead of the fabled commissary, there was now a sandwich shop across Canon Drive, which served salads and meat loaf.

In structure and operational design, the Canon Drive operation resembled an independent production company rather than a studio. The budget provided no studio amenities. When a star or a director arrived for meetings from New York or Europe, he or she was sent a minimalist budget covering their trips—no limos or private jets or lavish hotel suites.

It was this "independent production" style that aroused Yablans's suspicion. He was the president—the boss in New York—and he didn't want his Beverly Hills vassals to feel that they could set their own policies.

If Yablans was walking with an increasing swagger, he was not self-conscious about it. In an interview with *Time* magazine, he commented, "It's easy to be humble if you were born a prince. I came from the ghetto." He'd recently gotten his father a job as a cabdriver, Yablans said, but before that his dad had earned a living plucking chickens.

Yablans made no effort to thwart his growing reputation as a bully. Exhibitors gossiped that he'd once phoned a district manager at his hospital room on Christmas day, instructing him to check his theaters because *Love Story* was attracting sub-par audiences relative to other theaters in his region.

Yablans's fear of losing control over the studio was exacerbated by the delays in editing *The Godfather*.

When Evans took personal control of the editing process, and began complaining about his severe back pain, Yablans told him bluntly that his back wasn't the real problem. The issue was cocaine.

"We've all managed to climb a mountain but now we're getting altitude sickness," Yablans said. "Nothing in Hollywood is built to last. The whole town's on an ego trip. Everyone is coked up or smoking so much dope they don't know where they are."

The issue of drugs was becoming one of Yablans's favorite riffs—the moral decay of Hollywood. In Yablans's mind, he represented New York sanity trying to deal with an unruly bunch of Hollywood sybarites. "Bob Evans is the core of the problem," he railed. "It's all about coke."

Yablans's observations were mistakes, but prescient. Evans was rarely in his office anymore. He would check in once a day, saying he was in the editing room or at home. He sounded distracted, his sentences wandering off. His *Godfather* obsession had overtaken him.

Every few days he would ask me to visit him in the editing room to see a reel of *The Godfather* that he had been working on. Often he'd be stretched out on his gurney, his eyes hooded, his hair tangled. "You're becoming Howard Hughes," I challenged him once. "What's wrong with you?"

"It's my back," he would say. Back pain was his blanket explanation. And I felt a mounting frustration about how to intervene. I pondered calling Evans's personal physician, Dr. Lee Siegel, but I distrusted him as well. Though he seemed to be a responsible, matter-of-fact man, Lee Siegel was in fact a "Doctor Feel-good" who kept his star patients on a steady diet of dubious pharmaceuticals. Dr. Siegel frequently visited our office to give shots to Evans and on a couple of occasions he'd given me "treatments" to help me get over a bout of the flu. Siegel described them vaguely as "vitamin shots" but my entire body sizzled after the injections, as though I'd been injected with amphetamines (which was probably the case).

Frank Yablans, for one, was keenly aware of Dr. Siegel's treatments. On more than one occasion, Yablans demanded, "Doesn't Evans have a legitimate doctor somewhere in his Rolodex?" To the Paramount president, Evans's bizarre schedule was severely inhibiting his ability to run the studio, but with the fate of *The Godfather* on the line this was not the time to do anything about the problem.

Aside from Evans, Yablans was troubled by the story of another important player in the community whose career was being jeopardized by coke. Ted Ashley, the CEO of Warner Bros., a key Paramount rival, had been one of the industry's premier agents. Ashley, a short, scruffy but supremely self-confident man, had assembled a top production team at the studio headed by John Calley. They had turned his company around.

But lately Ashley's behavior had taken a dark turn. Once a family man, he was now showing up at parties with flashy young bimbos, and he was openly into coke.

While filmmakers, agents, and studio executives were usually surreptitious about their drug habits, Ashley's behavior represented a new, almost defiant openness. Following in the footsteps of Dennis Hopper, smoking pot was becoming commonplace on film sets. A Hal Ashby set without a cloud of marijuana smoke was unthinkable. Roman Polanski smoked not only pot but invited friends to join him at a friendly neighborhood opium den.

Julia Phillips, a gifted film producer and feminist who later wrote *You'll Never Eat Lunch in This Town Again*, became an admitted crack user. She once showed up in my office to protest my rejection of one of her producing projects. "You obviously don't trust women," she charged. "Otherwise you'd green-light my project."

"It has nothing to do with women," I responded. "Look at yourself. Half your hair looks like it was burned off."

"I torched myself. It was an accident."

I was dumbfounded. "So why should a studio entrust an expensive movie to a crack addict?" I asked. My comments had little impact. My alleged lack of confidence in women later was reiterated in her book.

Not surprisingly, Evans's long absences from the office changed the dynamic of both our personal and working relationships. There had always been a trust and openness in our interactions, but that was over.

Evans had always loved the spotlight. He coveted every photo op, but now he was retreating even from these public moments. He was avoiding dinners and industry functions. His weekend "tennis scene," whose participants had ranged from Teddy Kennedy to Henry Kissinger, not to mention random actresses and models, was canceled.

His wife, Ali, was also growing alienated by his behavior. Her career had stalled, and she was living with an absentee husband.

She, too, understood that while *The Godfather* had become an obsessive do-or-die mission, several other issues rankled him, and he was not the sort of man who concealed his irritation. First and foremost came his realization that he was now desperately behind schedule. Yablans had promised exhibitors that *The Godfather* would be the studio's big Christmas release. When Evans made the phone call that he needed at least two more months to deliver the finished picture, Yablans was furious. He left the shouting to Bluhdorn, who ranted. "Everyone on our distribution staff has seen the first cut and they think you're crazy to hold it back."

Evans's response: "If you want another *Paint Your Wagon*, release the movie in its present form."

The argument raged on for several days. Despite his fragile physical condition, Evans was unwavering. He threatened to quit. Bluhdorn declined. Bluhdorn and Yablans called Coppola, begging him to intervene, but the director said Evans had taken the movie away from him.

Bluhdorn felt stymied. The whole crisis stemmed from Evans's incompetence, Yablans told his boss.

The release of *The Godfather* was delayed until March. Meanwhile, Yablans stuck *Harold and Maude* in the empty Christmas slot, as though to tell his Hollywood executives, "This is what you hath wrought."

In Yablans's mind he had lost the battle but won the war. Charlie Bluhdorn would at last come to terms with the reality that the studio could not be left in the hands of an erratic production chief who believed he was Thalberg incarnate. Yablans was wrong. It was Yablans, not Evans, who was headed for trouble.

The record-shattering opening of *The Godfather*, in March, immediately reinforced Bluhdorn's faith in Bob Evans. The critics loved the movie. Audiences were lining up all over the world, and Francis Coppola was accepting the plaudits. Frank Yablans and Bob Evans posed for photo after photo, the perfect teammates in the eyes of the world.

The photos, with their show of effusive amity, only increased my own sense of foreboding. Yablans and Evans, in reality, were barely on speaking terms. When I spoke with Yablans I could tell he was all but overwhelmed with jealousy.

Evans was emerging as the Paramount hero, not Yablans. But I also realized that Yablans's suspicions about cocaine had now resurfaced, and this time they were valid. Released from the pressure of *The Godfather*, Evans seemed to be descending into the world of blow.

His back problems were the cause, he told me. An actress had noticed his agony and had advocated cocaine as its remedy. She even produced a small sample. When Evans mentioned that he had started using coke I didn't think much of it. Yet there was a curious naivete about his announcement—he seemed like a young boy trying his first cigarette.

Oddly, though Evans had grown up in Manhattan and had been keenly aware of the drug culture, he himself had never been a user. Efforts to smoke pot led him to coughing fits. Hard drugs simply had no appeal to him.

I myself had developed a casual fondness for cocaine, but to me it was a party drug—a once or twice a month plaything.

The notion of using cocaine on a habitual basis seemed outlandish to me, but mine was a nonaddictive personality, and Bob Evans was the mirror opposite. At a time when he should be wallowing in his new success and fame, he was, in fact, retreating from reality.

Meanwhile a new battle was about to envelope the Paramount hierarchy.

With Francis Coppola now enshrined among the world's elite directors, Charlie Bluhdorn was determined to elicit more movies from him. As it turned out, he and Coppola had been nurturing roughly the same idea—one that was inimical to Frank Yablans.

The scheme, in broadest terms, was to establish a new company, led by Coppola, which would have complete autonomy within a limited budget range and would effectively own its own product. The G & W chairman and the filmmaker decided that the deal would involve not only Coppola but also his two close friends, Peter Bogdanovich and Billy Friedkin.

Bluhdorn was ecstatic: Paramount would be mobilizing the talents of three of the hottest filmmakers in the world, and Coppola, having delivered a massively commercial mainstream movie, now wanted to get back to the genre that most interested him—low-budget independent films that he could totally control.

Excited by his concept, Bluhdorn summoned Yablans to deliver the news. "This will be regarded as a major coup for Paramount," Bluhdorn enthused. Knowing Yablans's bias against Evans, he added that the studio would have no role in the new entity, called the Directors Company—Coppola had demanded Evans's exclusion and Bluhdorn had consented.

Yablans was not appeased. "The idea is shit," he told his boss. "It's a dumb idea and I refuse to have anything to do with it."

The debate, once again, was acrimonious. Yablans told Bluhdorn he was giving away the store, that no filmmaker deserved this much autonomy, that these three in particular would use Paramount money to make esoteric films that audiences would reject.

Bluhdorn informed his president that he would move ahead with the company despite his opposition. In fact he planned to fly the three directors to New York for a friendly meeting the following week. Evans, Yablans, and Bart would attend, he said, and Yablans would have to be hospitable to the assemblage and pledge his support for their efforts.

The "peace meeting" took place but did not go as Bluhdorn had hoped. Several minutes into the discussion, Yablans raised a sensitive issue—exclusivity. Under the Bluhdorn-Coppola structure, the Directors Company was to become the primary focus of the three directors' activities, but each would still be free to accept offers from other entities.

Yablans disagreed with this. He felt strongly that the directors owed all their films to the new company. Billy Friedkin dissented; the notion of exclusivity was both impractical and offensive, he argued. Yablans reiterated his point of view even more forcefully. Friedkin, a famously volatile filmmaker, leapt to his feet. "I think you're an asshole," he told Yablans, and stalked out of the meeting.

Yablans was delighted, but Bluhdorn was undaunted. Despite the blowup, the Directors Company would go on to produce great movies, he decreed.

He turned out to be briefly correct. Over the next eighteen months, the first two films to emerge from the Directors Company, *Paper Moon* and *The Conversation*, perfectly fulfilled its mission—intelligent films made on modest budgets without studio interference. However, Bogdanovich's next offering, *Daisy Miller*, turned out to be exactly the sort of smugly onanistic effort that Yablans had forecast.

Friedkin, from the beginning, kept his distance; he declined to make any films at all for the venture of which he was a reluctant partner. Since Evans, too, was steadfast in his indifference, it was left for me to find a modus vivendi for the Directors Company. I developed the screenplay for *Paper Moon* with Alvin Sargent, a gifted screenwriter, as a mainstream Paramount project, but, to help jump-start the new entity, I submitted the project to Bogdanovich as a potential Directors Company film. Bogdanovich was reluctant at first to embrace what had been developed as a regular studio film, but, persuaded by his then-wife, Polly Platt, he decided to take it on. It turned out to be a smart decision.

I now found myself as the only Paramount executive who

regularly spoke with Bogdanovich and Coppola and was entrusted to watch dailies. I was enjoying our rapport, but, given the ever-growing atmosphere of fear and loathing, I knew the enterprise would be short-lived. Yablans was unrelenting in his opposition. And while Coppola would meet occasionally with Bluhdorn to spin grandiose plans for the company, he shortly became bogged down in the editing of *The Conversation*. It was a brilliant movie about topics dear to his heart—paranoia and the invasion of privacy—but he struggled for over a year in the editing room to find its narrative arc.

Meanwhile, the war between Yablans and Evans was finding a new hot spot—*Chinatown*. At its inception, *Chinatown* seemed like an inspired scheme to ameliorate tensions within the company and channel Evans's energies in a new, more productive direction. In the end, however, it turned out to be the final spark that would immolate Paramount's combustible management.

Written by Robert Towne, *Chinatown* was a Raymond Chandler–like detective story built around a dense thicket of a plot. It was Towne's aim to dramatize how corrupt developers contrived to create a boomtown in Los Angeles by diverting water from farm land, bribing any cops or local bureaucrats who tried to intervene. Towne envisioned his friend Jack Nicholson as ideal casting for the private eye, with Nicholson also serving as a consultant on the script.

The prospect of a Nicholson private-eye movie delighted Evans, especially given the terms of a new deal he was about to close with Bluhdorn.

Under his new arrangement, Evans would be free to personally produce one or two films a year under his own banner while still serving as chief of production, with profits to be divided fifty-fifty with the studio. The only previous production chief to be rewarded with a deal of this model was Darryl F. Zanuck some thirty years earlier.

In fact, the new Evans production deal represented a sort of peace treaty between Bluhdorn and Sidney Korshak, who had been dispatched by Evans to seek out an improved compensation package following the extraordinary success of *The Godfather*. The film had represented a windfall for Paramount, Korshak argued. Because of some deft dealmaking, the studio had retained fully 84 percent of the profits (neither Brando nor Coppola had negotiated significant profit participations). Hence, Korshak now demanded a major pay raise for Evans, who was making a paltry $350,000 a year. However, a big boost for Evans would also inevitably mean an improved package for Yablans, and Bluhdorn was intent on keeping the appetites of his young executives under control. The compromise: Evans would now become both a producer and a production head.

When Evans learned of the Korshak compromise—he'd hoped for an immediate pay increase—he was disappointed, but his consigliere persuaded him that he could turn the situation to his advantage. All he needed was one hit and his new banner would represent a coup. Besides, Evans would also have access to the best studio material and control over marketing resources.

Chinatown was thus a key to Evans's brave new world, but a problematic one. A notoriously slow writer, Towne agonized over every plot point of his script. The political complexities of water diversion did not interest Evans, nor did the subplot of incest involving Noah Cross, the corrupt developer, and his daughter, Evelyn. Evans knew Towne's father had tried his hand at being a developer and felt his writing might entail working out some familial neuroses that were clouding the plot.

When Towne finally delivered his script, Evans dispatched

it to me and our reactions were identical: The script was almost impossible to follow without resorting to the sort of chart you made in college when burrowing through a Tolstoy novel. Characters came and went. Layers of subtext appeared and disappeared. It was brilliant stuff, but it was also off-putting.

Evans was frustrated. His production banner was ready to start, he had his first script in hand, which he couldn't quite understand, but now he needed a stratagem to propel things forward.

His thoughts turned to his old friend Roman Polanski. Three years had passed since the Manson murders, and the filmmaker was still free-floating around Europe—his life unfocused. Polanski had always been drawn to convoluted plots. And he needed a job.

Even as Evans was reaching out to Polanski, Paramount went public with the announcement of his new deal. Predictably, Yablans was outraged. But his indignation was echoed by several important stars and directors who were prepping films at the studio. Among the protesters was Warren Beatty, a close friend of Evans, who told Bluhdorn that the deal meant that Evans's movies would always come ahead of all others when it came to ad spending or prime release dates.

Beatty and I had been working closely on *The Parallax View*—also based on a Bob Towne script—and Beatty was now infuriated that his film would be upstaged by *Chinatown*. "Bobby has to make a choice—either he runs the studio or he produces pictures," Beatty told me.

Not one to worry about consistency, Yablans now presented Evans with his own demands. *Chinatown*, he said, was a confusing mess of a script and Evans was crazy to make it his first film, but if that was his position, Yablans wanted to share in Evans's points. It would be a fifty-fifty split, and that was not a suggestion. It was a demand.

There was an additional demand as well. *Time* magazine was planning a cover story on Evans, and Yablans now insisted on a shared cover. A stunned Evans protested that he couldn't control *Time*'s editorial decisions, but Yablans warned, "If you don't deliver the cover I will make every hour of every day of your life so miserable you'll wish you were dead."

Evans surrendered on the fifty-fifty deal, but he alone decorated the cover of *Time*.

CHAPTER 12

The Outlaws

During the heyday of the studio system, in the thirties and forties, Hollywood directors clearly understood their place in the pecking order. The typical director was assigned his movies—he could turn them down but risked offending the studio chief. He was encouraged to work with writers to sharpen the shooting script, but only under the scrutiny of studio apparatchiks. Upon completion of principal photography, he awaited his next assignment while editors worked on the cut of his previous film. There was no question about the final cut. That resided in the hands of the studio.

At Paramount, I witnessed the final vestiges of that system. On *True Grit*, for example, Henry Hathaway, a salty old studio veteran, directed the actors and ran the set but the edit was supervised by his producer, Hal Wallis, a onetime production chief at Warner Bros.

Hathaway understood the old ground rules. He trusted Wallis's ability to supervise the editors and deliver a cut that would make both the performers and the director look good. Besides, that was the way the system worked.

But all that was soon to change. To the young filmmakers now making their impact, control was crucial. They wanted to edit their films and select the score and even have a say in the promotion. Their rallying cry was heard loud and clear: They wanted final cut.

In reality, a select circle of filmmakers had already achieved this objective. No distributor was going to mess around with a David Lean movie, for example. Alfred Hitchcock was not about to bend to corporate interference. I was having lunch with Hitchcock once when he informed me cheerfully how he'd preserved total secrecy during the making of *Psycho* (even to the point of buying up every copy of the book so no one would steal the plot). "Unless theater owners guaranteed me that no one would be admitted after the movie started, I would not let them show the film," he said, his eyes twinkling over his remembered success.

But the maverick young filmmakers now making their demands did not have the credentials of a Lean or Hitchcock. What they had going for them was brashness—and the luck of good timing. The old system was broken. The new rules were up for grabs.

It was the French auteurs, of course, who had effectively raised the ante. America's young filmmakers revered the work of Truffaut, Godard, and their contemporaries. They were in awe, not only of their creativity, but also of their control.

The French filmmakers, however, usually raised the money for their films, often recruiting their own private Medicis— wealthy businessmen who venerated the talents of the new auteur class. French directors thus became proprietors of their own work and, as copyright owners, exerted creative control.

The young Americans, by contrast, were funded by studios and the copyright belonged to the financier. Whatever their artistic ambitions, and however great their egos, they were, in fact, employees who worked at the pleasure of their employers, and their employers often showed their displeasure.

From my first moments at Paramount I could sense a growing tension. The revolution was at hand and I was to find myself regarded as both friend and enemy to each side.

Paramount was not the only studio at which these battles were being fought, but since Evans and I had been the most aggressive in recruiting a colorful young cast of filmmakers, it was inevitable that our studio would become a prime battleground.

The two filmmakers who marched into combat with the greatest swagger were Francis Coppola and Roman Polanski. Both were brought to the studio under the rules of the old regime but with promises of change. They were hired guns who nonetheless exuded confidence in their ability to expand the boundaries of cinema. But from the moment of their arrival, their ultimate goal was vividly apparent: they may have been our employees on paper, but in their minds, they were masters of their own fate.

And therein lay the paradox: Coppola and Polanski embodied both the most admirable and most self-destructive traits of their generation of filmmakers. Both were zealously creative and maniacally dedicated to their craft. Both had mastered the tools of filmmaking and understood their canvas. Yet both would ultimately fall victim to the most destructive traits of sixties filmmaking. Their egos would spin out of control. Their appetites would far exceed their talents. Their hatred of authority would become pathological. They came to think of themselves not merely as rebels but as outlaws. They viewed the studios, not as wellsprings of support, but as targets to be plundered.

The achievements of Coppola and Polanski in their time were extraordinary and their artistic courage admirable. Yet instead of a consistent growth of stature and achievement, there was rather a pattern of repeated flameouts—giant steps backward for every leap forward. Their personal lives, too, reflected a succession of near-operatic crises; they chose paths easily as risky as those of the protagonists in their films.

For better or worse their behavior served as a model for many of their contemporaries. The aim was to dance ever closer to the edge, defying both gravity and mortality. Only through that tortured process of defiance could their true artistic goals be satisfied.

When I first met Francis Coppola he was still a film student at UCLA. He was a homely, perpetually rumpled young man who seemed totally unconcerned about how he presented himself. A voracious reader, he was also a budding techno freak. He couldn't pass any device, even a vending machine, without imagining a redesign.

Frustrated that he lacked the money to shoot and edit his own movies as a film student, he created a minicareer of editing movies shot by friends—especially soft-core films that were then called "nudies." Sexually repressed, Coppola drew little enjoyment from this task—indeed, he found them embarrassing—but the efforts helped him hone his skills at filmic storytelling.

I didn't particularly care for Coppola on a personal level. He was a self-involved nerd, imprisoned by his own restless imagination. While a superb communicator on paper, his interest in personal communication was minimal. I don't think he cared for people, outside his own immediate family and the techno nerds with whom he worked. Strangers were of interest only if they could teach him something or pay him something or otherwise be of service.

After his UCLA years, Coppola and I kept in touch intermittently. I followed his incipient writing career with interest and faithfully read his scripts. I especially admired his screenplay of *Patton*, and when I went to Paramount, he was on my list of talents I wanted to bring into the studio.

Given his limited social skills, I was surprised that he was able to pull together backing for *You're a Big Boy Now* and even more amazed that Warner Bros. had backed him to direct *Finian's Rainbow*. Clearly Coppola was learning how to work the town.

While *Big Boy* conveyed a certain naive charm, *Finian's* was an abject failure. The demands of the musical were far beyond Coppola's skill set. Further, the decision to use a patrician but slightly decrepit Fred Astaire in a leading role was doomed.

When we met to discuss projects, Coppola announced that, following the *Finian's* experience, he was determined to focus on low-budget pictures in which he could more freely experiment with new ideas.

I entered into my notebook two tentative conclusions about Coppola: First, that I didn't trust him. But second, that if he were to be matched to the right material, he could emerge as a brilliant filmmaker. Months later, I felt I had found that material.

Though I'd never met Roman Polanski, I was equally hopeful of recruiting him to the Paramount stable. I had started hearing about the young Polish director on my initial trip to London on behalf of Paramount. Producers and agents already were praising his talents and his command of the camera. Though only thirty-four years old in 1967, Polanski had made a few experimental shorts in Poland, and had earned kudos for his first feature, *Knife in the Water*. A thriller about a married couple who pick up a young stranger, the film had won an Academy Award nomination for Best Foreign Language Film in 1963. He lost to Federico Fellini (for *8½*) but the kudo earned Polanski his first trip to Hollywood. His follow-up film, *Repulsion*, further amped up his reputation.

Polanski's instincts on subject matter were dark, which was hardly surprising to those who knew his background. As a child, he'd survived the Jewish ghetto in Krakow and saw his mother herded away to Auschwitz. In his teens he had to endure a new set of conquerors—the Russians.

Though short and skinny, Polanski had the instincts of a survivor. He trained himself to become an accomplished skier, fencer, and actor. Despite his lively intellect, friends took note of his ominous mood swings: Polanski could be upbeat one moment only to sink into a deep depression the next. He could veer from generosity to cruelty, and his relationships with women were especially troubled.

When I made inquiries about Polanski in London, one Polish producer warned me, "Roman is a great guy but he's also a sociopath."

Many in the film community, though eager to work with him, nonetheless circled him warily as though suspicious that an association would somehow burn them.

When I first came upon the manuscript of *Rosemary's Baby*, in 1967, I sensed it would be the right lure to bring Polanski to Hollywood. The thriller by Ira Levin exuded an aura of malevolence. Set in the Dakota apartments in Manhattan, the story focused on a young woman living with a loving husband and friendly neighbors. In fact, she has been impregnated with satanic seed and her neighbors turn out to be devil worshippers.

The novel, as improbable as it was spellbinding, had been optioned by a well-known producer of B-pictures named William Castle. Castle had achieved a certain infamy as a promoter. He had once offered to sell insurance policies to film-goers who paid to see his films, ostensibly because their plots were so frightening that they could induce heart attacks.

Under Castle's stewardship, *Rosemary's Baby* was destined to become another potboiler, and I was delegated the task of persuading him to step aside as the director while retaining his title of producer. The director Evans and I had in mind was Roman Polanski.

Bulky and silver-haired with the booming voice of a promoter, Castle received my news politely but protested that he had never heard of Roman Polanski. Did he speak English? Would he shoot the movie for $300,000—the customary William Castle B-picture budget?

The studio had a bigger budget in mind, I replied. In fact, it was our intention to go for broke—a big movie backed by a big ad campaign. "Your productions always made money, but this will be your giant hit," I assured him.

Puffing on a cigar, Castle seemed worried. "Let me meet this Polanski guy," he offered.

The "Polanski guy," meanwhile, was puzzling over the novel, which we had dispatched to him. "It's a Hollywood movie," he told me over the phone. "It's too commercial."

"Both of these are true," I said. Several conversations followed, but it was becoming apparent that I could not get Polanski off the dime. I decided to play the Evans card.

Bob Evans possessed unique powers of persuasion, as I'd quickly discovered at the studio. When dealing with actors or filmmakers, he could sense areas of vulnerability. He knew when to push and when to wait.

Evans learned that Polanski had enjoyed his one trip to Hollywood, despite his denials, and he decided on his strategy. "I want you to come to the studio and meet with us," Evans told him. "Talking about a movie on the phone is unproductive."

Polanski still hesitated. Dealing with a Hollywood studio, he confessed, was intimidating to him.

Evans played him expertly. Rather than pressing him on *Rosemary's Baby*, he also talked about *Downhill Racer*—a movie about one of his favorite hobbies, skiing. Polanski had a passion for skiing which also offered the exciting possibility of working with Robert Redford (the young filmmaker Michael Ritchie had already been hired to direct the movie at that point but Polanski didn't know that).

Then Evans zeroed in for the clincher. "Come to Hollywood for God's sake," he boomed into the phone. "What's the worst that can happen to you? You'll have the best pussy of your life."

Roman Polanski arrived the following week, and meetings on *Rosemary's Baby* were assembled. Polanski was quickly pursuing a busy and zestful social life, which Evans was happy to orchestrate. Indeed, the two were building a kinship. "I love Bob," Polanski told me. "He knows how to live well and he likes to make his friends happy."

With *Rosemary's Baby* now in serious discussion, the only skeptic was William Castle. "Roman is smart," Castle told me. "But we're entrusting a lot to a European director who is very arty but still is doing *Rosemary's Baby* for the money."

"The money and the sex," I corrected him. "He really likes this town."

"Couldn't we find a Hollywood director who'll do the job for money and sex?"

I had to smile. I knew William Castle didn't expect a serious answer to a frivolous question.

If Roman Polanski was initially skeptical about *Rosemary's Baby*, his disdain was easily matched by that of Francis Coppola when the latter was presented with *The Godfather*. The novel was trashy, he said. It lacked a contemporary attitude. It was peopled by stereotypes. "Why make another Mafia movie?" Coppola protested. "They don't work anymore. The audience has moved past all that."

If anything, Coppola seemed almost offended that the studio had submitted the material to him. His attitude did not surprise me; there was something reinforcing about its intensity.

Evans and I had asked ourselves the same questions about *The Godfather*, or *Mafia*, as it was originally titled. The novel had been sent to Evans and me by his story scout, George Wieser, whom Evans had employed during his brief career as an independent producer. Wieser's recommendations were consistently pulpy, yet relevant from a pure business standpoint—provocative topics, celebrity authors, and accessible story lines.

We had first seen *The Godfather* as a sixty-page outline. The early chapters were well written, but at midpoint the novel degenerated into a rough story sketch. William Targ, a top editor at Putnam who was editing the book, phoned me with a special appeal. "Mario Puzo is a really talented writer, but he's stone broke," Targ said. "He needs some option money to feed his family and finish the book." Puzo was a serious novelist, Targ explained, but his past novels hadn't sold well. This book represented his stab at writing a commercial novel. "I think it could be great," Targ said. "Please read it."

I respected Targ and appreciated that he'd made a special appeal. I read it promptly and then gave it to Evans. We reacted identically: Puzo's novel had some gripping characters and themes, but the notion of doing a Mafia movie was unappealing. A year earlier the studio had released *The Brotherhood*, a Mafia movie starring Kirk Douglas, and it had tanked. Our disposition was to pass.

But as we rode to work together a few days later, Puzo's novel came up again. Evans and I were both hung up on the central character—the formidable figure of the Godfather. "It's not just a Mafia novel," Evans told me. "It's too easy just to say 'no.'"

"It's a novel about the building of a dynasty," I said. "But what the hell do we do with it?" We dropped the subject for a few days, but it kept weighing on us both. "I want to give it to Francis Coppola," I volunteered at a production meeting. "Remember *Patton*. He's a brilliant writer and he loves telling stories about his Italian family. I think he'll fight it but I also think he may bring something to it."

Evans was leery. He had met Coppola a couple of times but had no strong impression of him. Evans, I knew, had already shown the novel to a couple of filmmakers who had quickly dismissed it. One had even reacted angrily, charging that Puzo's book was an attempt to glamorize the mob.

Given the stalemate, I decided to send the novel to Coppola with an admonition to read it quickly. I knew it would be an uphill fight.

Meanwhile there were glimmers of interest from other directors. Sam Peckinpah liked the book, but when he came to my office he was deliberative and cagey. Peckinpah was a charismatic, hard-drinking filmmaker who had made some remarkable but violent films—*The Wild Bunch*, most recently. "Give me the project and I will deliver a helluva picture," was the extent of his presentation.

I respected Peckinpah, but I had the impression he had not really thought it through. He was vamping and he looked like he hadn't slept for a few nights.

The young director Sidney J. Furie also wanted to talk about *The Godfather*. On the basis of the successful *Ipcress File* thriller, Furie had been given a studio deal at Paramount. It entailed a development fund, office, and secretary. When Evans and I went to see him to discuss *The Godfather*, however, Furie launched into a fifteen-minute rant about the modest size of his office. "The studio makes a deal with me and gives me this dump and I even have to go down the hall to pee," he complained.

Evans and I quickly departed, agreeing we did not intend to entrust *The Godfather* to someone whose highest priority was to have a private bathroom. Our decision was reinforced when, a day later, Furie's agent called to say he would agree to direct *The Godfather* provided he'd be paid $250,000. Learning this, Evans scoffed: "He's not worth a penny over $175,000. Besides, we don't want him."

Further conversations with Coppola meanwhile were reinforcing my interest. The Corleone chronicle was taking shape in Coppola's mind as a perverse metaphor for the growth of the capitalist dream. *The Godfather* was as much about a business empire as it was about a contentious family, and Coppola was fascinated by empire builders. The father-son elements of the novel also were intensely meaningful to him. Carmine Coppola, Francis's father, was a musician and composer of limited success, and the two had a close bond.

But other factors were also gnawing at him and melting his resistance. Coppola's early films had not been financially rewarding, yet he was a young man whose dreams chronically exceeded his resources. He had started a little company in San Francisco called Zoetrope to develop film projects with compadres like George Lucas and Walter Murch, and they needed money. Lucas in particular, though a quiet young man, persisted in reminding Coppola of his financial obligations. I, too, made it a point to bring up the high cost of private schools. "Your kids are going to be expensive," I told him. "So will your new company."

I don't remember Coppola ever uttering a declarative sentence along the lines of "I really have a passion to write and direct *The Godfather*." At some point he simply signed contracts and cashed checks.

"This guy isn't bringing conviction to this project," Evans remarked to me when he saw the deal memo. "I hope he at least helps Puzo deliver a decent script."

"I think he will. I have a hunch, even though I don't believe in hunches."

"He's Italian. Just remind him the story has to smell like great pasta. Can you trust him to do that? I mean, he's a friend of yours."

"He's not a friend of mine, Bob," I interrupted. "In his mind I'm the enemy, seducing him into making lowlife commercial movies. No matter what comes out of this venture, he'll never be a friend."

"OK, but Mario Puzo is already writing the screenplay and he's never written a screenplay. There's some orchestrating to do."

"Our asses are on the line, I know that," I mumbled.

Coppola and Mario Puzo instantly took a liking to each other. Coppola cooked his favorite pasta dish for the hefty writer and they exchanged recipes for their favorite sauces.

Puzo knew Coppola intended to add layers to his story and build up the character of the Godfather. In their initial conversations, both agreed that Marlon Brando would be ideal for the role. Puzo told me he was dubious about some of Coppola's ideas, but acknowledged, "The kid understands structure and I don't."

"A little bit of studio money is making everyone happy," I said to Evans. "Puzo's feeding his family again. Coppola's paying his bills. Everyone's working."

"*The Brotherhood* failed because Jews like Kirk Douglas and Martin Ritt thought they were making high drama about the Mafia," he replied. "Now we have a couple of wops who are just out to make a few bucks. Does that improve our chances?"

I knew Evans's skepticism was valid. But then the Puzo-Coppola draft started rolling in. Our lives were about to change.

From the moment Roman Polanski received his green light on *Rosemary's Baby*, tensions at the studio began to build. Paramount's resident bureaucrats did not appreciate Polanski's manner. "The little Polack thinks he owns the place," one department head complained to me. Accustomed to making small movies with minimal crews, the procedures of a major studio frustrated the young filmmaker. Sets weren't autocratically designed—meetings had to be held, budgets constructed, protocols followed.

But the first major battle, to my surprise, involved Evans. Though Evans and Polanski shared similar tastes in women (Polanski preferred them a little younger), their views on casting were sharply dissimilar. To Polanski, Tuesday Weld had the experience and gravitas to play Rosemary. Evans, to my surprise, was hung up on Mia Farrow.

"Tuesday is too healthy, Mia is ethereal. We need ethereal," Evans explained to me.

I trusted Evans's inclinations on casting, but I shared Polanski's reservations on Mia Farrow. "She's identified with *Peyton Place*." I explained. "She's got the TV stigma. It's Ryan O'Neal all over again. Besides, do you want to have to deal with the Sinatra nightmare?"

I'd had only a couple of minor run-ins with Sinatra over the years, but observed that his moods ran the gamut from rude to homicidal. Evans knew him better but shared my apprehensions. Coincidentally, Sinatra had just committed to star in a movie at Fox titled *The Detective*—the property that had launched Evans's brief and bumpy producing career. Suddenly his view of Sinatra seemed to brighten.

Polanski and Evans argued for a week, the director fretting that Mia's "ethereal" quality would fade on film. He also worried about his male lead. He had wanted to interest Redford in the role and had even met with the elusive Warren Beatty. One star after another turned the role down, however, fearing that the movie would belong to Rosemary. Besides, Redford urgently wanted to get *Downhill Racer* started—*Rosemary's Baby* came in a distant second.

Finally, John Cassavetes was selected to play Rosemary's husband, an unexpected choice on several counts. Cassavetes was himself a filmmaker. He had darting black eyes and his appearance was vaguely demonic; I feared he was a giveaway as the heavy.

But by the time *Rosemary's Baby* moved into its third week of production, it became clear that the biggest problem was not Mia Farrow or John Cassavetes, but rather Roman Polanski. He was such a perfectionist that he had barely finished one week's work by the end of week two and was shooting as many as thirty takes of every Mia Farrow scene, admonishing her again and again to become more emotive.

"Roman is the real horror story," advised Castle, who petitioned both Evans and me to let him take over the picture. "Come see for yourself what's going on."

I had steadfastly avoided visiting film sets. As a journalist I had been invited to several locations and had always been welcomed eagerly as a visitor from the *New York Times*. But now, as a studio suit, my visits were viewed as a veiled threat. If I was on hand, something must be going wrong; perhaps someone would be fired.

True to form, when I arrived at the soundstage and moved unobtrusively to the back of the set I could feel a stir. This was

a nervous crew; they knew they were already desperately behind schedule. Polanski did not acknowledge my presence. He
was working with Mia, but I felt he was really working her
over. She was close to tears. "He's trying to break her down,"
an assistant director whispered to me. "That's his idea of getting a performance. She's going to have a nervous breakdown
if this continues."

I left the set and went to Evans's office. "I want you to
come with me to the stage," I demanded. "We're in trouble."

Evans quickly made his phone call to Bob Goodfried, who
ran the publicity department. Any set visits had to be accom-
panied by a photographer, even in troubled times—that was
simply the way Evans, the ex-actor, did things. The photographer was instantly in place as we entered the stage, and Polanski looked exasperated to see unexpected visitors. Mia quickly
darted to her dressing room.

The meeting was amicable. Evans and his director lined
up for a photo. "I am moving as quickly as I can," Polanski said
reassuringly to his studio chief. "Mia is holding up well."

"The dailies look great," Evans lied. "But New York is raising the pressure. You've got to pick up time."

"Fuck New York," Polanski replied. "I'm making a movie."

After we left, Polanski went back to work, but again failed
to complete the schedule for the day. And Evans got a rant
from Bluhdorn about the overages.

Frank Sinatra's attorney, a ferocious pit bull named Mickey
Rudin, materialized in my office the next day to deliver a message. Rudin had not made an appointment; he felt he didn't
need to. "Frank has a rule on his pictures—two takes is the
limit," Rudin advised me abruptly. "That rule is going to apply
to Mia as well. Do I make myself clear?"

I was startled both by his message and the directness of

his delivery. "I'll convey Frank's suggestion to Polanski," I responded. "Candidly, I don't think it will have an impact."

"You don't understand—this is not a suggestion."

"Look, Mr. Rudin," I said, "why not drop down to Evans's office and give him your news. For that matter, tell Charlie Bluhdorn. I'm not going to be able to—"

"Frank and I know Polanski was your idea. You have the professional relationship. Evans is his pimp." Rudin wheeled around and left my office.

Evans was in New York that week. I tried to phone him but he was locked in meetings. Polanski meanwhile had broken his record—one scene with Mia required twenty-six takes. Mia had left the set in tears twice during the prolonged session.

When I viewed dailies that evening, the performances were brilliant. I understood what Polanski was up to, but agonized over his method of achieving it.

I was at dinner that night when Evans called. Sinatra himself had reached him directly where he was in New York with Bluhdorn. When he delivered his ultimatum, Evans had put him on the speakerphone so Bluhdorn could hear.

"The limit is two takes or I'm pulling Mia off the movie," he barked. "Polanski has four weeks to finish. Then she starts *The Detective* with me."

Evans explained that his demands were impossible, that Polanski needed at least eight additional weeks. Sinatra's response was predictable. He simply hung up. Bluhdorn for once was speechless.

Evans flew back to Los Angeles that night and the next morning Mia was in his office. This was a meeting I wanted no part of. It went on all morning and then through lunch.

Early in the afternoon I was watching dailies when Evans

sat down next to me in the dark. "Is she staying or leaving?" I asked as we both watched the images of Mia on screen.

"She's going to finish the movie," he replied, his voice hoarse with exhaustion. "She started out telling me she's pulling out. Old Blue Eyes was going to divorce her if she finished the movie."

"How did you turn her around?"

"She was weeping 'I want to be with Frank.' My only play was to appeal to her instincts as an actress. I told her that her performance is great, that she'll win an Academy Award. I showed her some of the dailies and she simply got up and returned to the set to get back to work."

Within a week, Mickey Rudin served up the promised divorce papers. A couple of nights later at Chasen's I almost collided with him as he was moving to his table. Rudin gave me a glancing gaze. "I'd watch my health if I were you, kid," he advised in a low snarl.

Polanski picked up his pace in the following weeks and Mia provided the performance he was looking for. Paradoxically, her real-life melodrama had apparently helped her deliver the appropriate subdued hysteria. A malevolent ring had indeed surrounded her, but it was Sinatra who had taken on that Mephistophelian aura. Instead of scuttling the movie, he seemed to have saved it.

From the moment *The Godfather* hit the bestseller list early in 1969, Bob Evans and I knew that the rules of the game would change. We had been dealing with this underdog project—a manuscript by an obscure author, Mario Puzo, which had been transformed into a gripping screenplay by a still-obscure writer-director, Francis Coppola. But now *The Godfather* had become, by Hollywood standards, a hot property. "I suppose we should be thrilled about this," I told Evans, "but I feel a chill, not a thrill."

Within days my chill seemed prescient. Million-dollar offers to buy the book arrived from top producers like Dino De Laurentiis and stars like Burt Lancaster. Their assumption was that, since Paramount hadn't assigned any major names to the project, we lacked the will or the funding to move it forward. Evans resolutely slammed the door on those discussions.

Next, and more ominous still, came the second-guessing from the hierarchs in New York. Every top executive at Paramount and at Gulf & Western, it seemed, was now poring through *The Godfather* and knew exactly who should direct the film and star in it. And given the company's institutional anarchy, several functionaries sent the novel to every name on their lists.

The landscape seemed all but covered with copies of *The Godfather*. Meetings were taking place all over the company about how best to get the project mobilized.

I was expecting the ubiquitous Bluhdorn to check in with his epiphanies, but he had suddenly gone silent. The reason, we learned, was that the Gulf & Western board of directors— a board supposedly friendly to Bluhdorn—had finally delivered an ultimatum: Sell Paramount or shut it down. Gulf & Western shares had been hammered by the appalling results of Bluhdorn's bombs. The death of the studio now seemed a fait accompli. And Evans and I would soon be out of a job.

He'd never really expected to find himself levitated into a Thalberg-like position in Hollywood, but now that he was there he had no intention of doing a fade-out. One evening, following a screening in his home projection room, he abandoned his guests and grabbed me by the arm, ushering me into his bedroom—the place where he did most of his thinking as well as most of his playing. "I'm flying to New York to speak to the board of directors," he said solemnly. "I'm going to tell them about the amazing product that we are about to release—about *Love Story* and *The Godfather* and all the rest."

"But none of it is finished. Or even close—"

"You'll help me write my speech. You're great at speeches," Evans said.

Evans was so excited I could practically feel the heat. "But will the board grant you time?"

"I'll beg. I don't mind begging. I'll fly in tomorrow and show them some footage. My speech will turn them around."

When informed of the eleventh-hour effort, Bluhdorn gruffly agreed to set aside thirty minutes at the board meeting, but he warned that the situation was dire.

It was a banner Evans performance—arguably his most persuasive acting job. The board of directors deliberated for fifteen minutes, and then agreed to give Paramount another chance.

Once again the pressure was now mounting to get *The Godfather* off the ground. Several more filmmakers who had been asked to read the book by the various corporate functionaries had weighed in with their assessments. All were negative. Franklin Schaffner, who directed *Patton*, said the book glamorized the Mafia and hence was immoral. Arthur Penn said he'd seen the movie before. Lewis Gilbert, who directed *Alfie* and *You Only Live Twice*, was drawn to the material, but disdained the meager budget.

When I reminded everyone that Francis Coppola was already working on the script, the news elicited a uniform indifference. Why put a lightweight director on a heavyweight film? I was asked. My colleagues had also conveniently forgotten that I had assigned the producing job to Albert S. Ruddy, a savvy young producer who I felt had the toughness and dedication to pull off what was becoming an increasingly controversial project.

Ruddy, a tall, shambling guy who affected a mobster-like voice, had a great appreciation of the absurd and a willingness to laugh off setbacks or insults. That trait would become a savior to us both.

When Ruddy first signed on, *The Godfather* had not yet hit the bestseller list, where it was to remain for sixty-seven weeks. Indeed, the book had just been published that very week, and Ruddy, famously cheap, had asked me for a free copy. I instructed him to set a precedent and buy his own.

If Ruddy was a penny-pincher, that too was a trait I coveted, because our plan was to bring in *The Godfather* for somewhere between $5 million and $6 million. The key was to forge an inexpensive deal with Marlon Brando, whose career was ice cold, then bring aboard some gifted young actors to fill out the cast.

When this plan became "public," other, "better" casting ideas again came pouring in. Charlie Bluhdorn proposed Carlo Ponti to play the Godfather. A revered Italian producer with an operatic personality, Ponti was not an actor nor was his English proficient. Various agents proposed everyone from Sonny Tufts to Anthony Quinn to play the Godfather. Predictably, Evans talked to Beatty about playing Michael. A persistent Burt Lancaster demanded a personal meeting with Bluhdorn, offering to give Paramount a $1 million profit over what the studio had originally paid for the rights.

As weeks of indecision rolled by, it became vividly clear that *The Godfather* had brought Paramount to its knees. The company had been immobilized by the dazzling worldwide success of the novel. "It's time to bite the bullet," I finally said to Evans. "Let's send Coppola to talk to Bluhdorn. Then let's send in Ruddy. We have a plan, so let's press all the buttons."

"A Charlie meeting will be a massacre," Evans replied.

"I talked with Francis. He really wants the job now. And

when he wants something he knows how to hustle. I think he will hustle Bluhdorn."

As it turned out, Bluhdorn, by now exasperated by the delays, reacted enthusiastically to both the director and the producer. Coppola eloquently spun out his approach to a father-son story, explaining how the creation of a Mafia dynasty was analogous to the building of America. Ruddy was typically more direct. "We're going to make a terrifyingly realistic movie about the kind of people you understand and love," he told the chairman. It was a calculated risk: Bluhdorn was sensitive about rumors that he was dealing on several fronts with shady financiers who had ties to the mob, but he took it in good humor.

With the New York executives' final acceptance of Coppola and Ruddy, the issue of casting remained the final barrier. At the first mention of Brando's name, Bluhdorn launched into a tirade that he was "box-office poison." When Coppola said he favored Al Pacino for the role of Michael, Stanley Jaffe, the thirty-year-old president of Paramount, snorted that "the Pacino kid" was too young and inexperienced. Evans advocated Jimmy Caan for the Michael role, Bluhdorn proposed Charlie Bronson for the Godfather, and, again, chaos prevailed. Offers went out to Jack Nicholson, David Carradine, even Danny Thomas. Screen tests were shot in New York encompassing a wide range of film and TV actors.

Eager to break the logjam, Coppola confided to me that he had organized his own surreptitious screen tests in San Francisco and had invited Jimmy Caan, Al Pacino, Robert Duvall, and Diane Keaton to participate. The tests were persuasive to Coppola—he had chosen the right cast. I felt he was correct.

Next Coppola tried an even shrewder ploy. He went to Brando's house on Mulholland Drive, atop Hollywood, with a skeleton crew, telling the actor that he wanted to shoot some trial footage in an effort to get a "take" on the character of the Godfather. He emphasized that this would not be a screen test: he was testing some equipment and also some character points.

Brando, attired in a kimono to conceal his girth, welcomed the young director. He had read the book again and felt that, whoever played the part, the actor should speak in a slurred manner—he had been shot in the throat at one time and his soft gravelly voice would carry more authority.

To Coppola's delight, Brando had started to get into the part. He stuffed Kleenex into his mouth, causing his jaw to jut out. He blackened his hair with shoe polish and put on a jacket with a rolled-back collar. When he started speaking his lines, Marlon Brando had become the Godfather.

I was not invited to witness the "Miracle on Mulholland," as Al Ruddy later described it. Learning about it a day later, however, I was intrigued by the paradox that both Coppola and Brando were resentful of Paramount, yet both had become enveloped in a love-hate relationship with the material. Brando knew Bluhdorn and Jaffe did not want him for the movie. Coppola was well aware that the project had been offered to several other filmmakers. Yet, from what I could glean, Brando had instinctively concluded that this would be a great role for him and, indeed, after the disastrous opening of *Burn*, he needed a great role. Coppola, meanwhile, had not exactly been deluged with offers from studios to direct other movies. He, too, needed money and, much as he resisted "commercial movies," he understood that *The Godfather*, based on the success of the novel, could be spectacularly successful. For Coppola and Brando alike, *The Godfather* had taken on the form of a literary narcotic.

The deals that were offered to them by the studio were less than enticing. The movie would be made on a modest budget, they were told. Brando was offered actor's scale up front and 5 percent of gross receipts when the film grossed $50 million. He would also have to put up a bond against any cost overruns caused by his bad behavior. Brando's attorney, Norman Gary, pleaded for at least $100,000 to help the actor avoid tax delinquency. In exchange Brando agreed to return his points in the movie—a deal which would ultimately cost Brando at least $11 million.

Even before Coppola's deal could be consummated, Warner Bros. put in a claim that his company, Zoetrope, owed the studio some $600,000 in overhead and development costs. Hence, whatever Coppola received for *The Godfather* would have to go first to that studio until this sum was paid off.

I felt a sense of elation that the initial blueprint for *The Godfather* was finally coming to fruition, yet was also concerned about the curtain of anger that hung over the project. And the tensions were soon to worsen. Bluhdorn's mandate was that the budget must be limited to $6 million, a spartan number even for 1971. This meant not only a rigorous shooting schedule, but also minimal salaries for supporting cast.

And, no one could agree on that cast. Coppola, having won on Brando, was vehemently demanding Al Pacino for the pivotal role of Michael. Evans reiterated that he wanted Jimmy Caan. Consistent with my earlier resolution, I removed myself from the casting battles, but watching Pacino's tests, I understood Evans's reservations. The young actor looked too clean-cut and immature. "The guy's no gangster," Evans told Coppola. With four weeks left before the start of shooting, the debate continued.

Evans realized he had no movie unless he gave his blessing to Pacino, but insisted that Caan get the role of Sonny. Coppola had already assigned that role to a rough-looking character named Carmine Caridi, reminding Evans of his objections to

The Brotherhood—that too much of the cast was Jewish, not Italian. Caan was also Jewish.

Coppola finally agreed to compromise on Sonny, only to learn that Pacino was no longer available for Michael. He had committed to a film called *The Gang That Couldn't Shoot Straight* at MGM on the assumption he would never land the *Godfather* role.

Mindful of his director's growing panic, Evans decided to play his Korshak card.

A day later word was flashed that Pacino had suddenly become available again.

Kirk Kerkorian was building his new hotel, the MGM Grand, in Las Vegas, and Korshak apparently reminded him about the risks of his potentially rising labor costs.

In March 1971, Coppola was finally given the green light to shoot his film. Coppola had won most of his casting battles, yet he still—understandably—felt under siege. His cinematographer, Gordon Willis, was innovative but cantankerous. His editor, Aram Avakian, was secretive and vaguely critical. Paramount's chief of physical production, Jack Ballard, felt the director was unprepared, faulting Coppola for devoting too much attention to testing actors, rather than scouting locations (the tests had been ordered by the studio, of course).

Then, too, there were rumblings from the very characters who were the subject of the film—the mob itself.

By and large, Italian-Americans admired the Puzo novel and Coppola had tried to fortify this affinity in his casting decisions. An actor named Gianni Russo with a mysterious background was cast as Carlo; he told fellow actors that Joe Colombo himself had urged the studio to give him the role. A massive, 320-pound bodyguard named Lenny Montana landed the role of Luca Brasi. During rehearsals, several of the bad boys found their way onto the set as observers.

If a sort of tacit peace treaty had been arranged, it seemed shaky. Evans received what he interpreted as a threatening phone call. Then a bomb threat from an unknown source triggered the evacuation of the Gulf & Western building.

A group surfaced calling itself the Italian-American Civil Rights League and began to issue vague admonitions about the content of the forthcoming movie. Though many felt this to be a faux organization, the corporate public relations men urged Al Ruddy to seek some sort of accommodation.

Responding to the pervasive nervousness, Ruddy met with representatives of the League to assure them that *The Godfather* would be what he called "an equal opportunity movie." The characters, he pointed out, would include a corrupt Irish cop and an equally dishonest Jewish producer. He even handed over a copy of the screenplay.

A League representative thumbed through the pages. He obviously had no intention of reading it, or no talent to do so. His one demand: That the word "Mafia" be deleted. In fact, "Mafia," which had once been the title, now appeared only once in the script, and Ruddy quickly promised its removal. Ruddy also pledged to contribute some of the proceeds from the premiere to benefit the League's charities.

However, an overzealous representative of the League saw to it that the story outlining Ruddy's concessions was leaked to a *New York Times* reporter. The ensuing story suggested that Ruddy, on behalf of Gulf & Western, had made concessions to the Mafia, and Charlie Bluhdorn's reaction was operatic. "Ruddy will have to go," Bluhdorn intoned. No one at Paramount knew at the time why Bluhdorn was hypersensitive to any suggestions that the producer of *The Godfather,* too, was negotiating with the mob.

His threats to fire Ruddy were quickly forgotten, however,

and amid all the noise, no one seemed to notice that Francis Coppola had quietly started shooting.

The preproduction period had been stormy for Coppola, and the rest of his ride would not prove any easier.

The atmosphere on the set of *The Godfather* during the first two or three weeks was at best chaotic. Coppola knew that he hadn't had enough prep time and hadn't studied his locations. His screenplay ran to 163 pages, which was roughly 40 pages too long. Al Ruddy was impatient with Coppola for being too protective of the dialogue. Much of it, Ruddy reminded him, had really been written by Puzo, not Coppola. Gordon Willis, his cameraman, was behaving disrespectfully toward his director. "You're not using your actors right," he declared in a loud voice. By contrast, Brando was mumbling his dialogue, still finding his way into his character.

The first flashpoint was prompted by the dailies. Coppola and Willis had agreed they wanted to shoot a dark, moody film, but the first few scenes were so dark that both Evans and I simultaneously removed our glasses, checking that we hadn't been wearing sunglasses by mistake. "I can't understand Brando and I can't see the actors—other than that the work is great," Evans commented, his voice laden with sarcasm.

Charlie Bluhdorn had also asked to see the dailies, and I was dreading his reaction. Fortunately, he was too distracted by his erupting quarrel with his young president, Stanley Jaffe, to focus on *The Godfather*. I liked Jaffe personally and was disappointed to see him implode. At the same time, it was helpful to keep Bluhdorn distracted until *The Godfather*'s problems could be sorted out.

As the movie moved into its second and third weeks, my primary concern was that Coppola was isolating himself. Even in the best of times Coppola was often uncommunicative, but now he had all but shut down his dialogue with the studio.

Jack Ballard was spending all his time on the set and was not happy. My own instinct was to stay away, but I called Coppola every day in an effort to extend support. "If you wanted to go for that exaggerated dark look, why didn't you prepare us for it?" I asked. "I'm on your side. I would have prepared my colleagues."

"I'm fixing it. Willis is an asshole."

"But he's your asshole. You hired him. Talk to people, Francis. This is not the time to brood; it's the time to lead."

"Things are getting better," he replied.

But they weren't. Members of the supporting cast were feeling the angst. Duvall told friends he was persuaded that Coppola would be fired within two or three weeks—he suspected the studio already had "planted" a replacement on the set. Pacino was drinking heavily every night, convinced he would be fired the following day.

The day after my conversation with Coppola, a palace coup broke out on the set. To my astonishment, Ballard announced on a conference call that Coppola "wasn't up to the job," that he wanted to designate Aram Avakian, the editor, as the new director. Al Ruddy had warned me that Avakian had been hovering around Ballard in a conspiratorial manner and that something dire was afoot.

"What the hell's going on?" I demanded of Evans. "I'm not willing to throw Coppola to the wolves, are you?"

Evans seemed distracted. "The Avakian rumors . . . I know about them."

"This whole situation is getting to be like a Mafia plot," I continued. "Ruddy's people in New York believe Avakian is sabotaging the dailies. The material we're seeing has been scrambled so that the scenes don't play."

"Francis can deliver. I know he can," Evans said. "We've got to restore order, otherwise the movie will unravel."

"Please call Coppola. Tell him that the studio is behind him. And I'm telling Jack Ballard to crawl into a fucking hole."

While Evans may have had mixed feelings about his director, he now sprang into firm support mode. Not only did he calm the edgy Coppola with the appropriate reassurances, but he also told the corporate team to back off. Rumors of the failed Avakian coup were now rife within the company and Evans knew they had to be silenced.

Coppola responded well to his vote of confidence. The actors, too, now rallied behind their director. Robert Duvall and Jimmy Caan in particular bonded with the other players; even the dour Brando flashed an occasional grin.

I visited the set fairly often now and was pleased by the emerging camaraderie. Coppola was managing Brando with special respect and patience. Since the actor refused to (or was incapable of) memorizing his lines, his dialogue for every scene was carefully printed out and placed in his sightline on set.

During the break in one scene, I approached Brando and put the question to him. "The lines—why do you want them printed out?"

Brando gazed at me, his expression purposefully ambiguous. "Because I can read them that way," he said. And clearly, that was the end of the discussion.

"Francis is starting to act like a director," Ruddy told me. "In good ways and bad ways."

Coppola, it seems, had already started renegotiating his deal with his producer. He now wanted "presentation" credit, which Ruddy had been accorded. He also asked Ruddy for a bigger share of his profits. Ruddy turned him down on both counts.

Toward the end of the shooting schedule, Coppola brought forth his final demand. He would prefer to edit the movie at his ministudio in San Francisco, not in Los Angeles.

The motivation behind that demand was readily apparent. Coppola wanted to go home. He wanted to insulate himself from the noise.

It was all perfectly understandable, but profoundly inept politically. For one thing, Coppola had never elicited a firm understanding about the length of the cut he was expected to deliver. His instructions were to deliver a cut of two hours ten minutes, he later claimed. Evans insisted his mandate was for two hours fifty minutes. Frank Yablans, the head of distribution who had just been appointed to succeed Stanley Jaffe as president, felt the proper length was two hours twenty minutes. He had set a Christmas release date on that premise. Yablans's release plan was a bold one: a wide release (for its time) in four hundred theaters. Though some exhibitors wanted to book the movie with an intermission, Yablans held firm, even canceling some bookings over the issue.

Yablans was furious when he received a phone call from Evans stating that the Christmas release was impossible and that he and Coppola had differences about running time. In fact, the "differences" were more of emotion than fact. When Evans ran Coppola's shorter cut—the one he claims he was asked to deliver—Evans correctly felt it was too stark. Coppola's curt response was that Evans simply wanted to add material that he had cut so he could claim credit for "saving" the movie.

My instinct was to try to serve as a middleman between the two. I had lured Coppola into this adventure and felt he deserved the right to exercise control over the cut, even though his contract did not specify final cut. I also felt it was imperative to preserve their working relationship, which was quickly deteriorating.

But Coppola was in an angry sulk, and Evans had become obsessive about the subtle moments and nuances in the film that the director had overlooked in his editing. He felt that if he could seclude himself in an editing room, his vision of *The Godfather* would be vastly superior to the one that Coppola had delivered.

The dialogue became nasty. "You've delivered a trailer, not a movie," Evans snapped at one point.

"Bob Evans's ego is running rampant," Coppola told anyone who would listen, including the press.

Adding to the muddle was a health issue. Though Evans had not previously suffered back pain, he was now in such agony that he needed to remain prone on a hospital-type gurney. The bed was wheeled in and out of the editing room, where Evans remained during eighteen-hour days. Back in San Francisco, Coppola read an item in a gossip column about Evans's new mission in life—that he was working night and day to salvage *The Godfather.* Coppola reacted by firing off an irate letter, insisting that his film did not require "salvaging."

Steadfast, Evans kept working. Now and then Coppola would glimpse some scenes and give his comments. Two or three times a week, Evans would summon me to the editing room and we would exchange ideas.

One evening Evans and I ran about ninety minutes of the reedited film.

After the screening we both sat in silence for a while. "I think it's becoming a movie," he said finally.

I was in a daze. I didn't want to respond. "It's really taking shape," I said in a noncommittal voice.

When I got home, I went to my den and tried to sort out my feelings. Amid all the noise and rancor, an absolutely brilliant movie was somehow coming together. Had I become lost in self-delusion? I wondered. Or was this nightmare somehow becoming a transcendent experience—one that could change the lives of everyone involved?

I decided not to share my ruminations with any of my colleagues. Especially not with Evans or Coppola.

But I couldn't help but wonder: Did they sense this too?

The banner reception accorded *Rosemary's Baby* among critics and filmgoers alike had a powerful impact on Roman Polanski. He was now the hot young director in Hollywood, hanging with Nicholson and Beatty, watching films at Evans's house with Sue Mengers and other "insiders" and fielding the inevitable offers from other studios. He could even gloat over the fact that *Rosemary's Baby* had outperformed Frank Sinatra's movie, *The Detective*, which costarred Lee Remick instead of Mia Farrow. Suddenly Polanski was no longer the outsider, the bad boy of cinema. He had positioned himself squarely in the middle of the fraternity he had once scorned.

Some of his old friends—shady characters from Eastern Europe—resented his metamorphosis. The young girls Polanski once favored were no longer receiving phone calls from him. The producer who regularly hosted opium parties in Malibu was no longer enjoying his prestigious company. Polanski now had a serious girlfriend, the actress Sharon Tate. Indeed, he intended to marry her.

When Polanski and his new bride, now pregnant, moved to a quiet house on Cielo Drive, a short trip up Benedict Canyon in Beverly Hills, one of his Polish friends told me outright, "Roman has gone bourgeois." He added, "Suddenly I get phone calls from him telling me, 'The baby is kicking, I'm going to be a father.'"

Sharon Tate was a beautiful girl whose sunny disposition seemed the perfect antidote to Roman's dark moods. Her movie career was blossoming after the release of *Valley of the Dolls*.

Polanski's relationship with Paramount had also levitated him to a new role as the patron of Polish cinema. An old friend,

Simon Hessera, had directed a mediocre movie called *A Day at the Beach*, which Polanski helped write, and Evans now persuaded Bluhdorn to advance $600,000 to finance its completion. Polanski and Evans went shopping together for a Rolls-Royce, which was to be a surprise present for Polanski's bride.

I had lunch with Polanski at a French bistro during this period, and was confounded by his new persona. He seemed self-assured and upbeat, and, as always, our conversation leapt from literature to music.

Over a second glass of wine, however, he told me of his sadness that his good friend Christopher Komeda had just died of a brain injury resulting from an automobile accident. Polanski had brought Komeda to Hollywood to compose the superb score for *Rosemary's Baby*. Too many of his friends, Polanski acknowledged, had suffered misfortune at the moment of their greatest success and that fact haunted him.

Three months later, on August 9, 1969, Polanski was in London when he received the phone call informing him that his wife, then eight-and-a-half-months pregnant, along with several other friends, had been found murdered at his home on Cielo Drive. Sharon Tate had been stabbed sixteen times and the word "PIG" had been written in her blood on the front door. Evans had been invited to join Sharon at the informal dinner she'd given that evening but had bowed out because Charlie Bluhdorn was arriving the next morning for meetings. Sharon's other guests had included Gibby Folger, the wealthy coffee heiress, and Folger's boyfriend, Wojciech Frykowski, who was one of Polanski's rogue pals from Poland.

Evans was numbed by the news and also furious over insinuations in the media that Polanski was himself a suspect. Even *Time* magazine observed that "Sharon and Polanski circulated in one of the film world's more offbeat crowds," suggesting that members of that "crowd" were somehow culpable.

Evans met Polanski when he arrived from London and installed him in a dressing room on the Paramount lot that had once been used by Julie Andrews during production of *Darling Lili*. He also arranged for his Doctor Feel-good friend to keep him sedated.

The image of the grief-stricken director sealed off from the world in an ornate dressing room struck me as grotesque. Evans shortly moved Polanski to his guest house which in turn meant round-the-clock guards. The Los Angeles Police Department tapped the phones. News of the filmmaker's whereabouts further prompted speculation that Evans, too, might somehow be implicated.

Polanski emerged from his daze and worked with the police on their investigation—a trail that soon led to the Manson family—but he felt his life had turned into a bad movie. Sharon Tate's funeral, he said, "was like some ghastly movie premiere."

Polanski spent most of his time in Europe following the Manson murders. In 1972 Evans persuaded him to direct *Chinatown*, which was to earn Polanski an Oscar nomination. The Academy Award would elude him, however. He would lose to Francis Coppola for *The Godfather Part II*.

CHAPTER 13

The Glitz Machine

As I assessed the lessons of my studio experience, it had become increasingly clear to me over time that the hits emerging from the Hollywood studios were the result of inadvertency, not strategy. The so-called blockbusters released by Paramount, such as *Love Story* or *The Godfather*, both started out with modest budgets and limited expectations. By contrast, extravaganzas like *On a Clear Day You Can See Forever* or even *Catch-22* were heralded from the start as future hits. At Twentieth Century-Fox, *Doctor Dolittle* was supposed to be a big smash, not *Patton*; Warner Bros. didn't even want to release either *Bonnie and Clyde* or *American Graffiti* (George Lucas had already informed Universal that he was prepping *Star Wars* as a "personal picture" with a modest budget).

A generation later, to be sure, Hollywood was to master the art of marketing the $200 million prepackaged "tentpole" pictures. In the seventies, however, this sort of know-how was a distant dream, and the recession mandated even further austerity to film budgets.

By 1973, fortified by the success of the two *Godfathers*, Bob Evans sensed it was time for a more aggressive strategy. For some years he had been nurturing the idea of remaking *The Great Gatsby*, based on the F. Scott Fitzgerald novel. In Evans's mind, *Gatsby* was more a legend than a novel—one that embodied style, mystery, and romance. If *Gatsby* were presented with the right showmanship, it would be a preordained blockbuster.

The *Gatsby* idea was actually fostered not by Evans, but rather by his wife, Ali MacGraw, who had been a devotee of the F. Scott Fitzgerald novel since discovering it in her teenage years (she said she had read it at least three times). Ali had given her husband a leather-bound copy of another Fitzgerald story, "Winter Dreams," as a wedding present—she had copied the story word for word in her own meticulous handwriting. Deeply touched, Evans decided that his gift to her in return would be the role of Daisy Buchanan.

The notion of remaking *The Great Gatsby* as a starring vehicle for Ali MacGraw was hardly popular within the company. Previous regimes at Paramount had already made two *Gatsby*s, both of them failures. From my jaundiced point of view, Fitzgerald's novel represented a literary trap. Though seductively stylized, the piece lacked a strong narrative, or even a true protagonist. Gatsby himself was an observer—a shadow rather than a presence. Events happened around him; he did not propel them.

There were business problems as well: the rights had reverted back to the Fitzgerald family, and his daughter, Scottie Lanahan Smith, had no desire to sell them to yet another Hollywood intruder.

Mindful of the skepticism within the studio, Evans persistently reminded his colleagues of all the players who had expressed interest in the project, Beatty to Nicholson to Sydney

Pollack. "This could be a great star vehicle," Evans maintained. "It's not just an Ali project."

The debate continued over several months, until Yablans laid down the gauntlet. "If you can deliver Jack Nicholson or Warren Beatty," he said, "I'll go with Ali."

Encouraged, Evans knew he first had to secure the rights. David Merrick, the curmudgeonly Broadway producer, had a social relationship with Scottie, so Evans quickly recruited him to the cause, promising him coproducer credit.

Merrick was renowned for his powers of persuasion, and Fitzgerald's daughter agreed to an option.

Evans decided on similarly Machiavellian tactics in choosing a screenwriter. Truman Capote had capitalized on his fame for writing *In Cold Blood* by becoming a chatty regular on the Johnny Carson show. His "act" was both tipsy and bitchy. Capote also had become a favored guest of Charlie Bluhdorn's salon in the Dominican Republic. The chairman felt he added social panache to his gatherings: Bluhdorn's guest list was otherwise a little heavy with shady financial types.

"Capote is perfect for *Gatsby*," Evans told me one morning, having just had his epiphany. "He's got the literary style, plus Charlie Bluhdorn loves him."

"Capote also has the best-publicized case of writer's block in literary history," I warned Evans. "That means that he is drinking too much. Way too much."

"Well, he better remember how to type," Evans responded. "Between Capote and the rights, I'm already in for $300,000 and have nothing to show for it."

It turned out Capote did remember how to type, but that was the extent of his talents at that moment. He willingly accepted his $150,000 fee and even showed up at Evans's house a few times to entertain guests with his scandalous anecdotes. When asked about his script, Capote promised that he was hard at work "improving" Fitzgerald's novel, which he humorously dismissed as "illiterate." His fabled agent, Irving "Swifty" Lazar, also called a couple of times to reassure us that the project was coming along swimmingly.

The script that Capote delivered, however, was both tragic and bizarre. I took it home on a Friday night and, after reading it, I poured myself a tall vodka and tried to put my thoughts together. It was about eleven at night when I phoned the news to Evans.

"You won't believe this, Bob, but the material Truman turned in—I don't know what it is, but it's not a screenplay."

"But I have it here. It looks like a script. I haven't read it yet . . ."

"All he did was type," I said. "He typed the dialogue from the book, typed Fitzgerald's descriptions and made them look like stage directions. He didn't contribute one original line or idea."

"But he delivered a script . . . ?" Evans stuttered.

"Technically it is formatted like a script, but it is not a script. It isn't anything," I reiterated. "It is just type."

Evans read the so-called script the next morning and was numb with disappointment. He admonished me not to tell anyone—not even anyone at Paramount. "What the hell are we going to do?" Evans demanded.

"We should get Swifty to return the money, for one thing," I blurted.

"But I need a script. I'm talking with Warren and Jack and I have to show them something soon. They are all interested, but I have to give them a screenplay." The whole *Gatsby* exercise, he realized, was becoming a con.

"I've talked about the project in the past with Francis," I said, grasping at straws. "He admires Fitzgerald and he may need the money—you know, he's always in financial trouble. Maybe a quick rewrite for a few hundred thousand . . . ."

I heard Evans gasp for a breath. "Coppola's *Gatsby*. Maybe it could work."

I immediately hated myself for suggesting the idea. I knew it was dangerous to try to retrace one's steps from an earlier journey. Over the next few days I called two or three people in the Coppola camp and learned that he, indeed, might be open to a healthy financial offer. However, I also knew Coppola still felt a bitter resentment toward Evans for grasping credit for *The Godfather*.

Knowing there would be static to overcome, I decided to phone Coppola directly. His response was predictably cool. Yes, he loved *Gatsby*. Yes, he was open to a job, but he wanted time to reread the novel and think it over.

He called back in a few days to list his demands. He refused to work directly with Evans. Further, he did not believe Ali MacGraw could master the role of Daisy. In fact, the Daisy character itself needed work. Rereading the novel, he found there were no true scenes between Gatsby and Daisy—nothing that could define their cinematic relationship. He would have to create a major scene—perhaps one where they talked through the night and truly engaged one another. He had been working on just such a scene.

I could tell Coppola was intrigued and also that he needed the money. It was time to pass the baton to Evans. They would have to talk on the phone and make their peace.

Evans would offer Coppola a $350,000 payday. He would also emphasize how important this was to him, how desperately he needed Coppola to rescue his pet project.

A deal was made.

Braced with Coppola's commitment, Evans resumed his

conversations with his list of proposed stars. He and Ali also started running films night after night, reviewing the possibilities and weighing their attributes. They were joined by some tough critics—Sue Mengers, the agent, and her husband, Jean-Claude Tramont, Roman Polanski, Warren Beatty, Jack Nicholson, Dustin Hoffman, and, on occasion, Cary Grant and Mike Nichols would all be invited to the screenings. Mengers in particular, was acerbic in her critiques of the performances on display. No one was good enough for Gatsby—except, of course, the actors in the screening room.

But then, inevitably, came the moment of truth. Despite all the warm rhetoric, all the florid praise for Fitzgerald's writing, none of the actors wanted the role. Money was not the issue. They all were offered top dollar. But no one wanted to star in a movie opposite Ali MacGraw. Not Nicholson or Beatty or any other "bankable" star.

As usual, the most diplomatic turndown came from Beatty, who a few years earlier had himself tried to secure the screen rights to *Gatsby*.

"The only person to play Gatsby is Bob Evans," Beatty declared.

Evans was confounded. He knew his limitations as an actor. He also knew that, as head of the studio, he could not take an acting sabbatical.

"Evans is Gatsby," Beatty reiterated to me one night as we stood at the tennis court adjacent to the Evans screening room. "Maybe I'd produce it and give him line readings, if necessary."

I didn't believe him for a moment. Warren Beatty had a whimsical sense of humor—I had witnessed it many times. In addition, he was famously self-protective; there was no way he would produce a *Gatsby* with Ali MacGraw and Bob Evans starring.

But now, yet another star name was tossed into the equation—one whose entry would trigger a dizzying series of events. Steve McQueen was looking for his next movie, and *Gatsby* surprisingly held his interest. Several possible projects were also looming, but they were all encumbered. He liked a screenplay written by Walter Hill titled *The Getaway*, but I, coincidentally, had already offered it to Peter Bogdanovich to direct, and Bogdanovich felt it would be a good role for his girlfriend, Cybill Shepherd. But Bogdanovich had confided to me that he couldn't commit to *The Getaway* or to McQueen until yet another project had resolved itself, which he described as a once-in-a-lifetime opportunity. Bogdanovich, a big fan of westerns, felt he could bring John Wayne, Henry Fonda, and Jimmy Stewart together one more time on a project that was being written by Larry McMurtry. This would truly be a coup, Bogdanovich said, and he would be the first to see the finished script because McMurtry had written *The Last Picture Show*—a big success for them both.

The movie dominoes were lined up, and I was excited to see how they would fall.

The upshot was not at all as I expected. Wayne read the McMurtry script and passed. This unsettled the other two stars—Fonda and Stewart—and both pulled out. Bogdanovich then informed us that he was ready to do *The Getaway*, but Evans told him that Paramount would not do it with Cybill Shepherd. Ali MacGraw had just become available because, he announced, *The Great Gatsby* wasn't coming together as expected. "She would be perfect for *The Getaway*," said Evans.

Bogdanovich was dumbfounded, and so was I. *The Getaway* was about a trucker and his trashy Southern girlfriend—not exactly a fit for Ali. Besides, Steve McQueen was suddenly now passionate about *The Getaway* and it was becoming clear to me that Ali MacGraw was equally passionate about Steve McQueen.

Assimilating all these elements one evening, I took Sue Mengers aside for a reality check. Mengers was already angry because her client, Bogdanovich, was in a huff—he had no intention of making *The Getaway* with Ali MacGraw. Mengers's antenna had also picked up on the budding McQueen-Ali flirtation. The two had met at dinner parties and screenings, but had never spent one-on-one time together. Ali, we knew, had been complaining to friends that her relationship with Evans was becoming wobbly. McQueen, a prototypical diamond-in-the-rough, was immensely attractive to her. Her lovers in the past had been smoothly urbane men—never a McQueen type.

Most perplexing of all, despite the McQueen rumors, Evans was now trying to persuade his wife to take *The Getaway*. "*Gatsby* will take a long time to come together," he told her. "*The Getaway* will keep you in the middle of the action."

"I don't want to be in the action," she responded. It was a different sort of action she was coveting.

"What the hell's going on?" I asked Mengers. "Why is Evans persuading her to do a movie with McQueen? Doesn't he get it?"

But Mengers, too, had conflicting agendas. Her former boss at the CMA talent agency, Freddie Fields, was now chief of a company called First Artists, which was co-owned by McQueen, Paul Newman, Barbra Streisand, Dustin Hoffman, and Sidney Poitier. And Fields had told Mengers that he wanted to produce *The Getaway* at First Artists with McQueen and MacGraw. The legendary Sam Peckinpah was standing by to direct the film and it had "hit" written all over it.

For Mengers, this solved lots of problems. Two of her clients, MacGraw and McQueen, would instantly get big paychecks—her friend Freddie would see to that. Bogdanovich would be out of a job, but it had been his decision to walk away.

The problem child was Evans: Was Evans into his own head to such a degree that he didn't sense the electricity between Ali and McQueen? Further, was he unaware of Freddie Fields's plot to steal *The Getaway* away from Paramount and set it up for his own company?

When I tried to question Evans, I found him evasive. *Gatsby* had created a distance between us. Evans's growing dependence on cocaine was making him fuzzy. He was seeing situations from another perspective or from no perspective at all.

Yablans, meanwhile, was furious at Evans for losing *The Getaway* to a rival studio. Bluhdorn was yelling at him for blowing a Steve McQueen movie. I myself was feeling a growing frustration: The Bogdanovich *Getaway* that I had been developing was, in my view, a far better movie—with or without Ali. And *Gatsby* seemed a blatant waste of money and energy.

Six weeks into production of *The Getaway* in El Paso, Evans, following the hugely successful premiere of *The Godfather*, decided impulsively to fly down to visit his wife. The reception was predictably chilly. Ali was forthright about her involvement with her costar. McQueen had quickly left the location, refusing to shoot until Evans disappeared. Sam Peckinpah barked at Evans to go away so he could finish shooting. Evans saw that both Ali and their son, Joshua, then a year old, were distraught over the confrontations. Devastated, he headed home.

The confrontation in El Paso was perfect grist for the gossip columnists—a helpless Evans, a victorious McQueen. The accounts in the press were so melodramatic that even Henry Kissinger, an occasional visitor to the Evans compound, called from Washington to offer his services as a negotiator. When Evans told me of the phone call, I responded, "He's messing up in Vietnam, Bob; I don't think he'll do any better with Evans and MacGraw."

Bob Evans was a single man once again. Despite the dramatics, I sensed that this status better suited him. As a creature of the movies, Evans had been playing a role as husband and daddy. He'd done a good job at it for a brief period of time, but it was still role-playing

Meanwhile, Coppola, the man who had won his first Oscar for *Patton*, had restructured *Gatsby* into a coherent movie. The characters actually interacted with one another, though they still seemed tantalizingly out of reach. Coppola had managed to preserve Fitzgerald's impeccably stylish veneer but at the same time had created a narrative drive.

There was a movie here—possibly a commercial movie—and I understood what Bob Evans wanted *Gatsby* to be. He had come out of the fashion business, and he saw in the Gatsby-Fitzgerald aura a chance to build what would be closer to a fashion brand than a movie—a consummate triumph of style over substance. And his friends got that, too. A then-emerging young designer named Ralph Lauren was eager to create the wardrobe, and others of his ilk also were stepping forward.

Indeed, throughout Paramount, there seemed to be a building obsession with the *Gatsby* brand. And there was no doubt anymore that this would be a blockbuster in the making. The only doubt, that is, seemed to be harbored by me.

To my mind, if *Gatsby* were to be made at all, the key to putting it together was to pay Francis Coppola another million bucks to direct it and sign Brando to play Gatsby. Neither was stepping forward, I realized, but money—big money—could change their minds. Both desperately resented their meager back-end deals on *The Godfather*. Both were susceptible to creative bribes.

And Brando would add a menace to the character of Jay

Gatsby. It would be an older, more battle-scarred Gatsby, but a fascinating one nonetheless.

But now a new prospective candidate entered the *Gatsby* derby. Robert Redford was willing to cut his price drastically to play Gatsby, and to my colleagues this was star casting. Redford's Gatsby would be younger and better looking. A Redford vehicle would appeal to a wider audience.

Redford's main concern was dialogue. "In the book, Gatsby didn't speak like a real person. His dialogue bordered on the absurd," he told one interviewer. While the Gatsby character was "not fleshed out," Redford admitted he was fascinated by the subtle implications about his past.

Was Redford's commitment real? Those of us at the studio who had lived through *Blue* were dubious about yet another Redford adventure. He had walked out on *Blue* and had done little to sell *Little Fauss and Big Halsy*. Still, he was a star and he seemed resolute about *Gatsby*.

Redford was also the first choice of the several directors who seemed interested in the film. The leading candidate to direct in Evans's mind was a Brit named Jack Clayton, whose reputation rested on a small English film titled *Room at the Top*.

Clayton seemed an odd choice. I had known him for several years, and liked him, but he had never directed a studio film. Still, with Clayton at the helm, *Gatsby* could be shot in London and structured to qualify for generous subsidies. And Redford and Clayton had met and found that their views of the material meshed.

If Redford were Gatsby, then who would be his costar? Several top actresses were being tested for the part and the idea was to run the tests before a "committee" in New York to achieve a final judgment. I begged off the New York trip; my colleagues knew I was distressed that my Coppola-Brando scenario had been shunted aside. The committee consisted of Evans, the producer David Merrick and his chief aide Alan DeLynn, plus Clayton, Yablans, and Bluhdorn.

After running the tests, Clayton cast a vote for Mia Farrow. Merrick, to everyone's surprise, voted for Ali MacGraw, and said he wanted McQueen to play Gatsby. At this point Evans stammered objections, but Merrick, an intimidating presence, snapped, "Let's start being professional here, Evans."

Charlie Bluhdorn had had enough. He stood up and roared, "I agree with Clayton. It's Mia." Merrick was apoplectic. "You're turning down MacGraw and McQueen for Mia Farrow . . . ?"

But Bluhdorn would not budge. Other actresses had been tested, including Candice Bergen, Katharine Ross, and Faye Dunaway, but discussion was cut off.

What neither Bluhdorn nor Clayton knew at the time was that Mia Farrow, who was married to the conductor André Previn, was pregnant, and hence a stretch to play Fitzgerald's teasing sparrow of a character (her wardrobe was continually expanded and ruffles added during the shoot).

Hoping to mollify the gathering, Clayton meekly said, "Can we move on to the part of Jordan? I'd like to go with Lois Chiles."

Chiles was a former girlfriend of Evans's and this proved too much for Yablans. "We keep talking about Evans's wives, now his girlfriends. Are we running a lonely-hearts club or a movie company?"

Evans tried to protest that he had not proposed Chiles, but Bluhdorn was quickly on his feet again, demanding an apology from Yablans. Instead the president of Paramount simply walked out of the room.

Lois Chiles won the part. *Gatsby* would be a Mia-Redford movie, lavishly stylized but frugally budgeted. Every actor in the cast dutifully agreed to cut his price. Despite the gorgeous sets, elaborate party scenes, and period wardrobes, the final production cost of the film was an austere $6.4 million.

As a dissenter to the basic scheme, I decided to distance myself from the production. I rarely watched dailies and left the usual crisis meetings to Evans.

When I finally saw the first cut I felt a profound disappointment. The movie seemed inert. There was no chemistry between Redford and Mia Farrow. Jack Clayton had delivered what the studio demanded: a big, glamorous star vehicle that could be promoted as a symbol of Old Hollywood.

Of all Paramount releases of the decade, few, if any, would be accorded the promotional push of *Gatsby*. Its opening was more a celebration than a premiere—a celebration of style (the chic wardrobe), of glamour (the star cast), and of opulence (a chance to revisit the glories of wealth). By two weeks before opening, the movie, which cost $6.4 million to produce, had brought in advances of $18.6 million from exhibitors. "It's the most talked about movie since *Gone with the Wind*, Evans proclaimed in *Time* magazine.

By the moment of opening, so many brands had jumped on the *Gatsby* bandwagon that the spectacle became comical. *Women's Wear Daily* proclaimed the emergence of a new "Gatsby look." Tie-ins were orchestrated with Ballantine scotch, Robert Bruce sportswear, Kenzo tennis sweaters and white flannel pants—even a chain of hairdressers. Inevitably, rebellion set in. Redford refused to model suits for *Vogue*. Scottie Lanahan Smith told reporters that Paramount "was turning *Gatsby* into pots and pans."

With *Gatsby* awaiting release, the tensions between Yablans and Evans provided a vivid sideshow. A sixteen-page advertising flyer was put out by Yablans listing upcoming productions, but there was no mention of Evans. All interview requests with Evans were rejected by studio publicists unless Yablans was included in the session. "I don't want any confusion about who is running Paramount," Yablans told *Time* magazine. "His name is Yablans." Yablans acknowledged to *Time* that he wanted ultimately to run for elective office, adding, "Yes, I'd like to be president of the United States."

Evans told me his response to all this. "Call it 'the sounds of silence,'" he said.

Gatsby's release seemed almost anticlimactic. As a commercial vehicle, most industry insiders concluded it was an inspired creation. Artistically, however, the movie was a disappointment.

In reality, this *Gatsby* represented a clumsy coalescing of the Eurocentric art cinema of the seventies with Hollywood values of the thirties. The finished product was at once arty and vulgar. The smooth, silvery dialogue, which flowed so elegantly across the pages of Fitzgerald's novel, played stilted on the screen.

When I saw *The Great Gatsby* thirty years later on DVD I found myself even more impatient with the film, with its lack of narrative drive, the interminable party scenes of random frivolity, and the long stretches of voice-over backstory that told you little about the characters. Robert Redford was utterly miscast as Gatsby—far too young and callow for a man with a complex backstory in war and business. Mia Farrow played Daisy as a semihysteric young woman who would break into tears when Gatsby discarded piles of his Turnbull & Asser custom shirts. For the sexualized seventies, *The Great Gatsby* stands out as an astonishingly sexless movie.

Gatsby thus has failed three times as a movie, but filmmakers will still toy with it again, seduced by its graceful prose and tantalized by the tenuousness of its central character.

From time to time I find myself speculating on what the Coppola-Brando *Gatsby* film would have been like, had it been

made. Would it have worked as a film about a tough, somewhat mysterious gangster who conceals his past and falls in
love with a beautiful plaything in the roaring twenties—a
movie about social class in America, about the vulgarity of
wealth? It might have been dark and sexy. But Coppola possibly would have backed away from the project at the eleventh
hour. After completing the script and collecting the badly
needed money, he had, I suspected, lost his faith in the project. I cannot produce a document to support my thesis, but after delivering his script, Coppola simply vaporized. He did not
want to discuss casting or rewrites or any other issues and certainly never visited the set.

And while he had delivered a fine, literate script, it had
still raised the basic questions: What is *The Great Gatsby* really
about? And why should we care about these characters?

The Great Gatsby was not a disaster for Paramount—in
fact, it made a modest profit. The impact on the studio, however, was a negative one. Paramount had been delivering
films of substance, but *Gatsby* was all glitz—an empty movie
that revealed growing emptiness at the studio.

CHAPTER 14

Reckoning

A stunned silence greeted the premiere screening of *The Godfather* at the Loew's State Theater in New York on March 14, 1972. It was quickly followed by a wellspring of applause. The expectations of disaster were now drowned out by the shock of success. Even as the audience rose, I could hear virtually everyone ask the question of the night: How could this brilliant, brooding masterpiece of storytelling have emerged from a pop gangster novel?

The mood of surprise and celebration further intensified at the post-premiere party at the St. Regis Hotel, which instantly became a glittering media circus. In its vortex were Evans and MacGraw, the glitz machine's perfect couple, holding hands, kissing, embracing, their images aglow. And at their side was the eminence gris Henry Kissinger, who had braved a fierce snowstorm to fly in from President Nixon's side in Washington so that his aura of power could fleetingly connect with the Evans aura of celebrity and sexual adventure.

It was the perfect Paramount moment—the quintessential collision of the real and the surreal, with careers being born, marriages ending, myths imploding, all amid a hallucinogenic melee of hubris and self congratulation.

When Evans and MacGraw rose from their table to dance, every head in the room turned to watch and marvel. It was a magazine cover come to life, two extraordinarily attractive people dancing out their fantasies: He had just presided over a mythic movie; she was costarring in a Steve McQueen romantic action film.

I took refuge at one side of the ballroom and tried to steal some perspective. Was I the only person in the room who understood the subtext of what seemed like magic moments? Ali MacGraw had just reminded me that she didn't want to be here: she yearned to fly back to El Paso to be with her new lover, McQueen. And Evans knew their relationship was a lie. Even as he smiled for the camera he was trying to figure out how he could extricate himself without looking like a jilted fool.

The dance was over. The music stopped. They kissed. The crowd could feel the love.

By the fall of 1974, Paramount was clearly broken. Frank Yablans was embittered that he had not been accorded the money and attention that he felt he deserved. Charlie Bluhdorn, frazzled by the unrelenting SEC onslaught, was now determined to find a successor to Yablans—someone who would actually run the company. Having completed *Chinatown*, Bob Evans spent much of his time sulking at home, communicating with only a small circle of allies.

By the time *Chinatown* was completed, in mid 1974, the relationships at Paramount had deteriorated to such a degree that hardly anyone was on speaking terms with anyone else. The enthusiastic responses of critics and other opinion leaders did not

ameliorate the tension. The night of the premiere, Bluhdorn decided he would make a final stab at camaraderie, inviting his
two warring executives to a late dinner at a New York steak
house called Pietro's. The chairman toasted the movie and
the partnership of Yablans and Evans that had made it possible. Yablans interrupted, his voice resonating through the
room, "Forget the partnership shit," he snapped. "The world
consists of 'haves' and 'have-nots' and you're the only 'have'
at this table."

Bluhdorn cast a withering stare at his president; he had
fought off the inevitable decision for some time, but he had
to accept it now. Frank Yablans was history.

Bluhdorn later acknowledged to me that he had not
been aware that Evans had surrendered to Yablans's threats
and had signed over half his points in *Chinatown*. Nor was
Bluhdorn witness to Yablans's tantrums about the *Time* cover.

What neither Yablans nor Evans knew at the time was
that Bluhdorn had begun serious talks with Barry Diller about
Diller assuming a top position at Paramount. What they also
didn't know was that Bluhdorn had instructed his financial
team to quietly probe Yablans's expense account to determine
if any improprieties had taken place. Did Yablans tell his London office to purchase some first editions of Charles Dickens's
works, which he presented to his wife as a birthday present?
The cost of the purchase had appeared on the books as "The
Charles Dickens Project," suggesting that a film was being developed by that name. No one in London could confirm such
a project had ever existed.

While Bluhdorn was doing his detective work, the Diller
conversations were picking up in intensity.

The two had first become acquainted when Diller, as a
twenty-three-year-old junior executive at ABC, had started
bidding for the TV rights to several Paramount movies. The

TV aftermarket had not gained importance at the time and Bluhdorn was surprised and impressed that a network kid would show any interest in his product—films that no one else from the aftermarkets had seemed interested in.

Bluhdorn liked Diller. He was short and already bald and had no movie experience, but the chairman admired his self-confidence and agility. By 1974, he sat down with Diller and explained that he urgently needed him at Paramount. Gulf & Western had become too big and diverse, he said, and the board of directors felt strongly that Bluhdorn was devoting too much time to the entertainment assets. Given the discordant relationship between Yablans and Evans, the problem had become even more acute. Bluhdorn made his offer over lunch: that Diller assume a senior management job reporting directly to Yablans.

The response was forthright: "I'd rather be a waiter in this restaurant than work for Frank Yablans," Diller declared.

Within days the proposal was importantly modified: Bluhdorn would now agree to have Yablans and Evans both report to Diller.

The young TV executive was surprised by how quickly the situation had changed, but was still reluctant. "I didn't really know the movie business," he told me later.

Diller took the job, but his apprehensiveness was soon validated. During Diller's first official trip to the studio, Yablans was twenty minutes late for the first staff meeting, and then regaled the executives with a crude story about a presumed sexual encounter the night before.

Back in New York the inevitable confrontation quickly took place. Yablans issued instruction to the senior executives that they would continue to report to him. Diller summoned Yablans to his office to clarify the reporting lines: top executives at Paramount would report to Diller, as would Yablans.

Yablans flushed and said nothing, but when he exited Diller's office he slammed the door so loudly that a painting fell from the wall and its frame shattered.

Within weeks a token production deal for Frank Yablans was announced. Evans, too, would now focus on production and would no longer have responsibility for studio films.

Paramount's success story had come to a sour end. And I was (gratefully) out the door.

The decision-making process had ground to a halt. The studio had become an all-but-deserted battlefield. There were a few casualties strewn here and there, but most of the combatants had simply moved on.

At the box office, paradoxically, the studio was displaying greater success than ever before. More than twenty films were to be put into release in the following months; an eclectic mix both artistically and commercially. Not only would *The Godfather Part II* be even more richly acclaimed than its predecessor, but filmgoers also rallied to *The Longest Yard*, starring Burt Reynolds, *Chinatown*, with Jack Nicholson, and *The Great Gatsby*, with Robert Redford. Several smaller-budget films also reaped critical praise, if more modest acceptance commercially—*Lady Sings the Blues*, starring Diana Ross, *The Gambler*, starring James Caan and directed by Karel Reisz, *White Dawn*, directed by Philip Kaufman, *The Parallax View*, starring Warren Beatty, *The Apprenticeship of Duddy Kravitz*, starring Richard Dreyfuss and directed by Ted Kotcheff, *Murder on the Orient Express*, starring Sean Connery and Lauren Bacall and directed by Sidney Lumet, and *The Conversation*, from Francis Coppola.

In addition, several promising films were about to go into release, such as *Friends of Eddie Coyle*, starring Robert Mitchum and directed by Peter Yates, *Paper Moon*, starring Tatum and Ryan O'Neal from Bogdanovich, and *Save the Tiger*, starring Jack Lemmon and directed by John Avildsen.

To be sure, the list included some formidable clunkers—most prominently the final offering from Lerner and Loewe, the lifeless musical called *The Little Prince*. Stanley Donen, an accomplished director, managed to destroy the classic story by Antoine de Saint-Exupéry.

On the surface, Paramount had become astonishingly prolific both in terms of quality and commerce. This was a formidable slate of films, even by the prolific standards of the seventies.

But in Charlie Bluhdorn's mind, the moment had come to wipe the slate clean. The corporate announcements were crisply formal. Yablans and Evans were stepping down from their respective management positions. Their contracts would be converted into production deals, calling for Paramount to finance and distribute their future films. Final approvals would, of course, reside with the new president of the studio, Barry Diller.

Both men seemed oddly relieved by the announcements. They knew that they had lost the confidence of their leader. Buoyed by their recent successes, both were supremely confident that success and wealth would continue to favor them—indeed that their fortunes would be enhanced. Their friends and acolytes reinforced this sense of hubris.

Their forecasts were wrong.

Few of Paramount's leading players would ever recapture their glory days. While Evans's producing career started promisingly with *Marathon Man*, some of his subsequent films, like *Popeye* and *The Players*, were deeply troubled, and his career finally ran aground in 1983 with the catastrophic production of *The Cotton Club*. The film reunited Evans with Coppola in a nightmare rerun of *The Godfather*. Both men at the time were strung out on cocaine, which further exacerbated their toxic relationship.

Coppola acknowledged in later years that he never decided

what story he wanted to tell in *Cotton Club*, suggesting that Evans had somehow dragooned him into the project against his better judgment. Evans, meanwhile, desperate for funds to cover his $25 million overage, fell in with two sleazy hustlers named Roy Radin and Laynie Jacobs, who promised funding but delivered only deceit and danger. When Radin suddenly disappeared, Evans found himself a potential murder suspect. In the end, Jacobs went to prison for Radin's murder.

When *Cotton Club* opened, on December 8, 1984, it was all but hooted off the screen. Evans's long-standing Paramount relationship was canceled.

A couple of years later Evans tried to revisit *Chinatown* with the production of *The Two Jakes*. The plan was for Bob Towne to direct and for Evans to play the lead, under the coaching of Jack Nicholson. After the project imploded, Evans went into a prolonged period of retreat, re-establishing himself in 1994 with the publication of his memoir, *The Kid Stays in the Picture*.

Yablans's career after Paramount was similarly volatile. While *The North Dallas Forty* was a hit at Paramount, *Mommie Dearest*, released by Fox, was a gauche soap opera about Joan Crawford and her daughter that all but ended Yablans's production credibility. Learning that Kirk Kerkorian, the longtime proprietor of MGM, was planning to pump new capital into his studio, Yablans brashly courted the Las Vegas billionaire, landing the job as president in 1983.

By the end of 1984, after a series of misfires, the rug was pulled out from under Yablans as Kerkorian put his studio back into play, triggering a series of exotic deals involving Ted Turner and lesser luminaries.

After the MGM debacle, Yablans returned to production as head of Promenade Pictures, a small firm that focuses on the Christian evangelical market.

Having miraculously survived crisis after crisis, Charlie Bluhdorn's decline began with a *Godfather*-like betrayal. Joel Dolkart, the smart but duplicitous attorney who'd been Gulf & Western's general counsel for twenty years, was found to be systematically stealing from the company, writing fraudulent checks and banking the proceeds. Only two executives in the company knew about Dolkart's thievery—Martin Davis, the G & W president, and Art Barron, the chief financial officer. When summoned to a crisis meeting in Bluhdorn's office, the three disagreed sharply over how to proceed. Davis, who had been jealous of Dolkart's influence over his boss, advocated throwing the book at Dolkart. "He's an embezzler," Davis said. "Let's fry him."

Barron, a stubby man with a stoic temperament, pointed out the dangers of this attack. Facing a certain jail sentence, Dolkart would cooperate with the authorities and bring forth some embarrassing facts. A safer course, he argued, might be to simply fire him and demand repayment. Probably only $2.5 million was at stake.

Bluhdorn briefly weighed the alternatives. Then, as was often the case in his deliberations, his anger got the best of him. He opted for Davis's attack mode.

Dolkart ultimately pleaded guilty to an eighty-nine-count indictment and was sentenced to a jail term of up to three years. Not surprisingly, he started talking.

Within weeks Gulf & Western was again the target of a fusillade of investigations. One probed possible organized-crime links, another looked into secret transactions involving corporate securities, yet another at the manipulation of its pension funds. Stanley Sporkin, who headed the SEC's division of enforcement, declared that Joel Dolkart's revelations were "reliable and objective." Jeremiah B. McKenna, general counsel of a New York State Senate committee on crime, announced that "we are coming at the organized crime aspect of it from a different angle."

Bluhdorn's reaction was to transform G & W headquarters into his personal bunker. Once a regular on the speaking circuit, Bluhdorn now talked to no one. His habit of trading securities moment by moment—especially G & W securities—was now abandoned as he watched his shares fall by 20 percent in a month. A snarky piece in *Time* magazine in July 1977 noted that "Bluhdorn's truculent, toothy grin" had vanished.

By now, Sydney Korshak was not around to provide crisis advice. Afflicted with Alzheimer's disease, Korshak had slowly retreated into semiretirement, dressing in his dark blue suit and tie each morning to sit alone in front of a TV set in his den. Korshak died in 1996. None of his onetime friends from the dark side were in attendance at the memorial, nor was Lew Wasserman. Bob Evans delivered the eulogy.

Bluhdorn was never the same after the Dolkart fiasco. Having lost his bravado, his final days in 1983 were shrouded in mystery. An initial report suggested that he died at his estate in the Dominican Republic, but that was quickly corrected, perhaps for legal or tax reasons, to a revisionist report that he'd died in flight, on his private jet, on his way back to New York. There were rumors that he'd been murdered, but they were never investigated.

Not surprisingly, Bluhdorn did not leave behind a clean path of succession. After a brief but bitter battle, Martin Davis was named the new CEO, having marshaled the support of Bluhdorn's widow, Yvette, and of Barry Diller. Both were later to declare their regret as Davis quickly cut off Yvette Bluhdorn's corporate perks, even her use of the G & W plane.

Though Diller proved to be a skilled corporate president, he and Davis clashed frequently, especially over issues of compensation. After one especially stormy week, Diller quit to become president of Twentieth Century-Fox. His two principal aides also bolted, Michael Eisner becoming the new boss of Disney with Jeffrey Katzenberg later joining him there. All three would have stellar careers, even as Davis struggled to solidify his corporate power.

In contrast to the Evans-Yablans melodramas, my own odyssey at Paramount came to a quiet end. I had been tracking the Bluhdorn-Diller dialogues and knew that a big change was imminent. I also knew that I didn't want to be part of a studio makeover. I'd had my fill of corporate intrigues and had lost any residual respect for Charlie Bluhdorn. Though Diller would bring new ideas, all roads would still lead to Bluhdorn and, to my mind, they were roads of no return.

I paid a visit to Evans's house to tell him I wanted out. "You promised a great ride, and you delivered," I said. "But I know when it's time to get off."

Evans gave me a wan smile. "I'd like to go with you," he said. "But I can't." Evans, I knew, had to wait out the rituals of termination. There would be a flowery announcement of a new production deal and appropriate euphemisms about commitments for the future. As he predicted, all of it was to unfold over the next two weeks. I still felt a great fondness for Evans and I knew it was mutual. I also knew our time of working together was over—he had his demons to overcome.

Meanwhile, I wasn't ready to turn my back on the movie business. Indeed, two studios had approached me about potential jobs, but the years of infighting at Paramount had left me wary of new corporate entanglements.

For some time I had been talking with a billionaire named Max Palevsky about starting a new entity. A pioneer in the burgeoning computer world, Palevsky had just sold his company, Scientific Data Systems, to Xerox and proposed formation of a partnership to independently develop and cofinance a small slate of movies. I admired Palevsky's taste in films and I also welcomed the fact that his personality was the mirror opposite of Bluhdorn's. Palevsky was committed but cautious; having helped conquer the computer, he had no interest in conquering the world.

My association with Palevsky resulted in two films, *Islands in the Stream*, which reteamed George C. Scott and the director Franklin Schaffner, who had worked together on *Patton*, and *Fun with Dick and Jane*, starring Jane Fonda and George Segal and directed by Ted Kotcheff, who was responsible for *The Apprenticeship of Duddy Kravitz*.

Open heart surgery forced Palevsky to cut back his activities and we closed the company after three years. I was to move on to two other movie jobs: Frank Yablans recruited me to join him in an effort to resuscitate the fading MGM. Yablans had assumed the presidency of that legendary studio and had been pledged hundreds of millions in new capital to support his ambitious slate. The funding proved less long-term than advertised, however, and Yablans's erratic leadership stirred the mistrust of Kirk Kerkorian, MGM's majority shareholder. The MGM adventure was to last only one year.

I was then recruited to join a smaller yet seemingly far more promising company called Lorimar, which had hatched several of the most successful TV shows of the eighties, including *The Waltons*, *Eight Is Enough*, and *Dallas*. Merv Adelson and Les Rich, who controlled the company, were determined to expand into film production and asked me to become president of a new division to pursue that objective. Again, the Lorimar scheme was short-lived. Several estimable films emerged from my first eighteen months, including *Being There*, directed by Hal Ashby, and *The Postman Always Rings Twice*, starring Jack Nicholson. Adelson and Rich clashed constantly about programming and finance, however, and their feuding destabilized their company's operations. Not long after my departure, Lorimar was sold to Warner Bros.

Soon thereafter, a headhunter approached me with an unexpected proposal. The century-old show business newspaper *Variety* had just been sold by the Silverman family, whose control of the company had spanned four generations. The new owner was a New England–based publisher of trade publications, Cahners Publishing Company, which in turn was part of a multinational corporation, Reed Elsevier.

According to the headhunter, the new owners had concluded that *Variety* was on shaky financial ground—the daily newspaper in Hollywood was making money but the weekly, published in New York, was dipping into the red. New leadership was needed—preferably someone who had worked both in journalism and in the movie business. The list of individuals who met those criteria was a limited one—indeed, mine was the only name on it.

I had always enjoyed reading *Variety*; the prospect of introducing new coverage and new design elements was exciting to me. Further, despite the traumas at Paramount, the entertainment business seemed poised for a period of exponential growth. *Variety* would be a beneficiary of that expansion if it was appropriately reinvigorated.

Happily, my prognostication proved to be correct. My stint as editor in chief of *Variety* was to endure twenty years, during which the paper was to thrive in prestige and in revenues. My timing proved fortuitous: the end of my tenure in 2009 coincided with the sharp economic downturn across the entire landscape of journalism.

Looking back, I realize that I was the beneficiary of good timing both at *Variety* and at Paramount. It is hard to imagine a new era of growth in print journalism comparable to that of the eighties and nineties. Similarly, it would be all but impossible to re-create a major film studio today that embodied the reckless swagger of Paramount in the seventies. Hollywood's dream factories today operate within rigid corporate discipline more akin to those of Proctor & Gamble. The mandate for studio regimes is to perpetuate tent-pole franchises like *Spider-Man* and *Iron Man* for the consumption of global audiences, not to subsidize the cinematic mind games of a new generation of Coppolas and Lucases. The business of Hollywood is that of building brands, not fostering imagination.

With rare exceptions, the generation of filmmakers from that earlier era is no longer around to witness the transformation. Spielberg and Lucas still reign supreme within their spectrums, but their colleagues and contemporaries, by and large, have faded from sight.

At the end of *Easy Rider*, the character called Wyatt tells his friend Billy, "We blew it . . ." The line is cited importantly in Peter Biskind's thoughtful book titled *Easy Riders, Raging Bulls*, in explaining the devastating casualty rate among the leading players in seventies Hollywood. The careers of many artists seemed to capsize shortly after reaching their zenith— Bogdanovich, Arthur Penn, Bob Rafelson, Paul Schrader, among others.

Undeniably, indiscriminate drug use shortened many careers, and so did rampant egomania. But the hit movies of the sixties and seventies were themselves narcotics, and their mythic success transformed immature filmmakers into rock stars, with all the attendant risks and rewards. The suddenness of their rise seemed to mandate their instant obsolescence.

Filmmakers have always tended to accomplish their greatest success with their earliest one or two works, and the crazed acclaim accorded their films during this epoch accelerated this phenomenon. Sure, they "blew it," but it was all but impossible to hold onto "it"—the instant celebrity, the unimaginable financial rewards.

Without consciously doing so, they had reached for the moon and come away with vastly more than they had bargained for. Nor had they bargained for the long night that awaited them.

Bob Evans, too, had reached for the moon. Today he still lives in the same elegant house in Beverly Hills that he purchased when he first came to Paramount. The screening room, which was the scene of so many grand and historic moments, burned down in 2001. The furnishings of the main house have not been changed since the seventies. The trees lining the driveway, now bent with age, branches in need of trimming, lean ominously close to the pavement. The proud cock at the front fountain looks a tad forlorn. The home is filled with memorabilia, including photos of its famous visitors. Especially prominent is a framed front page of *Daily Variety* dated May 18, 1972. Its banner shouts: PAR DISPLACES 20TH AS NO. ONE. The story details the studio's astonishing rise from last place to first place in five short years. Few, if any, studios in Hollywood history have accomplished such a remarkable turnaround.

"I still get a charge when I pass the page," Evans told me wistfully over lunch not long ago.

"I do, too," I replied, but even as I said it I asked myself why I had never framed that page, or had even saved it. Was it an acknowledgment of its evanescence? That moment seems so brief and so distanced. So very long ago.

PARAMOUNT SLATE OF FILMS

TITLE	DIRECTOR	PRODUCER
1967		
Hurry Sundown	Otto Preminger	Otto Preminger
The Busy Body	William Castle	William Castle
El Dorado	Howard Hawks	Howard Hawks
Barefoot in the Park	Gene Saks	Hal B. Wallis
Africa—Texas Style	Andrew Martin	Andrew Martin
The Stranger	Luchino Visconti	Dino De Laurentiis
The Last Safari	Henry Hathaway	Henry Hathaway
The Penthouse	Peter Collinson	Harry Fine
Oh Dad, Poor Dad, . . .	Richard Quine	Ray Stark– Stanley Rubin
The Spirit Is Willing	William Castle	William Castle
Waterhole No. 3	William Graham	Joseph Steck
Hostile Guns	R. G. Springsteen	A. C. Lyles
Warning Shot	Buzz Kulik	Buss Kulik– Bob Banner
The President's Analyst	Theodore Flicker	Stanley Rubin
Tarzan and the Great River	Robert Day	Sy Weintraub
Funeral in Berlin	Guy Hamilton	Charles Kasher
Red Tomahawk	R. G. Springsteen	A. C. Lyles
Chuka	Gordon Douglas	Rod Taylor– Jack Jason
C'mon, Let's Live a Little	David Butler	June Starr– John Hertelandy
The Deadly Bees	Freddie Francis	Max Rosenberg– Milton Sobotsky
Easy Come, Easy Go	John Rich	Hal B. Wallis
Fort Utah	Lesley Selander	A. C. Lyles
The Gentle Giant	James Neilson	Ivan Tors
Gunn	Blake Edwards	Owen Crumo
The Hired Killer	Frank Shannon	F. T. Gay
The Long Duel	Ken Annakin	Ken Annakin
The Sea Pirate	Roy Rowland	Roy Rowland
Smashing Time	Desmond Davis	Carlo Ponti– Ray Millichip
Two Weeks in September	Serge Bourguignon	Francis Cosne– Kenneth Harper
The Upper Hand	Denys de la Patelliere	Maurice Juaquin
The Vulture	Lawrence Huntington	Lawrence Huntington
1968		
Benjamin	Michael Deville	Mag Bodard

Targets	Peter Bogdanovich	Peter Bogdanovich
Sebastian	David Greene	Michael Powell–
		Herbert Brodkin
The Bliss of Mrs. Blossom	Joseph McGrath	Joseph Shaftel
Inadmissable Evidence	Anthony Page	Ronald Kinnoch
The Strange Affair	David Greene	Stanley Mann–
		Howard Harrison
Rosemary's Baby	Roman Polanski	William Castle
The Odd Couple	Gene Saks	Howard W. Koch
Danger: Diabolik	Mario Bava	Dino De Laurentiis
Tarzan and the	Robert Gordon	Sy Weintraub–
Jungle Boy		Robert Day
Villa Rides!	Buzz Kulik	Ted Richmond
Romeo and Juliet	Franco Zeffirelli	Anthony
		Havelock-Allen–
		John Brabourne
Uptight	Jules Dassin	Jules Dassin
Will Penny	Tom Gries	Fred Engel–
		Walter Seltzer
No Way to Treat a Lady	Jack Smight	Sol C. Siegel
Up the Junction	Peter Collinson	Anthony
		Havelock-Allen–
		John Brabourne
Long Day's Dying	Peter Collinson	Harry Fine
Anyone Can Play	Luigi Zampa	Gianni Hecht Lucari
Arizona Bushwackers	Lesley Selander	A. C. Lyles
Blue	Silvio Narizzano	Judd Bernard
Buckskin	Michael Moore	A. C. Lyles
Fever Heat	Russell Doughton Jr.	Russell Doughton Jr.
Maroc 7	Gerry O'Hara	John Gale–
		Leslie Phillips
Project X	William Castle	William Castle
The Treasure of	Dino Risi	Vetra-Lyre-Roxy
San Gennaro		
The Violent Four	Carlo Lizzani	Dino De Laurentiis

1969

My Side of the Mountain	James B. Clark	Robert Radnitz
Downhill Racer	Michael Ritchie	Richard Gregson
Medium Cool	Haskell Wexler	Tully Friedman–
		Haskell Wexler
If	Lindsay Anderson	Michael Medwin
Fraulein Doktor	Alberto Lattuada	Dino De Laurentiis
Once upon a Time	Sergio Leone	Sergio Leone–
in the West		Sergio Donati
Ace High (Revenge	Giuseppe Colizzi	Giuseppe Colizzi–
in El Paso)		Bino Cicogna

Paint Your Wagon	Joshua Logan	Alan Jay Lerner
True Grit	Henry Hathaway	Hal B. Wallis
The Sterile Cuckoo	Alan J. Pakula	Alan J. Pakula
The Italian Job	Peter Collinson	Michael Deeley
Oh! What a Lovely War	Richard Attenborough	Richard Attenborough–Brian Duffy
Only When I Larf	Basil Dearden	Len Deighton—Brian Duffy
Riot	Buzz Kulik	William Baker
The Assassination Bureau	Basil Dearden	Michael Relph
Goodbye, Columbus	Larry Peerce	Stanley Jaffe
Adalen 31	Bo Widerberg	Bo Widerberg
The Brain	Gerard Oury	Alain Poire
Hello Down There	Jack Arnold	George Sherman
Those Daring Young Men in Their Jaunty Jalopies	Ken Annakin	Ken Annakin

1970

WUSA	Stuart Rosenberg	John Forman–Paul Newman
The Adventurers	Lewis Gilbert	Lewis Gilbert
Darling Lili	Blake Edwards	Blake Edwards
Catch-22	Mike Nichols	Martin Ransohoff–John Calley
Borsalino	Jacques Deray	Alain Delon
The Molly Maguires	Martin Ritt	Martin Ritt–Walter Bernstein
The Out-of-Towners	Arthur Hiller	Paul Nathan
On a Clear Day You Can See Forever	Vincente Minnelli	Howard W. Koch
The Lawyer	Sidney J. Furie	Brad Dexter
Love Story	Arthur Hiller	Howard Minsky
Tell Me You Love Me, Junie Moon	Otto Preminger	Otto Preminger
The Confession	Constantin Costa-Gavras	Robert Dorfman–Bertrand Javal
Little Fauss and Big Halsy	Sidney J. Furie	Albert S. Ruddy
Norwood	Jack Haley Jr.	Hal B. Wallis
Tropic of Cancer	Joseph Strick	Joseph Strick

1971

Waterloo	Sergei Bondarchuk	Dino De Laurentiis
Friends	Lewis Gilbert	Lewis Gilbert
The Deserter	Burt Kennedy	Norman Baer–Dino De Laurentiis–Ralph Serpe

Plaza Suite	Arthur Hiller	Howard W. Koch
Such Good Friends	Otto Preminger	Otto Preminger
Deep End	Jerzy Skolimowski	Helmut Jedele
A New Leaf	Elaine May	Joe Manduke
Unman, Wittering and Zigo	John Mackenzie	Gareth Wigan
Harold and Maude	Hal Ashby	Charles Mulvehill–Colin Higgins
The Bear and the Doll	Michael Deville	Mag Bodard
Been Down So Long It Looks Like Up to Me	Jeffrey Young	Robert Rosenthal
Black Beauty	James Hill	Peter Andrews–Malcolm Hayworth
The Conformist	Bernardo Bertolucci	Maurizio Lodi-Fe
Desperate Characters	Frank D. Gilroy	Frank D. Gilroy
A Gunfight	Lamont Johnson	A. Ronald Rubin–Harold Jack Bloom
Joe Hill	Bo Widerberg	Bo Widerberg
Let's Scare Jessica to Death	John Hancock	Charles B. Moss Jr.
Murphy's War	Peter Yates	Michael Deeley
The Red Tent	Mikail K. Kalatozov	Franco Cristaldi
The Star-Spangled Girl	Jerry Paris	Howard W. Koch
T.R. Baskin	Herbert Ross	Peter Hyams
Willy Wonka and the Chocolate Factory	Mel Stuart	David Wolper–Stan Margulies

1972

A Separate Peace	Larry Peerce	Robert Goldston
The Man	Joseph Sargent	Lee Rich
The Pied Piper	Jacques Demy	David Puttnam–Sanford Lieberson
Bad Company	Robert Benton	Stanley R. Jaffe
Lady Sings the Blues	Sidney J. Furie	Jay Weston–James S. White
Child's Play	David Merrick	Sidney Lumet
Last of the Red Hot Lovers	Gene Saks	Howard W. Koch
Play It Again, Sam	Herbert Ross	Arthur Jacobs
The Godfather	Francis Ford Coppola	Albert S. Ruddy
Four Flies on Grey Velvet	Dario Argento	Salvatore Argento
Hannie Caulder	Burt Kennedy	Patrick Curtis
The Legend of Nigger Charley	Martin Goldman	Larry G. Spangler
The Possession of Joel Delaney	Waris Hussein	Martin Poll
ZPG: Zero Population Growth	Michael Campus	Thomas F. Madigan

1973

Ash Wednesday	Larry Peerce	Dominick Dunne
A Doll's House	Patrick Garland	Hillard Elkins
Don't Look Now	Nicolas Roeg	Peter Katz
Bang the Drum Slowly	John Hancock	Maurice Rosenfield
Badge 373	Howard W. Koch	Howard W. Koch
Serpico	Sidney Lumet	Dino De Laurentiis– Martin Bregman
Innocent Bystanders	Peter Collinson	George H. Brown
Charlotte's Web	Charles Nichols– Iwao Takamoto	Joseph Barbera– William Hanna
Save the Tiger	John G. Avildsen	Steve Shagan
Paper Moon	Peter Bogdanovich	Peter Bogdanovich
The Friends of Eddie Coyle	Peter Yates	Paul Monash
Brother Sun, Sister Moon	Franco Zeffirelli	Luciano Perugia
Jonathan Livingston Seagull	Hall Bartlett	Hall Bartlett
Alfredo, Alfredo	Pietro Germi	Pietro Germi
Charley One-Eye	Don Chaffey	James Swann
Fear Is the Key	Michael Tuchner	Alan Ladd Jr.– Jay Kanter
The First Circle	Alexander Ford	Mogens Skot-Hansen
Hit	Sidney J. Furie	Harry Korshak
Hitler: The Last Ten Days	Ennio D. Concini	John Heyman
The Mattei Affair	Francesco Rosi	Franco Cristaldi
The Optimists	Anthony Simmons	Adrian Gaye– Victor Lyndon
Save the Children	Stan Latham	Matt Robinson
Scalawag	Kirk Douglas	Anne Douglas
The Soul of Nigger Charley	Larry G. Spangler	Larry G. Spangler
Superfly T.N.T.	Ron O'Neil	Sig Shore
Tales That Witness Madness	Freddie Francis	Norman Priggen

1974

The Longest Yard	Robert Aldrich	Albert S. Ruddy
Death Wish	Michael Winner	Hal Landers– Bobby Roberts
The Great Gatsby	Jack Clayton	David Merrick
The Conversation	Francis Ford Coppola	Francis Ford Coppola– Fred Roos
Daisy Miller	Peter Bogdanovich	Peter Bogdanovich
Chinatown	Roman Polanski	Robert Evans
Murder on the Orient Express	Sidney Lumet	John Brabourne– Richard Goodwin

Paul and Michelle	Lewis Gilbert	Lewis Gilbert
Man on a Swing	Frank Perry	Howard Jaffe
The Godfather Part II	Francis Ford Coppola	Francis Ford Coppola
The Gambler	Karel Reisz	Irwin Winkler– Robert Chartoff
The Parallax View	Alan J. Pakula	Alan J. Pakula
The White Dawn	Philip Kaufman	Martin Ransohoff
The Little Prince	Stanley Donen	Stanley Donen
The Apprenticeship of Duddy Kravitz	Ted Kotcheff	John Kemeny
Captain Kronos, Vampire Hunter	Brian Clemens	Brian Clemens– Albert Fennell
The Education of Sonny Carson	Michael Campus	Irwin Yablans
Frankenstein and the Monster from Hell	Terence Fisher	Roy Skeggs
The Klansman	Terence Young	William Alexander
Malizia	Salvatore Samperi	Silvio Clementelli
Phase IV	Saul Bass	Paul B. Radin
Shanks	William Castle	Steve North
Three Tough Guys	Duccio Tessari	Dino De Laurentiis

1975

Sheila Levine Is Dead and Living in New York	Sidney J. Furie	Harry Korshak
Posse	Kirk Douglas	Kirk Douglas
Mandingo	Richard Fleischer	Dino De Laurentiis
Once Is Not Enough	Guy Green	Howard W. Koch
The Day of the Locust	John Schlesinger	Jerome Hellman
Nashville	Robert Altman	ABC–Altman
Hustle	Robert Aldrich	Robert Aldrich
Three Days of the Condor	Sydney Pollack	Stanley Schneider– Dino De Laurentiis
Bug	Jeannot Szwarc	William Castle
Dog-Pound Shuffle	Jeffrey Bloom	Jeffrey Bloom
The Dove	Charles Jarrott	Gregory Peck
Framed	Phil Karlson	Mort Briskin– Joel Briskin
Mahogany	Berry Gordy	Rob Cohen– Jack Ballard

1976

Lifeguard	Daniel Petrie	Ron Silverman
The Shootist	Don Siegel	M. J. Frankovich– William Self
King Kong	John Guillermin	Dino De Laurentiis
Bugsy Malone	Alan Parker	Alan Marshall

The Tenant	Roman Polanski	Andrew Braunsberg
The Bad News Bears	Michael Ritchie	Stanley R. Jaffe
The Big Bus	James Frawley	Fred Freemen– Lawrence J. Cohen
Face to Face	Ingmar Bergman	Ingmar Bergman
Marathon Man	John Schlesinger	Robert Evans– Sidney Beckerman
Lipstick	Lamont Johnson	Freddie Fields– Dino De Laurentiis
Won Ton Ton: The Dog Who Saved Hollywood	Michael Winner	Michael Winner– David Picker– Arnold Schulman
The Last Tycoon	Elia Kazan	Sam Spiegel
Emmanuelle: The Joys of a Woman	Francis Giacobetti	Yves Rousset-Rouard
The First Nudie Musical	Mark Haggard	Jack Reeves– Bruce Kimmel
Leadbelly	Gordon Parks	Marc Merson
The Memory of Justice	Elia Kazan	Sam Spiegel
Mikey and Nicky	Elaine May	Michael Hausmann
Survive!	René Cardona	René Cardona

1977

1900	Bernardo Bertolucci	Alberto Grimaldi
Sorcerer	William Friedkin	Paramount–Universal
Islands in the Stream	Franklin J. Schaffner	Peter Bart– Max Palevsky
Citizens Band	Jonathen Demme	Freddie Fields
Looking for Mr. Goodbar	Richard Brooks	Freddie Fields
Saturday Night Fever	John Badham	Robert Stigwood
Black Sunday	John Frankenheimer	Robert Evans
The Bad News Bears in Breaking Training	Michael Pressman	Leonard Goldberg
First Love	Joan Darling	Lawrence Turman– David Foster
Fraternity Row	Thomas J. Tobin	Charles Gary Allison
Orca	Michael Anderson	Luciano Vincenzoni
Race for Your Life, Charlie Brown	Bill Melendez	Bill Melendez– Lee Mendelson
Thieves	John Berry	George Barrie

Index

Accardo, Tony, 97, 104
Adams, Frank, 3
Adelson, Merv, 258–59
Adonis, Joe, 101
Adventurers, The, 37
Allen, Woody, 155, 162
Andrews, Julie, vii–viii, 5, 46, 51–59, 93, 154
Arvey, Jake, 104
Ashby, Hal, 120–29, 186, 190
Ashley, Ted, 190
Atherton, William, 150
Aubrey, Jim, 4, 87
Avakian, Aram, 223, 226, 227

Baker, Stanley, 45, 46, 47
Balaban, Barney, 100
Balaban, Bob, 122
Ballard, Jack, 52–53, 55, 223, 226, 227
Barefoot in the Park, 135, 159, 161, 178
Barron, Art, 255
Baum, Martin, 46–47
Bautzer, Greg, 11–12, 42
Beatty, Warren, 41, 42–43, 94–95, 151, 157–72, 174, 184, 198, 213, 219, 230, 234–36, 238, 252
Being There, 129
Benton, Robert, 164
Bernard, Judd, 135–37, 138, 178
Bertolucci, Bernardo, 89
Bioff, Willie, 100
Black, Karen, 150
Blue, 134–38, 145, 179, 181, 243
Bluhdorn, Charles, ix, 11–16, 24–37, 43, 45–52, 55–59, 65, 67–68, 74, 78–79, 88, 91, 98–99, 103, 108–11, 119, 130–31, 136–38, 141, 142, 145, 146, 150, 152, 155–56, 171, 185–87, 192–97, 214, 215, 217–22, 224, 225, 231, 235, 241, 244, 249–51, 253, 255–58
Bluhdorn, Yvette, 51, 52, 256
Bogdanovich, Peter, 20, 186, 194, 195–96, 239–41, 252, 260
Bonnie and Clyde, 133, 163–66, 169, 233
Boswell, John, 20–21
Brando, Marlon, viii, 89, 111, 156–57, 158, 197, 211, 219–22, 225, 227, 242–43, 246–47

Brooks, Richard, 63
Burstyn, Ellen, 88, 89
Butch Cassidy and the Sundance Kid, 167, 181, 182

Caan, James, 220, 222–23, 227, 252
Caffey, Frank, 21–22
Cagney, James, 8, 62, 101
Caine, Michael, 47
Canby, Vincent, 64, 171
Capone, Al, 100, 101, 108
Capote, Truman, 235–36
Cassavetes, John, 180, 213
Castle, William, 205–6, 207, 213
Catch-22, 186, 233
Catledge, Turner, 3
Champlin, Charles, 173–74
Chaney, Lon, 8
Chayefsky, Paddy, 61, 63, 128
Chicago Sun-Times, 3, 5
Childers, Michael, 151, 152
Chiles, Lois, 244
Chinatown, 152, 171–72, 196–98, 232, 249, 250, 252, 254
Christie, Julie, 92–95, 148, 151, 167
Christmas, Eric, 125
Clayton, Jack, 243–45
Coburn, James, 143
Coco, 59, 65
Cohen, Mickey, 101, 102
Cohn, Harry, 100, 102, 105
Cohn, Joan, 105
Coppola, Carmine, 210
Coppola, Francis, viii, 111, 144, 186, 192–97, 202–4, 207–12, 216, 218–30, 232, 236–37, 242, 246–47, 252–54
Cort, Bud, 122, 125
Costello, Frank, 102
Cotton Club, The, 253–54
Crane, Cheryl, 102
Crowley, Mart, 137
Crowther, Bosley, 161, 166
Crump, Owen, 54, 56, 57

Dalitz, Moe, 97
Daniel, Clifton, 3, 4–6, 18

Dann, Mike, 4
Darling Lili, vii–viii, 36, 46, 51–58, 61, 109, 140, 154
Davidson, Martin, 72–73, 75–76
Davis, Martin, 12, 25–26, 35, 47, 79, 88, 90, 91, 119, 141, 255, 256
Davis, Sammy, Jr., 102
Day of the Locust, 148–52
Deeley, Michael, 45–47
Deep Throat, 90–91, 102–3, 119
Delon, Alain, 41, 81, 131
De Niro, Robert, 112
Detective, The (Thorp), 10–11
Diller, Barry, 250–53, 256–57
Dirty Harry, 177, 184
Dolkart, Joel, 99, 255–56
Dominican Republic, 28–29, 109, 235, 256
Donen, Stanley, 253
Don't Look Now, 92–95, 167
Downhill Racer, 179–82, 207, 213
Duvall, Robert, 220, 226, 227

Eastman, Andrea, 88
Eastman, Charles, 182
Eastwood, Clint, 33, 46, 62–64, 128, 157–59, 172–77, 184
Easy Rider, 260
Edwards, Blake, viii, 51–57, 61, 65, 117
Eisner, Michael, 257
Elkins, Hillard, 145
Emmett, Jay, 103
Emperor of the North Pole, 155
Ephron, Nora, 71
Esquire, 71, 164
Evans, Robert, ix, 3, 8–18, 21, 22, 35, 36, 55, 58, 65, 83, 84, 86–89, 94–95, 96, 98–99, 106–8, 110–12, 115, 117, 130–34, 137, 138, 140, 142–47. 150, 152, 155–57, 168, 171–72, 182, 186–99, 202, 230–32, 239, 245–46, 253–54, 256, 257, 261; *Darling Lili* and, 51, 52; *Funny Girl* and, 48–50; *The Godfather* and, 189,

191–93, 197, 208–12, 216–18, 222–29; *The Great Gatsby* and, 234–38, 243–44; *Harold and Maude* and, 119, 121–24, 126; *Love Story* and, 66, 68, 69, 72–82, 186, 218; MacGraw and, 72, 77, 186, 191, 234–35, 238–42, 244, 248–49; *The Odd Couple* and, 29–33; *Paint Your Wagon* and, 58–63, 175; *Rosemary's Baby* and, 206–7, 212–16; salon of, 39–44

Fade In, 137–38
Farrow, Mia, 112, 154–55, 212–16, 244–46
Fehmiu, Bekim, 155–56
Feldman, Charlie, 48, 160, 162
Fields, Freddie, 42, 240–41
Fistful of Dollars, A, 173
Flicker, Theodore, 143
Fonda, Peter, 162
Forman, John, 143
Forster, Robert, 140
Frankfurt, Stephen, 128
Friedkin, Billy, 194, 195
Funny Girl, 48–50, 59, 155
Fun with Dick and Jane, 258
Furie, Sidney J., 183, 209–10

Gersh, Phil, 75
Getaway, The, 239–41
Giancanna, Sam, 97, 100, 101
Godard, Jean-Luc, 164, 201
Godfather, The, viii–ix, xii, 2, 78, 79, 101, 111–13, 127, 170–71, 185, 186, 189–93, 197, 207–12, 216–30, 233, 234, 237, 241, 242, 248, 252
Godfather Part II, The, 232, 234, 252
Good, the Bad and the Ugly, The, 173–74
Goodbye, Columbus, 2, 22, 34–35, 38, 72–74, 128, 146
Gordon, Ruth, 122–23
Graduate, The, 133, 166, 179
Great Gatsby, The, 73, 234–47, 252

Greenberg, Alex, 104
Greenspun, Roger, 177
Gregson, Richard, 179–80, 181
Gulf & Western, viii–ix, 24–29, 57–58, 78, 90, 108, 109, 141, 217–18, 224, 251, 255–56
Gunderson, Karen, 59

Halberstam, David, 6, 18
Half a Sixpence, 14, 47
Hang 'Em High, 174–75, 176
Harold and Maude, 2, 78, 79, 117–29, 192
Hathaway, Henry, 200–201
Hawks, Howard, 101
Hellman, Jerome, 149, 150
Hepburn, Katharine, 59
Hersh, Seymour, 99
Higgins, Colin, 117–21, 122
Hiller, Arthur, 68, 74–77, 79–82
Hirshan, Leonard, 30–33
Hitchcock, Alfred, 16, 201
Hoffa, Jimmy, 97, 105
Hoffman, Dustin, 179, 238, 240
Holiday, 64
Hoover, J. Edgar, 143–44
Hopper, Dennis, 190
Hudson, Rock, vii–viii, 53–55, 56, 93, 154, 158
Hughes, Howard, 97, 101, 104
Humphreys, Murray, 104

Inge, William, 160, 161
Islands in the Stream, 258
Is Paris Burning?, 15, 49
Italian Job, The, 47

Jaffe, Leo, 34
Jaffe, Stanley, 34–38, 73, 74, 88, 146, 147, 186–87, 220, 221, 225, 228
Jewison, Norman, 120, 121
John, Elton, 121
Jones, Tommy Lee, 77

Kael, Pauline, 151, 166, 174, 177
Katzenberg, Jeffrey, 257

Kefauver, Estes, 102
Kennedy, John F., 101
Kennedy, Robert, 43, 167
Kennedy, Ted, 41, 43, 191
Kerkorian, Kirk, 108, 111–12, 223, 254, 258
Kissinger, Henry, ix, 42, 191, 241–42, 248
Koch, Howard W., 15, 17–18, 29, 33, 145–46, 170
Komeda, Christopher, 231
Korda, Michael, 25, 26
Korshak, Harry, 97–98, 106–8
Korshak, Marshall, 103
Korshak, Sidney, 96–99, 102, 103–13, 197, 223, 256

Lai, Francis, 81
Lanchester, Elsa, 119
Landlord, The, 120
Lansky, Meyer, 101
Last Tango in Paris, 89
Lauren, Ralph, 242
Lazar, Irving "Swifty," 236
Lemmon, Jack, 30–33, 75, 252
Leone, Sergio, 159, 173, 175
Lerner, Alan Jay, 59–65, 117, 175, 176, 253
Lewis, Edward, 118–19
Lilith, 162
Little Fauss and Big Halsy, 182–83, 243
Little Prince, The, 65, 253
Loden, Barbara, 137, 138
Loewe, Fritz, 59, 60, 61, 64, 176, 253
Logan, Josh, 61–64
Los Angeles Times, 63, 173, 176
Love Story, 2, 38, 66–82, 186, 189, 218, 233
Lucas, George, 210, 233, 260
Luciano, Lucky, 100, 101, 102

MacGraw, Ali, 38, 42, 67, 69, 72–77, 80–82, 186, 191, 234–35, 237–42, 244, 248–49

Mafia, ix, 2, 90–91, 97–105, 208, 220, 223–24
Mann, Abby, 8, 9, 10
Mann, William J., 152
Man of a Thousand Faces, 8
Marley, John, 77
Marvin, Lee, 46, 62–64, 135, 154
Matthau, Walter, 29–32, 145, 146
May, Elaine, 144–48
Mayer, Louis B., 60, 100, 153
McEwen, Walter, 165–66
McGovern, George, 167
McQueen, Steve, 8, 158, 239–41, 249
Medium Cool, 139–42, 143
Mengers, Sue, 41, 230, 238, 240
Merrick, David, 235, 244
Mickey One, 162, 164–65
Mikey and Nicky, 98
Milland, Ray, 77
Miller, Henry, 89
Minsky, Howard, 69, 72
Molly Maguires, The, 46, 154, 186
Mommie Dearest, 254
Montgomery, Robert, 101
Mulvehill, Charles, 122, 123, 124, 126
Murphy, Art, 23, 127

Narizzano, Silvio, 135, 136, 138, 145, 179
New Leaf, A, 79, 144–48
Newman, David, 164
Newman, Paul, 8, 142–43, 156–57, 158, 177, 181, 240
Newsweek, 71
Newton, Helmut, 42
New Yorker, 166, 174, 177
New York Times, 1, 3–8, 11, 14, 16–18, 23, 64, 71, 99, 142, 161, 163, 166, 171, 177, 213, 224
Nichols, Mike, 144, 179, 238
Nicholson, Jack, 41, 42, 196, 220, 230, 234–36, 238, 252, 254
Nixon, Richard, ix, 6, 167, 168, 248
Novak, Kim, 102

Odd Couple, The, 22, 29–33
On a Clear Day You Can See Forever,
    59, 65, 233
O'Neal, Ryan, 68–69, 71, 77, 80–81,
    212, 252
O'Toole, Peter, 162–63
Out-of-Towners, The, 75, 76

Pacino, Al, 111–12, 220, 222–23,
    226
Paint Your Wagon, 36, 46, 58–65,
    109, 154, 175–76, 192
Pakula, Alan J., 168–72
Palevsky, Max, 257–58
Paper Moon, 195, 252
Parallax View, The, 168–72, 198, 252
Peckinpah, Sam, 209, 240, 241
Peerce, Larry, 38, 73–75
Penn, Arthur, 162, 165, 218, 260
Peraino, Lou, 103
Phillips, Julia, 191
Picker, David, 165
Pickles, Vivian, 123
Playboy, 174
Play It Again, Sam, 155
Play Misty for Me, 176–77
Poitier, Sidney, 240
Polanski, Roman, 154, 180, 186,
    190, 198, 202–7, 212–16, 230–
    32, 238
Pollack, Sydney, 234–35
Pollard, Michael J., 183
Ponti, Carlo, 219
Post, Ted, 175
Preminger, Otto, 131–32, 133
President's Analyst, The, 22, 143–44
Presley, Elvis, 5, 20, 115, 116, 133
Previn, André, 61
Puzo, Mario, 112–13, 208, 209,
    211–12, 216, 223, 225

Raft, George, 101
Reagan, Ronald, 97, 106
Redford, Robert, 135–36, 137,
    157–59, 161, 177–84, 207, 213,
    243–46, 252

Redstone, Sumner, 25, 187
Reed, Rex, 64
Reisz, Karel, 186, 252
Reynolds, Burt, 137, 138
Rich, Les, 258–59
Ritchie, Michael, 181, 207
Robbins, Harold, 37, 156
Roeg, Nicolas, 92–95, 186
Roselli, Johnny, 100, 102
Rosemary's Baby, xii, 2, 78,
    112, 123, 128, 154–55,
    180, 186, 205–7, 212–16,
    230, 231
Rosenberg, Stuart, 142
Ross, Herb, 155
Rossen, Robert, 162
Roth, Philip, 34, 73, 74
Rubinstein, John, 119–20, 122
Ruddy, Albert S., 182–83, 218–21,
    224–27
Rudin, Mickey, 214–15, 216

Saks, Gene, 32, 33
Salter, James, 180
Sargent, Alvin, 195
Sarris, Andrew, 173
Scarface, 101
Schenck, Nicholas, 100
Schlesinger, John, 148–52
Schloss, Irwin, 27
Schneider, Maria, 89
Schulman, Arnold, 34
Seberg, Jean, 62, 63, 64, 162
SEC, 26–29, 109, 110, 249, 255
Segal, Erich, 68, 70–72, 74, 80
Sellers, Peter, 163
Selznick, Joyce, 156–57
Shaw, Tom, 63
Shearer, Norma, 8
*Sheila Levine is Dead and Living in
    New York,* 106–7
Siegel, Bugsy, 97
Siegel, Don, 61, 174, 175, 177
Siegel, Lee, 189–90
Simon, Neil, 29, 32, 76
Simon & Schuster, 25, 26

Sinatra, Frank, 29, 101, 102, 112–13, 154–55, 177, 212–16, 230
Sindona, Michele, 103, 109–10
Sitton, Claude, 3, 6, 18
Splendor in the Grass, 159, 160–61
Sporkin, Stanley, 255
Stamp, Terence, 136, 138
Stark, Ray, 48, 49, 50
Steele, Tommy, 14, 47, 154
Stevens, Cat, 121, 124, 125, 126
Stompanato, Johnny, 101–2
Streisand, Barbra, 49–50, 59, 71, 167, 240
Strick, Joseph, 89
Sun Also Rises, The, 8–9
Sutherland, Donald, 92–95, 150, 151, 167

Targ, William, 208
Tate, Sharon, 230–32
Taylor, Jud, 137
Tell Me That You Love Me, Junie Moon, 132, 154
Thalberg, Irving, 8, 9, 11, 43, 78, 100, 192, 217
Time, 70–71, 81, 82, 161, 188, 199, 231–32, 245, 246, 250, 256
Towne, Robert, 169, 170, 196–98, 254
Tropic of Cancer, 88–89
True Grit, 116–17, 186, 200–201
Truffaut, Francois, 131, 163–64, 201
Turner, Lana, 101–2

Valley of the Dolls (Susann), 10
Variety, 22–23, 127, 164, 259

Wales, Ken, 54–57
Wallis, Hal, 115–17, 200–201
Wall Street Journal, 3, 5
Warner, Jack, 16, 116, 153, 161, 165–66
Wasserman, Lew, 16, 97, 99, 105–6, 108–9, 256
Wayne, John, 116–17, 239
Webb, Jimmy, 81
Weld, Tuesday, 212
Wexler, Haskell, 139–41
What's New Pussycat?, 162–63
What's Up, Doc?, 71
Where's Jack?, 46–47, 154
Wieser, George, 10, 208
Wilder, Billy, 31, 32, 81, 160
Willis, Gordon, 170–71, 223, 225, 226
Wood, Natalie, 159, 160, 161
Woodward, Joanne, 142
WUSA, 142–43

Yablans, Frank, 35–36, 98, 127, 128, 143, 145, 150, 152, 170, 172, 186–99, 228, 235, 241, 244–46, 249–54, 258
Yablans, Irwin, 187
Yates, Peter, 186

Zanuck, Darryl F., 8–9, 58, 197
Zanuck, Richard, 9, 58, 155
Ziegler, Evarts, 115